World Drama

HOLT, RINEHART AND WINSTON

A Harcourt Education Company

Orlando • **Austin** • New York • San Diego • Toronto • London

Staff Credits

EDITORIAL

Editorial Director
Ralph Tachuk

Executive Editor
Patricia McCambridge

Senior Editor
Amy Strong

Copyediting: Michael Neibergall, *Copyediting Manager;* Mary Malone, *Senior Copyediting Supervisor;* Elizabeth Dickson, Christine Altgelt, *Senior Copyeditors;* Emily Force, Stephanie Jones, *Copyeditors*

Project Administration: Marie Price, *Managing Editor;* Elizabeth LaManna, *Associate Managing Editor;* Betty Gabriel, *Editorial Coordinator*

Editorial Permissions: Sally Garland, *Supervisor of Copyrights & Permissions*

DESIGN

Senior Design Director
Betty Mintz

Image Acquisitions
Mary Monaco

PRODUCTION

Carol Trammel, *Senior Production Manager*
Cynthia Muñoz, *Senior Production Coordinator*

MANUFACTURING/INVENTORY

Shirley Cantrell, *Manufacturing Supervisor*
Mark McDonald, *Inventory Planner*
Amy Borseth, *Media Manufacturing Coordinator*

ISBN 0-03-041084-3
6 7 018 07

Contents

Introduction to World Drama

People seem to be storytellers by nature. You might be surprised to find, though, that the oldest stories in the world probably took the form of what we now call plays, or drama. Many scholars believe that drama existed even among prehistoric people. (We can imagine early humans acting out scenes of the hunt in their fire-illuminated caves.) The first plays we know about in Western literature were staged in Greece in the fifth century B.C. Some form of drama was performed in India and China many years earlier than that—so long ago that no one can pinpoint exactly when drama began.

A **drama** is simply a story acted out. Today we see dramas on TV and in the movies, as well as on the stage, but for centuries plays were acted out in front of live audiences. All plays, whether from the East or the West, share certain characteristics, though each culture puts its unique stamp on its dramatic productions.

Drama Began in Religious Ritual

In both the East and the West, the very first dramas probably originated in religious rituals. The ancient Egyptians, for example, performed ritual plays as part of celebrations involving the coronations or deaths of pharaohs, who were seen as divine. Thousands of years ago in China, religious rites involving music and dance dramatized people's occupations and the accompanying sensations of joy, fatigue, and contentment. In ancient Greece drama began in the fifth century B.C. with rituals honoring the god Dionysus. The impulse to fuse religious ritual with drama continued in medieval England with mystery and miracle plays—plays about biblical stories or saints' lives performed on certain feast days.

From the Divine to the Human

Plays are about **characters**—the actors in the drama. Characters in plays, as in stories and novels, are usually human. Even those characters who are not human—like the animals in animated films—represent human qualities, often exaggerated for effect: A hungry, man-eating plant might represent outrageous greed, for example. Great plays from everywhere in the world are ultimately about human beings, people more or less like ourselves.

The "Bare Bones" of Drama

Most plays in Western culture share a few key elements of structure—what we might call the "bare bones," or essential framework, of drama. Plays usually begin with characters who find themselves in a situation where they want something very much—perhaps even desperately. They might want to win the love of another person, find a murderer, save a relationship, or resist the pull of some destructive force. The part of the play that "sets up" the main characters and situation is called the **exposition.**

The **action** of the play begins when the main character—the **protagonist**—takes steps to get what he or she wants. In taking action, the character encounters a **conflict**—a clash or struggle between two forces. A conflict can take place between two or more people, between a person and a force of nature (an animal, a hurricane, the void of space), or between warring desires or needs in the protagonist's mind. Often, the protagonist struggles against another character—the **antagonist.** When the clash is physical—or, at least, outwardly directed—we have an **external conflict;** when the clash takes the form of a struggle within the central character's mind, we have an **internal conflict.**

During the plot's **rising action,** as the character takes steps to resolve the conflict, **complications** develop in which the protagonist may face one roadblock after another. Eventually the drama reaches a **turning point,** when the protagonist makes a choice from which there is no turning back. At this point, the audience experiences **suspense**—and, if the play is well written and feels "true" to us, we will begin to care a great deal about the characters and hope they made the right choice.

The actions in the play eventually move to a **climax**—an intensely suspenseful moment when the action of the play can go either one way or another, toward either a happy ending or a sad one. This emotionally charged moment is when we know the protagonist is either going to win or lose the struggle.

After the climax comes the **denouement,** a winding down of the plot in which loose ends come together and the conflict finally comes to a **resolution.**

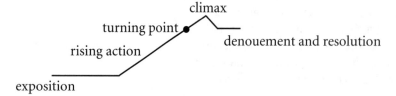

If the protagonist prevails in the conflict, the audience is usually satisfied and may feel uplifted; if the protagonist loses, the audience usually feels sad, though this reaction too can be oddly satisfying. Whatever the outcome, the experience of seeing a live play with live people acting out a story can be exhilarating. When audiences leave a play that has been well written, well directed, and well performed, they feel that they have participated in a genuine human experience. Whether it ends happily or sadly, the play has revealed to them something about our lives here on earth.

Two Main Types of Dramas: Tragedy and Comedy

In the Western tradition, starting in ancient Greece, drama has taken two basic forms: tragedy and comedy.

Tragedy

Tragedy traditionally has focused on a dignified, courageous, often high-ranking hero or heroine who fails to win what he or she wants. Often, what brings about the fall of this great figure is some tragic flaw in character—pride, perhaps, or too much ambition, or jealousy. At the end of most tragedies, we do not feel depressed; instead we feel pity and relief, having watched a potentially great human being who has lost everything but has also gained wisdom and self-knowledge.

Two of the world's greatest tragedies are included in this book: *Antigone* by Sophocles and *Medea* by Euripides, both of which were performed for festivals of Dionysus in ancient Greece. In case you've thought that women were not well represented in ancient drama, note that each of these masterpieces focuses on a woman who must make agonizing choices. The heroines of these tragedies are very different, however, and debate has raged over the centuries about whether Medea is a tragic heroine at all— or just a depraved murderer.

Comedy

Unlike tragedy, **comedy** is a drama with a happy ending. The word *comedy* derives from the Greek work *komos*, or revelry; and, indeed, many classical comedies end in boisterous celebrations—banquets, dances, and above all, marriages. Often the plot of a comedy involves a love story that can be summed up in this way: boy meets girl, boy loses girl, boy wins girl. (Substitute *girl* for *boy* and *boy* for *girl* in this summation, and you have the same story.) *The Flying Doctor*, by the French dramatist known as Molière, uses this comic plot as an excuse to engage in a mad farce. **Farce** involves broadly comic characters maneuvering in ridiculous, convoluted plots. Farce often involves physical comedy. The farces that you see in old movies, for example, might have characters slipping on banana peels, tossing pies in people's faces, and hiding in closets or under someone's bed.

Although the tragedy-comedy classification is a Western concept, the idea of moving an audience's emotions to pity or to laughter seems to be universal. For example, the traditional Noh drama of Japan appeals to some of the same emotions found in Western tragedy—courage and vengeance, sorrow and guilt. (In between the several dramas that make up a typical Noh performance, lighthearted farces called *kyógen* provide comic relief.) In India, classical Sanskrit drama has been judged by its ability to produce a range of *rasas*, moods or emotions, in the audience. Playgoers everywhere share the desire to participate in the range of emotions that occur when human dramas are acted out on stage.

Variations and Innovations

Like all writers, dramatists are innovators—that is, they experiment all the time with the basic forms of drama. In this book you will find plays by dramatists who were schooled in the tradition of Greek drama and Shakespeare, yet who wrote plays that are neither fully tragic nor fully comic. For example, in *A Doll's House*, a **realistic drama** by Norwegian playwright Henrik Ibsen, the heroine is not, well, very heroic. Nora, unlike Antigone or Medea, is someone very like ourselves—an ordinary woman who is sometimes admirable but often less than noble.

Since the early twentieth century, drama has often taken the form of social protest, in which the dramatist's purpose is to expose a social or political problem. In fact, in world literature today, you will find many works of literature that could be called social protest—novels, poems, short stories, and drama. This book includes a short play of social protest by the great German dramatist Bertolt Brecht. *The Spy* is set in Nazi Germany, in a world where children are trained to turn parents in to the police.

Another important technique that revolutionized modern drama in the twentieth century is the use of what is called the **absurd.** In dramas of the absurd, characters move in a world that fails to make sense even on the most elemental level. In one famous absurdist drama by the Irish dramatist Samuel Beckett, we watch two characters carry on their dialogue while buried up to their necks in sand. You will find that some of the modern plays in this book use elements of the absurd to dramatize the problems people face in an inhuman, corrupt society. For example, in *The Man Who*

Turned into a Dog, by the Argentinean writer Osvaldo Dragún, an unemployed man gets a job as a watchdog—literally.

The Power of the Theater

Most plays are meant to be presented on a stage, using all the arts of the theater: costumes, sets, props, lights, music, and even sound and visual effects. When these arts are put to use by an imaginative director, a play works a kind of magic, enabling us to suspend our disbelief no matter how otherworldly or outlandish the concept may be. The people who help to bring the play to life—the director, actors, set designer, costume designer, light technician—are often called the playwright's collaborators.

In the prologue of *Henry V*, the great British playwright William Shakespeare points to another collaborator when he asks the audience to

Sit and see
Minding true things by what their mockeries be.

Today, a play may take the form of an elaborate costume drama with lavish sets and lighting techniques; it may just as easily take the form of a bare stage with one black-clad actor, her face alone highlighted by the piercing focus of a single light. In the end, it is the audience members' imaginations that lift the dramatist's efforts above the level of mere imitation—mere "mockery"—and into the realm of "true things."

The Greek Theater

Like drama from many parts of the world, Greek drama grew out of religious rituals. During celebrations honoring Dionysus, the god of wine and fertility, worshipers would dance around an altar, singing hymns to the wild, passionate accompaniment of the flute.

At some point during the sixth century B.C., these Dionysian celebrations became an annual festival held in Athens at a large outdoor amphitheater. Eventually, the dancing choruses of worshipers began competing for prizes—usually a bull or a goat. Tradition has it that a man named Thespis transformed these hymns into songs that still honored Dionysus but also told the story of a famous hero or even another god. Then Thespis added another innovation: One chorus member would step away from the others to play the part of that hero or god. Drama as we know it was born when the playwright Aeschylus added a second individual actor to the performance, creating the possibility of conflict. (Thespis is immortalized in our word *thespian*, which refers to an actor or actress.)

The Theater of Dionysus

By the end of the fifth century B.C., this annual festival, called the Dionysia, had become an extravaganza taking place over a period of days. Public business was suspended; prisoners were released on bail. The main festivities took place in the Theater of Dionysus.

The Theater of Dionysus looked like a semicircular football stadium. The seats were carved out of stone on a hillside; at the bottom was a performance area where the actors spoke their lines from behind huge masks. These masks had exaggerated mouthpieces that amplified the actors' voices. Many masks were stylized into familiar character types that were easily recognized by the audience: a king, a messenger, a prophet, a queen, or a nurse, for example. All the actors were men, and the choruses were well-trained boys. By switching masks, each actor could play several roles.

The Dionysia: Dueling Dramatists

As many as fourteen thousand spectators gathered in the open-air theater to watch as playwrights competed for prizes in tragedy and comedy. Three dramatists in each category presented their plays over three days. Each day, one of the playwrights presented a comedy and another playwright presented three tragedies and a satyr play. The **comedies** featured ordinary people as characters and had happy endings. The **satyr plays** were comic versions of the same themes presented in the tragedies. But the **tragedies** themselves—serious treatments of mythic questions with heroic characters and unhappy endings—dominated the program.

Tragedy and the Tragic Hero

In his *Poetics*, the Greek philosopher Aristotle (384–322 B.C.) makes observations about Greek tragedy that people still use to talk about drama, both ancient and modern. Some of his observations follow:

- **The function of tragedy is to arouse pity and fear in the audience so that we may be purged, or cleansed, of these unsettling emotions.** Aristotle's term for this emotional purging is the Greek word *catharsis:* the strangely pleasurable sense of emotional release we experience after watching a great tragedy.

- **A true tragic hero should be someone "highly renowned and prosperous."** If the hero doesn't experience a tremendous reversal of fortune, the thinking goes, we won't feel such pity. We feel fear because the hero is *better* than we are, and *still* he failed.

- **The tragic hero is responsible for his or her downfall because of some "error or frailty."** Aristotle called this weakness *hamartia* (hä′mär·tē′ə), which is often translated as "tragic flaw." Some critics believe Aristotle considered a single error of judgment to be a tragic flaw. Others say that the tragic hero must have a fundamental character weakness, such as destructive pride or obsessive jealousy. Indeed, the tragic flaw in Greek drama is often *hubris* (hyo͞o′bris), or arrogant pride. According to Aristotle, the tragic hero recognizes his or her own error and accepts its tragic consequences.

BEFORE YOU READ

Antigone

Meet the Playwright

Sophocles (496?–406 B.C.)

Sophocles is generally considered the greatest of the ancient Greek playwrights. Few writers from any period have had a greater impact on drama, and few have been better loved in their own lifetimes.

A prominent citizen of Athens, Sophocles was known for his musical, poetic, and dramatic talents. He also took an active role in public life, serving as general, political leader, and priest. He is said to have been extremely handsome and graceful. At the age of about seventeen, he was the *choragos*, or chorus leader, in a dramatic celebration of Greece's victory over Persia. When he was twenty-eight, he caused a sensation by winning first prize for tragedy at the festival of Dionysus, defeating Aeschylus, the leading playwright of the day. Later, Sophocles served as a general under Pericles. Over the next sixty-two years, Sophocles won twenty-four first prizes and seven second prizes in thirty-one competitions—the best record of any Greek playwright. Late in his life he was one of the elder statesmen who organized the recovery of Athens after its defeat at Syracuse.

Moralist and Innovator

Sophocles made good use of a remarkably long life, writing more than one hundred and twenty tragedies, of which only seven survive. A religious conservative, he was deeply concerned with the individual's need to find a place in the existing moral and cosmic order. His plays always contain a moral lesson—usually a caution against pride and religious indifference. Sophocles was also a great technical innovator: He added a third actor to Aeschylus's original two, introduced painted sets, and expanded the size of the chorus to fifteen.

Few plays are more widely admired than Sophocles' "Theban" plays—three tragedies about King Oedipus of Thebes and his family. Sophocles wrote these plays over a forty-year period, and he actually began with the third and chronologically last part of the story, *Antigone*, first performed in 442 B.C. Twelve years later, Sophocles backtracked and wrote the first part of the story, *Oedipus Rex*, which tells the myth of King Oedipus. It wasn't until the last year of his life that Sophocles wrote the middle segment, *Oedipus at Colonus*, which recounts the death and redemption of Oedipus in exile and old age.

Background to *Antigone*

The basic plot of *Antigone* is part of a long myth that was as familiar to Athenian audiences as stories about the Pilgrims are to Americans today: the myth of Oedipus the King.

A Tragic Myth: The House of Thebes

The myth of Oedipus begins with King Laius and Queen Jocasta of Thebes learning from an oracle that their newborn son will one day kill his father and marry his mother. Horrified by this prediction, they give their baby to a shepherd, with orders to leave the infant to die on a lonely mountainside with his ankles pinned together. The shepherd, however, takes pity on the baby. Instead of abandoning him, he gives him to a Corinthian shepherd, who in turn gives the baby to the childless king and queen of Corinth. They name him Oedipus, which means "swollen foot" or "club foot," and raise him as their son.

When Oedipus is a young man, he learns of the oracle's prophecy. Believing the king and queen of Corinth to be his real parents, he runs away from home in horror. In the course of his wanderings, he encounters an arrogant old man who tries to run him off the road with his chariot. Because honor is at stake, the two men fight, and Oedipus kills the stranger. He then continues on his journey to the city of Thebes.

Meeting the Monster Sphinx

At the outskirts of the city, Oedipus encounters the Sphinx, a terrible monster with the wings of an eagle, the body of a lion, and the face of a woman. This Sphinx has been menacing Thebes by ambushing travelers going to the city and challenging them to answer a riddle. If the unfortunate travelers can answer the riddle correctly—which no one has been able to do—they can proceed; if not, the Sphinx devours them. Famine is near at hand: No goods can come into the city of Thebes.

The Sphinx's riddle goes like this: "What creature goes on four legs in the morning, two legs in the afternoon, and three legs in the evening?" Oedipus immediately guesses that the answer to the riddle is "man," who crawls on all fours as an infant, walks on two legs as an adult, and leans on a cane in old age. Upon hearing Oedipus's answer, the defeated Sphinx leaps off a high rock. Thebes is saved.

A Hero's Welcome in Thebes

When Oedipus arrives in Thebes, the city where (unknown to him) he had been born, the people welcome him as their savior. Since Laius, their king, has recently been killed, the Thebans offer Oedipus their throne and the widowed queen, Jocasta, as his bride. So Oedipus becomes king of Thebes, marries Jocasta, and has four children with her: two sons, Polynices and Eteocles; and two daughters, Antigone and Ismene. All goes well for many years until a plague strikes Thebes. Desperate to learn the cause, Oedipus sends Jocasta's brother, Creon, to consult the great oracle at Delphi.

A Horrible Discovery

The oracle warns that the plague will not end until Thebes has punished the murderer of King Laius. Oedipus vows to find this murderer. After questioning several people, including the blind prophet Tiresias, he discovers that the man he had killed on the road years before was none other than King Laius. Furthermore, he learns that Laius and Jocasta were his original parents. Thus Oedipus has unwittingly fulfilled the oracle's prophecy—he has killed his father and married his mother. When Oedipus and Jocasta discover this horrible truth, she kills herself and he gouges out his eyes to punish himself for having been blind to the truth.

After these disasters, Creon takes over as regent (acting ruler) of Thebes, and after several years he decides to exile Oedipus. Accompanied only by his daughter Antigone (in some versions of the myth, also by Ismene), Oedipus wanders the countryside as a beggar until he reaches the sanctuary of Colonus, where he dies.

Antigone's Story: The Gods' Laws or Man's?

Antigone returns to Thebes, where her two brothers have agreed to rule in alternate years. Eteocles' turn comes first, but when it ends, he refuses to give up his throne to Polynices. Polynices flees to the city of Argos, where he raises an army; he then returns with his men and attacks Thebes. The Thebans repulse the attack, but in the course of battle, Eteocles and Polynices kill each other. Creon then becomes king of Thebes and gives Eteocles a hero's burial. Creon considers Polynices a traitor, so he decrees that Polynices' body be left unburied, to rot outside the city gates. To the Greeks, this was a terrible punishment: Their holiest laws demanded that certain burial rites be performed, or else the soul of the dead person would be condemned to eternal unrest. This is the basis of Creon's conflict with the strong-willed Antigone. As you will see, she believes that spiritual laws must be obeyed, whatever the consequences.

Antigone

Sophocles

Translated by **Robert Fagles**

> **CHARACTERS**
>
> **Antigone** (an·tig′ə·nē′), daughter of Oedipus and Jocasta
> **Ismene** (is·men′ē), sister of Antigone
> **A Chorus** of old Theban citizens and their **Leader**
> **Creon,** king of Thebes, uncle of Antigone and Ismene
> **A Sentry**
> **Haemon** (hā′mən), son of Creon and Eurydice
> **Tiresias** (tī·rē′sē·əs), a blind prophet
> **A Messenger**
> **Eurydice** (yōō·ri′də·sē), wife of Creon
> Guards, attendants, and a boy

Time and Scene: The royal house of Thebes. It is still night, and the invading armies of Argos have just been driven from the city. Fighting on opposite sides, the sons of Oedipus, Eteocles and Polynices, have killed each other in combat. Their uncle, Creon, is now king of Thebes.

Enter ANTIGONE, *slipping through the central doors of the palace. She motions to her sister,* ISMENE, *who follows her cautiously toward an altar at the center of the stage.*

Antigone.
My own flesh and blood—dear sister, dear Ismene,
how many griefs our father Oedipus handed down!
Do you know one, I ask you, one grief
that Zeus will not perfect for the two of us
while we still live and breathe? There's nothing,
no pain—our lives are pain—no private shame,
no public disgrace, nothing I haven't seen
in your griefs and mine. And now this:
an emergency decree, they say, the Commander
10   has just declared for all of Thebes.
What, haven't you heard? Don't you see?
The doom reserved for enemies
marches on the ones we love the most.

Ismene.
Not I, I haven't heard a word, Antigone.
Nothing of loved ones,
no joy or pain has come my way, not since
the two of us were robbed of our two brothers,
both gone in a day, a double blow—
not since the armies of Argos vanished,
20   just this very night. I know nothing more,
whether our luck's improved or ruin's still to come.

Antigone.
I thought so. That's why I brought you out here,
past the gates, so you could hear in private.

Ismene.
What's the matter? Trouble, clearly . . .
you sound so dark, so grim.

Antigone.
Why not? Our own brothers' burial!
Hasn't Creon graced one with all the rites,

disgraced the other? Eteocles, they say,
has been given full military honors,
rightly so—Creon's laid him in the earth
and he goes with glory down among the dead.
But the body of Polynices, who died miserably—
why, a city-wide proclamation, rumor has it,
forbids anyone to bury him, even mourn him.
He's to be left unwept, unburied, a lovely treasure
for birds that scan the field and feast to their heart's content.

Such, I hear, is the martial law our good Creon
lays down for you and me—yes, me, I tell you—
and he's coming here to alert the uninformed
in no uncertain terms,
and he won't treat the matter lightly. Whoever
disobeys in the least will die, his doom is sealed:
stoning to death inside the city walls!

There you have it. You'll soon show what you are,
worth your breeding, Ismene, or a coward—
for all your royal blood.

Ismene.
My poor sister, if things have come to this,
who am I to make or mend them, tell me,
what good am I to you?

Antigone.
                                        Decide.
Will you share the labor, share the work?

Ismene.
What work, what's the risk? What do you mean?

Antigone. (*Raising her hands.*)
Will you lift up his body with these bare hands
and lower it with me?

Ismene.
                                What? You'd bury him—
when a law forbids the city?

Antigone.
                                Yes!
He is my brother and—deny it as you will—
your brother too.
No one will ever convict me for a traitor.

Ismene.

So desperate, and Creon has expressly—

Antigone.

No,

he has no right to keep me from my own.

Ismene.

60   Oh my sister, think—

think how our own father died, hated,

his reputation in ruins, driven on

by the crimes he brought to light himself

to gouge out his eyes with his own hands—

then mother . . . his mother and wife, both in one,

mutilating her life in the twisted noose—

and last, our two brothers dead in a single day,

both shedding their own blood, poor suffering boys,

battling out their common destiny hand-to-hand.

70   Now look at the two of us, left so alone . . .

think what a death we'll die, the worst of all

if we violate the laws and override

the fixed decree of the throne, its power—

we must be sensible. Remember we are women,

we're not born to contend with men. Then too,

we're underlings, ruled by much stronger hands,

so we must submit in this, and things still worse.

I, for one, I'll beg the dead to forgive me—

I'm forced, I have no choice—I must obey

80   the ones who stand in power. Why rush to extremes?

It's madness, madness.

Antigone.

I won't insist,

no, even if you should have a change of heart,

I'd never welcome you in the labor, not with me.

So, do as you like, whatever suits you best—

I'll bury him myself.

And even if I die in the act, that death will be a glory.

I'll lie with the one I love and loved by him—

an outrage sacred to the gods! I have longer

to please the dead than please the living here:

90   in the kingdom down below I'll lie forever.

Do as you like, dishonor the laws

the gods hold in honor.

Ismene.
>   I'd do them no dishonor . . .
> but defy the city? I have no strength for that.

Antigone.
> You have your excuses. I am on my way,
> I'll raise a mound for him, for my dear brother.

Ismene.
> Oh Antigone, you're so rash—I'm so afraid for you!

Antigone.
> Don't fear for me. Set your own life in order.

Ismene.
> Then don't, at least, blurt this out to anyone.
> Keep it a secret. I'll join you in that, I promise.

Antigone.
100
> Dear god, shout it from the rooftops. I'll hate you
> all the more for silence—tell the world!

Ismene.
> So fiery—and it ought to chill your heart.

Antigone.
> I know I please where I must please the most.

Ismene.
> Yes, if you can, but you're in love with impossibility.

Antigone.
> Very well then, once my strength gives out
> I will be done at last.

Ismene.
>   You're wrong from the start,
> you're off on a hopeless quest.

Antigone.
> If you say so, you will make me hate you,
> and the hatred of the dead, by all rights,
110
> will haunt you night and day.
> But leave me to my own absurdity, leave me
> to suffer this—dreadful thing. I'll suffer
> nothing as great as death without glory.

> *[Exit to the side.]*

Ismene.
> Then go if you must, but rest assured,
> wild, irrational as you are, my sister,
> you are truly dear to the ones who love you.

[Withdrawing to the palace.]

[Enter a CHORUS, the old citizens of Thebes, chanting as the sun begins to rise.]

Chorus.
>   Glory!—great beam of the sun, brightest of all
>   that ever rose on the seven gates of Thebes,
>   you burn through night at last!
>   Great eye of the golden day,
120   mounting the Dirce's banks° you throw him back—
>   the enemy out of Argos, the white shield, the man of bronze—
>   he's flying headlong now
>   the bridle of fate stampeding him with pain!
>
>   And he had driven against our borders,
>   launched by the warring claims of Polynices—
>   like an eagle screaming, winging havoc
>   over the land, wings of armor
>   shielded white as snow,
130   a huge army massing,
>   crested helmets bristling for assault.
>
>   He hovered above our roofs, his vast maw gaping
>   closing down around our seven gates,
>   his spears thirsting for the kill
>   but now he's gone, look,
>   before he could glut his jaws with Theban blood
>   or the god of fire put our crown of towers to the torch.
>   He grappled the Dragon none can master—Thebes°—
>   the clang of our arms like thunder at his back!
>
140   Zeus hates with a vengeance all bravado,
>   the mighty boasts of men. He watched them
>   coming on in a rising flood, the pride
>   of their golden armor ringing shrill—
>   and brandishing his lightning
>   blasted the fighter just at the goal,
>   rushing to shout his triumph from our walls.°
>
>   Down from the heights he crashed, pounding down on the earth!

121. Dirce's banks: Dirce (dʉr′sē) is a stream near Thebes, named for a queen of Thebes who was thrown into the stream after she was murdered.

138. the Dragon . . . Thebes: Thebes is identified with the dragon because a dragon once guarded the field where Thebes was founded. The teeth of the dragon turned into warriors who helped establish the city.

140–146. Zeus . . . walls: Zeus, who sided with the Thebans, struck the first Argive attacker with a thunderbolt.

And a moment ago, blazing torch in hand—
    mad for attack, ecstatic
150   he breathed his rage, the storm
    of his fury hurling at our heads!
But now his high hopes have laid him low
and down the enemy ranks the iron god of war
    deals his rewards, his stunning blows—Ares°
    rapture of battle, our right arm in the crisis.

154. Ares (er′ēz′): god of war.

Seven captains marshaled at seven gates
seven against their equals, gave
their brazen trophies up to Zeus,
god of the breaking rout of battle,
160   all but two: those blood brothers,
one father, one mother—matched in rage,
spears matched for the twin conquest—
clashed and won the common prize of death.

But now for Victory! Glorious in the morning,
joy in her eyes to meet our joy
    she is winging down to Thebes,
our fleets of chariots wheeling in her wake—
    Now let us win oblivion from the wars,
thronging the temples of the gods
170   in singing, dancing choirs through the night!
    Lord Dionysus, god of the dance
    that shakes the land of Thebes, now lead the way!

[*Enter* CREON *from the palace, attended by his guard.*]

But look, the king of the realm is coming,
Creon, the new man for the new day,
whatever the gods are sending now . . .
what new plan will he launch?
Why this, this special session?
Why this sudden call to the old men
summoned at one command?

Creon.
                   My countrymen,
180   the ship of state is safe. The gods who rocked her,
after a long, merciless pounding in the storm,
have righted her once more.

                                        Out of the whole city
I have called you here alone. Well I know,
first, your undeviating respect
for the throne and royal power of King Laius.
Next, while Oedipus steered the land of Thebes,
and even after he died, your loyalty was unshakable,
you still stood by their children. Now then,
since the two sons are dead—two blows of fate
190   in the same day, cut down by each other's hands,
both killers, both brothers stained with blood—
as I am next in kin to the dead,
I now possess the throne and all its powers.

Of course you cannot know a man completely,
his character, his principles, sense of judgment,
not till he's shown his colors, ruling the people,
making laws. Experience, there's the test.
As I see it, whoever assumes the task,
the awesome task of setting the city's course,
200   and refuses to adopt the soundest policies
but fearing someone, keeps his lips locked tight,
he's utterly worthless. So I rate him now,
I always have. And whoever places a friend
above the good of his own country, he is nothing:
I have no use for him. Zeus my witness,
Zeus who sees all things, always—
I could never stand by silent, watching destruction
march against our city, putting safety to rout,
nor could I ever make that man a friend of mine
210   who menaces our country. Remember this:
our country *is* our safety.
Only while she voyages true on course
can we establish friendships, truer than blood itself.
Such are my standards. They make our city great.

Closely akin to them I have proclaimed,
just now, the following decree to our people
concerning the two sons of Oedipus.
Eteocles, who died fighting for Thebes,
excelling all in arms: he shall be buried,
220   crowned with a hero's honors, the cups we pour
to soak the earth and reach the famous dead.°

220–221. the cups . . . dead: In
ancient Greek custom, wine
(sometimes mixed with honey,
milk, or water) was poured on
the ground to honor the gods
and, in many cases, to satisfy
the dead buried below. This
ritual pouring of wine is called
a libation (lī·bā′shən).

But as for his blood brother, Polynices,
who returned from exile, home to his father-city
and the gods of his race, consumed with one desire—
to burn them roof to roots—who thirsted to drink
his kinsmen's blood and sell the rest to slavery:
that man—a proclamation has forbidden the city
to dignify him with burial, mourn him at all.
No, he must be left unburied, his corpse
230   carrion for the birds and dogs to tear,
an obscenity for the citizens to behold!

These are my principles. Never at my hands
will the traitor be honored above the patriot.
But whoever proves his loyalty to the state:
I'll prize that man in death as well as life.

Leader.

If this is your pleasure, Creon, treating
our city's enemy and our friend this way . . .
The power is yours, I suppose, to enforce it
with the laws, both for the dead and all of us,
the living.

Creon.

240   Follow my orders closely then,
be on your guard.

Leader.

                    We're too old.
Lay that burden on younger shoulders.

Creon.

                          No, no,
I don't mean the body—I've posted guards already.

Leader.

What commands for us then? What other service?

Creon.

See that you never side with those who break my orders.

Leader.

Never. Only a fool could be in love with death.

Creon.

Death is the price—you're right. But all too often
the mere hope of money has ruined many men.

[*A* SENTRY *enters from the side.*]

Sentry.

My lord,

    I can't say I'm winded from running, or set out
250   with any spring in my legs either—no sir,
    I was lost in thought, and it made me stop, often,
    dead in my tracks, wheeling, turning back,
    and all the time a voice inside me muttering,
    "Idiot, why? You're going straight to your death."
    Then muttering, "Stopped again, poor fool?
    If somebody gets the news to Creon first,
    what's to save your neck?"

And so,

    mulling it over, on I trudged, dragging my feet,
    you can make a short road take forever . . .
260   but at last, look, common sense won out,
    I'm here, and I'm all yours,
    and even though I come empty-handed
    I'll tell my story just the same, because
    I've come with a good grip on one hope,
    what will come will come, whatever fate—

Creon.

    Come to the point!
    What's wrong—why so afraid?

Sentry.

    First, myself, I've got to tell you,
    I didn't do it, didn't see who did—
270   Be fair, don't take it out on me.

Creon.

    You're playing it safe, soldier,
    barricading yourself from any trouble.
    It's obvious, you've something strange to tell.

Sentry.

    Dangerous too, and danger makes you delay
    for all you're worth.

Creon.

    Out with it—then dismiss!

Sentry.

    All right, here it comes. The body—
    someone's just buried it, then run off . . .
    sprinkled some dry dust on the flesh,
    given it proper rites.

Creon.

280 What?

What man alive would dare—

Sentry.

I've no idea, I swear it.
There was no mark of a spade, no pickaxe there,
no earth turned up, the ground packed hard and dry,
unbroken, no tracks, no wheelruts, nothing,
the workman left no trace. Just at sunup
the first watch of the day points it out—
it was a wonder! We were stunned . . .
a terrific burden too, for all of us, listen:
you can't see the corpse, not that it's buried,
290 really, just a light cover of road-dust on it,
as if someone meant to lay the dead to rest
and keep from getting cursed.
Not a sign in sight that dogs or wild beasts
had worried the body, even torn the skin.

But what came next! Rough talk flew thick and fast,
guard grilling guard—we'd have come to blows
at last, nothing to stop it; each man for himself
and each the culprit, no one caught red-handed,
all of us pleading ignorance, dodging the charges,
300 ready to take up red-hot iron in our fists,
go through fire, swear oaths to the gods—
"I didn't do it, I had no hand in it either,
not in the plotting, not the work itself!"

Finally, after all this wrangling came to nothing,
one man spoke out and made us stare at the ground,
hanging our heads in fear. No way to counter him,
no way to take his advice and come through
safe and sound. Here's what he said:
"Look, we've got to report the facts to Creon,
310 we can't keep this hidden." Well, that won out,
and the lot fell to me, condemned me,
unlucky as ever, I got the prize. So here I am,
against my will and yours too, well I know—
no one wants the man who brings bad news.

Leader.

My king,
ever since he began I've been debating in my mind,

could this possibly be the work of the gods?
Creon.

                                            Stop—
before you make me choke with anger—the gods!
You, you're senile, must you be insane?
You say—why it's intolerable—say the gods

320   could have the slightest concern for that corpse?
Tell me, was it for meritorious service
they proceeded to bury him, prized him so? The hero
who came to burn their temples ringed with pillars,
their golden treasures—scorch their hallowed earth
and fling their laws to the winds.
Exactly when did you last see the gods
celebrating traitors? Inconceivable!

No, from the first there were certain citizens
who could hardly stand the spirit of my regime,

330   grumbling against me in the dark, heads together,
tossing wildly, never keeping their necks beneath
the yoke, loyally submitting to their king.
These are the instigators, I'm convinced—
they've perverted my own guard, bribed them
to do their work.

                        Money! Nothing worse
in our lives, so current, rampant, so corrupting.
Money—you demolish cities, root men from their homes,
you train and twist good minds and set them on
to the most atrocious schemes. No limit,

340   you make them adept at every kind of outrage,
every godless crime—money!

                          Everyone—
the whole crew bribed to commit this crime,
they've made one thing sure at least:
sooner or later they will pay the price.
(*Wheeling on the* SENTRY.)   You—
I swear to Zeus as I still believe in Zeus,
if you don't find the man who buried that corpse,
the very man, and produce him before my eyes,
simple death won't be enough for you,
not till we string you up alive

350   and wring the immorality out of you.
Then you can steal the rest of your days,

better informed about where to make a killing.
You'll have learned, at last, it doesn't pay
to itch for rewards from every hand that beckons.
Filthy profits wreck most men, you'll see—
they'll never save your life.

Sentry.

                    Please,
may I say a word or two, or just turn and go?

Creon.

Can't you tell? Everything you say offends me.

Sentry.

Where does it hurt you, in the ears or in the heart?

Creon.

360   And who are you to pinpoint my displeasure?

Sentry.

The culprit grates on your feelings,
I just annoy your ears.

Creon.

               Still talking?
You talk too much! A born nuisance—

Sentry.

                    Maybe so,
but I never did this thing, so help me!

Creon.

                 Yes you did—
what's more, you squandered your life for silver!

Sentry.

Oh it's terrible when the one who does the judging
judges things all wrong.

Creon.

             Well now,
you just be clever about your judgments—
if you fail to produce the criminals for me,
370   you'll swear your dirty money brought you pain.

[*Turning sharply, reentering the palace.*]

Sentry.

I hope he's found. Best thing by far.
But caught or not, that's in the lap of fortune;
I'll never come back, you've seen the last of me.
I'm saved, even now, and I never thought,

I never hoped—
dear gods, I owe you all my thanks!

[*Rushing out.*]

Chorus.

Numberless wonders
terrible wonders walk the world but none the match for man—
that great wonder crossing the heaving gray sea,
driven on by the blasts of winter
380   on through breakers crashing left and right,
holds his steady course
and the oldest of the gods he wears away—
the Earth, the immortal, the inexhaustible—
as his plows go back and forth, year in, year out
with the breed of stallions turning up the furrows.

And the blithe, lightheaded race of birds he snares,
the tribes of savage beasts, the life that swarms the depths—
with one fling of his nets
woven and coiled tight, he takes them all,
390   man the skilled, the brilliant!
He conquers all, taming with his techniques
the prey that roams the cliffs and wild lairs,
training the stallion, clamping the yoke across
his shaggy neck, and the tireless mountain bull.

And speech and thought, quick as the wind
and the mood and mind for law that rules the city—
all these he has taught himself
and shelter from the arrows of the frost
when there's rough lodging under the cold clear sky
400   and the shafts of lashing rain—
ready, resourceful man!
Never without resources
never an impasse as he marches on the future—
only Death, from Death alone he will find no rescue
but from desperate plagues he has plotted his escapes.

Man the master, ingenious past all measure
past all dreams, the skills within his grasp—
he forges on, now to destruction

now again to greatness. When he weaves in
410   the laws of the land, and the justice of the gods
that binds his oaths together
                    he and his city rise high—
                            but the city casts out
that man who weds himself to inhumanity
thanks to reckless daring. Never share my hearth
never think my thoughts, whoever does such things.

[*Enter* ANTIGONE *from the side, accompanied by the* SENTRY.]

Here is a dark sign from the gods—
what to make of this? I know her,
how can I deny it? That young girl's Antigone!
420   Wretched, child of a wretched father,
Oedipus. Look, is it possible?
They bring you in like a prisoner—
why? did you break the king's laws?
Did they take you in some act of mad defiance?
Sentry.
She's the one, she did it single-handed—
we caught her burying the body. Where's Creon?

[*Enter* CREON *from the palace.*]

Leader.
Back again, just in time when you need him.
Creon.
In time for what? What is it?
Sentry.
                    My king,
there's nothing you can swear you'll never do—
430   second thoughts make liars of us all.
I could have sworn I wouldn't hurry back
(what with your threats, the buffeting I just took),
but a stroke of luck beyond our wildest hopes,
what a joy, there's nothing like it. So,
back I've come, breaking my oath, who cares?
I'm bringing in our prisoner—this young girl—
we took her giving the dead the last rites.
But no casting lots this time; this is *my* luck,
my prize, no one else's.

Now, my lord,
here she is. Take her, question her,
cross-examine her to your heart's content.
But set me free, it's only right—
I'm rid of this dreadful business once for all.

Creon.
Prisoner! Her? You took her—where, doing what?

Sentry.
Burying the man. That's the whole story.

Creon.
What?
You mean what you say, you're telling me the truth?

Sentry.
She's the one. With my own eyes I saw her
bury the body, just what you've forbidden.
There. Is that plain and clear?

Creon.
What did you see? Did you catch her in the act?

Sentry.
Here's what happened. We went back to our post,
those threats of yours breathing down our necks—
we brushed the corpse clean of the dust that covered it,
stripped it bare . . . it was slimy, going soft,
and we took to high ground, backs to the wind
so the stink of him couldn't hit us;
jostling, baiting each other to keep awake,
shouting back and forth—no napping on the job,
not this time. And so the hours dragged by
until the sun stood dead above our heads,
a huge white ball in the noon sky, beating,
blazing down, and then it happened—
suddenly, a whirlwind!
Twisting a great dust-storm up from the earth,
a black plague of the heavens, filling the plain,
ripping the leaves off every tree in sight,
choking the air and sky. We squinted hard
and took our whipping from the gods.

And after the storm passed—it seemed endless—
there, we saw the girl!
And she cried out a sharp, piercing cry,
like a bird come back to an empty nest,

peering into its bed, and all the babies gone . . .
Just so, when she sees the corpse bare
she bursts into a long, shattering wail
and calls down withering curses on the heads
of all who did the work. And she scoops up dry dust,
handfuls, quickly, and lifting a fine bronze urn,
lifting it high and pouring, she crowns the dead
with three full libations.

480   Soon as we saw
we rushed her, closed on the kill like hunters,
and she, she didn't flinch. We interrogated her,
charging her with offenses past and present—
she stood up to it all, denied nothing. I tell you,
it made me ache and laugh in the same breath.
It's pure joy to escape the worst yourself,
it hurts a man to bring down his friends.
But all that, I'm afraid, means less to me
than my own skin. That's the way I'm made.

Creon.
(*Wheeling on* ANTIGONE.)
                                         You,

490   with your eyes fixed on the ground—speak up.
Do you deny you did this, yes or no?

Antigone.
I did it. I don't deny a thing.

Creon.
(*To the* SENTRY.)
You, get out, wherever you please—
you're clear of a very heavy charge.

[*He leaves;* CREON *turns back to* ANTIGONE.]

You, tell me briefly, no long speeches—
were you aware a decree had forbidden this?

Antigone.
Well aware. How could I avoid it? It was public.

Creon.
And still you had the gall to break this law?

Antigone.
Of course I did. It wasn't Zeus, not in the least,
500   who made this proclamation—not to me.

Nor did that Justice, dwelling with the gods
beneath the earth, ordain such laws for men.
Nor did I think your edict had such force
that you, a mere mortal, could override the gods,
the great unwritten, unshakable traditions.
They are alive, not just today or yesterday:
they live forever, from the first of time,
and no one knows when they first saw the light.

510
These laws—I was not about to break them,
not out of fear of some man's wounded pride,
and face the retribution of the gods.
Die I must, I've known it all my life—
how could I keep from knowing?—even without
your death-sentence ringing in my ears.
And if I am to die before my time
I consider that a gain. Who on earth,
alive in the midst of so much grief as I,
could fail to find his death a rich reward?
So for me, at least, to meet this doom of yours

520
is precious little pain. But if I had allowed
my own mother's son to rot, an unburied corpse—
that would have been an agony! This is nothing.
And if my present actions strike you as foolish,
let's just say I've been accused of folly
by a fool.

Leader.
        Like father like daughter,
passionate, wild . . .
she hasn't learned to bend before adversity.

Creon.
No? Believe me, the stiffest stubborn wills
fall the hardest; the toughest iron,

530
tempered strong in the white-hot fire,
you'll see it crack and shatter first of all.
And I've known spirited horses you can break
with a light bit—proud, rebellious horses.
There's no room for pride, not in a slave,
not with the lord and master standing by.

This girl was an old hand at insolence
when she overrode the edicts we made public.

But once she'd done it—the insolence,
twice over—to glory in it, laughing,
540   mocking us to our face with what she'd done.
I'm not the man, not now: she is the man
if this victory goes to her and she goes free.

Never! Sister's child or closer in blood
than all my family clustered at my altar
worshiping Guardian Zeus—she'll never escape,
she and her blood sister, the most barbaric death.
Yes, I accuse her sister of an equal part
in scheming this, this burial.
(*To his attendants.*)
                           Bring her here!
I just saw her inside, hysterical, gone to pieces.
550   It never fails: the mind convicts itself
in advance, when scoundrels are up to no good,
plotting in the dark. Oh but I hate it more
when a traitor, caught red-handed,
tries to glorify his crimes.

Antigone.
Creon, what more do you want
than my arrest and execution?

Creon.
Nothing. Then I have it all.

Antigone.
Then why delay? Your moralizing repels me,
every word you say—pray god it always will.
So naturally all I say repels you too.
560   Enough.
Give me glory! What greater glory could I win
than to give my own brother decent burial?
These citizens here would all agree,
(*To the* CHORUS.)
they'd praise me too
if their lips weren't locked in fear.
(*Pointing to* CREON.)
Lucky tyrants—the perquisites of power!
Ruthless power to do and say whatever pleases *them*.

Creon.
You alone, of all the people in Thebes,
see things that way.

Antigone.
                    They see it just that way
570   but defer to you and keep their tongues in leash.
Creon.
        And you, aren't you ashamed to differ so from them?
        So disloyal!
Antigone.
                Not ashamed for a moment,
        not to honor my brother, my own flesh and blood.
Creon.
        Wasn't Eteocles a brother too—cut down, facing him?
Antigone.
        Brother, yes, by the same mother, the same father.
Creon.
        Then how can you render his enemy such honors,
        such impieties in his eyes?
Antigone.
        He'll never testify to that,
        Eteocles dead and buried.
Creon.
                            He will—
580   if you honor the traitor just as much as him.
Antigone.
        But it was his brother, not some slave that died—
Creon.
        Ravaging our country!—
        but Eteocles died fighting in our behalf.
Antigone.
        No matter—Death longs for the same rites for all.
Creon.
        Never the same for the patriot and the traitor.
Antigone.
        Who, Creon, who on earth can say the ones below
        don't find this pure and uncorrupt?
Creon.
        Never. Once an enemy, never a friend,
        not even after death.
Antigone.
590   I was born to join in love, not hate—
        that is my nature.

Creon.

             Go down below and love,
if love you must—love the dead! While I'm alive,
no woman is going to lord it over me.

[*Enter* ISMENE *from the palace, under guard.*]

Chorus.

                        Look,
Ismene's coming, weeping a sister's tears,
loving sister, under a cloud . . .
her face is flushed, her cheeks streaming.
Sorrow puts her lovely radiance in the dark.

Creon.

                      You—
in my own house, you viper, slinking undetected,
sucking my life-blood! I never knew
I was breeding twin disasters, the two of you
rising up against my throne. Come, tell me,
will you confess your part in the crime or not?
Answer me. Swear to me.

Ismene.

               I did it, yes—
if only she consents—I share the guilt,
the consequences too.

Antigone.

            No,
Justice will never suffer that—not you,
you were unwilling. I never brought you in.

Ismene.

But now you face such dangers . . . I'm not ashamed
to sail through trouble with you,
make your troubles mine.

Antigone.

                Who did the work?
Let the dead and the god of death bear witness!
I've no love for a friend who loves in words alone.

Ismene.

Oh no, my sister, don't reject me, please,
let me die beside you, consecrating
the dead together.

Antigone.

           Never share my dying,

don't lay claim to what you never touched.
My death will be enough.

Ismene.

What do I care for life, cut off from you?

Antigone.

Ask Creon. Your concern is all for him.

Ismene.

Why abuse me so? It doesn't help you now.

Antigone.

620
                                           You're right—
if I mock you, I get no pleasure from it,
only pain.

Ismene.

           Tell me, dear one,
what can I do to help you, even now?

Antigone.

Save yourself. I don't grudge you your survival.

Ismene.

Oh no, no, denied my portion in your death?

Antigone.

You chose to live, I chose to die.

Ismene.

                              Not, at least,
without every kind of caution I could voice.

Antigone.

Your wisdom appealed to one world—mine, another.

Ismene.

But look, we're both guilty, both condemned to death.

Antigone.

630
Courage! Live your life. I gave myself to death,
long ago, so I might serve the dead.

Creon.

They're both mad, I tell you, the two of them.
One's just shown it, the other's been that way
since she was born.

Ismene.

               True, my king,
the sense we were born with cannot last forever . . .
commit cruelty on a person long enough
and the mind begins to go.

Creon.

                    Yours did,

when you chose to commit your crimes with her.

Ismene.

How can I live alone, without her?

Creon.

            Her?

640 Don't even mention her—she no longer exists.

Ismene.

What? You'd kill your own son's bride?

Creon.

           Absolutely:

there are other fields for him to plow.

Ismene.

           Perhaps,

but never as true, as close a bond as theirs.

Creon.

A worthless woman for my son? It repels me.

Ismene.

Dearest Haemon, your father wrongs you so!

Creon.

Enough, enough—you and your talk of marriage!

Ismene.

Creon—you're really going to rob your son of Antigone?

Creon.

Death will do it for me—break their marriage off.

Leader.

So, it's settled then? Antigone must die?

Creon.

650 Settled, yes—we both know that.

(*To the guards.*)

Stop wasting time. Take them in.

From now on they'll act like women.

Tie them up, no more running loose;

even the bravest will cut and run,

once they see Death coming for their lives.

[*The guards escort* ANTIGONE *and* ISMENE *into the palace.* CREON

remains while the old citizens form their chorus.]

Chorus.

Blest, they are the truly blest who all their lives

have never tasted devastation. For others, once

the gods have rocked a house to its foundations

the ruin will never cease, cresting on and on

660 from one generation on throughout the race—
like a great mounting tide
driven on by savage northern gales,
      surging over the dead black depths
roiling up from the bottom dark heaves of sand
and the headlands, taking the storm's onslaught full-force,
roar, and the low moaning
              echoes on and on
                     and now
as in ancient times I see the sorrows of the house,
the living heirs of the old ancestral kings,
piling on the sorrows of the dead

670   and one generation cannot free the next—
some god will bring them crashing down,
the race finds no release.
And now the light, the hope
      springing up from the late last root
in the house of Oedipus, that hope's cut down in turn
by the long, bloody knife swung by the gods of death
by a senseless word
        by fury at the heart.
                 Zeus,
yours is the power, Zeus, what man on earth
can override it, who can hold it back?

680 Power that neither Sleep, the all-ensnaring
    no, nor the tireless months of heaven
can ever overmaster—young through all time,
mighty lord of power, you hold fast
    the dazzling crystal mansions of Olympus.
And throughout the future, late and soon
as through the past, your law prevails:
no towering form of greatness
      enters into the lives of mortals
           free and clear of ruin.
               True,

690 our dreams, our high hopes voyaging far and wide
bring sheer delight to many, to many others
    delusion, blithe, mindless lusts
and the fraud steals on one slowly . . . unaware
till he trips and puts his foot into the fire.
    He was a wise old man who coined

the famous saying: "Sooner or later
foul is fair, fair is foul
to the man the gods will ruin"—
  He goes his way for a moment only
700   free of blinding ruin.

[*Enter* HAEMON *from the palace.*]

  Here's Haemon now, the last of all your sons.
  Does he come in tears for his bride,
  his doomed bride, Antigone—
  bitter at being cheated of their marriage?
Creon.
  We'll soon know, better than seers° could tell us.
  (*Turning to* HAEMON.)
  Son, you've heard the final verdict on your bride?
  Are you coming now, raving against your father?
  Or do you love me, no matter what I do?
Haemon.
  Father, I'm your *son* . . . you in your wisdom
710   set my bearings for me—I obey you.
  No marriage could ever mean more to me than you,
  whatever good direction you may offer.
Creon.
                                        Fine, Haemon.
  That's how you ought to feel within your heart,
  subordinate to your father's will in every way.
  That's what a man prays for: to produce good sons—
  households full of them, dutiful and attentive,
  so they can pay his enemy back with interest
  and match the respect their father shows his friend.
  But the man who rears a brood of useless children,
720   what has he brought into the world, I ask you?
  Nothing but trouble for himself, and mockery
  from his enemies laughing in his face.
                                        Oh Haemon,
  never lose your sense of judgment over a woman.
  The warmth, the rush of pleasure, it all goes cold
  in your arms, I warn you . . . a worthless woman
  in your house, a misery in your bed.
  What wound cuts deeper than a loved one
  turned against you? Spit her out,

705. seers (sirz): people who claim to see into the future by interpreting certain signs or events.

like a mortal enemy—let the girl go.
730   Let her find a husband down among the dead.

Imagine it: I caught her in naked rebellion,
the traitor, the only one in the whole city.
I'm not about to prove myself a liar,
not to my people, no, I'm going to kill her!
That's right—so let her cry for mercy, sing her hymns
to Zeus who defends all bonds of kindred blood.
Why, if I bring up my own kin to be rebels,
think what I'd suffer from the world at large.
Show me the man who rules his household well:
740   I'll show you someone fit to rule the state.
That good man, my son,
I have every confidence he and he alone
can give commands and take them too. Staunch
in the storm of spears he'll stand his ground,
a loyal, unflinching comrade at your side.

But whoever steps out of line, violates the laws
or presumes to hand out orders to his superiors,
he'll win no praise from me. But that man
the city places in authority, his orders
750   must be obeyed, large and small,
right and wrong.

                Anarchy—
show me a greater crime in all the earth!
She, she destroys cities, rips up houses,
breaks the ranks of spearmen into headlong rout.
But the ones who last it out, the great mass of them
owe their lives to discipline. Therefore
we must defend the men who live by law,
never let some woman triumph over us.
Better to fall from power, if fall we must,
760   at the hands of a man—never be rated
inferior to a woman, never.
Leader.
                  To us,
unless old age has robbed us of our wits,
you seem to say what you have to say with sense.

Haemon.
Father, only the gods endow a man with reason,
the finest of all their gifts, a treasure.
Far be it from me—I haven't the skill,
and certainly no desire, to tell you when,
if ever, you make a slip in speech . . . though
someone else might have a good suggestion.

770 Of course it's not for you,
in the normal run of things, to watch
whatever men say or do, or find to criticize.
The man in the street, you know, dreads your glance,
he'd never say anything displeasing to your face.
But it's for me to catch the murmurs in the dark,
the way the city mourns for this young girl.
"No woman," they say, "ever deserved death less,
and such a brutal death for such a glorious action.
She, with her own dear brother lying in his blood—
780 she couldn't bear to leave him dead, unburied,
food for the wild dogs or wheeling vultures.
Death? She deserves a glowing crown of gold!"
So they say, and the rumor spreads in secret,
darkly . . .
            I rejoice in your success, father—
nothing more precious to me in the world.
What medal of honor brighter to his children
than a father's growing glory? Or a child's
to his proud father? Now don't, please,
be quite so single-minded, self-involved,
790 or assume the world is wrong and you are right.
Whoever thinks that he alone possesses intelligence,
the gift of eloquence, he and no one else,
and character too . . . such men, I tell you,
spread them open—you will find them empty.
                                    No,
it's no disgrace for a man, even a wise man,
to learn many things and not to be too rigid.
You've seen trees by a raging winter torrent,
how many sway with the flood and salvage every twig,
but not the stubborn—they're ripped out, roots and all.
800 Bend or break. The same when a man is sailing:
haul your sheets too taut, never give an inch,

you'll capsize, go the rest of the voyage
keel up and the rowing-benches under.

Oh give way. Relax your anger—change!
I'm young, I know, but let me offer this:
it would be best by far, I admit,
if a man were born infallible, right by nature.
If not—and things don't often go that way,
it's best to learn from those with good advice.

Leader.

You'd do well, my lord, if he's speaking to the point,
to learn from him,
(*Turning to* HAEMON.)
             and you, my boy, from him.
You both are talking sense.

Creon.

                   So,
men our age, we're to be lectured, are we?—
schooled by a boy his age?

Haemon.

Only in what is right. But if I seem young,
look less to my years and more to what I do.

Creon.

Do? Is admiring rebels an achievement?

Haemon.

I'd never suggest that you admire treason.

Creon.

                       Oh?—
isn't that just the sickness that's attacked her?

Haemon.

The whole city of Thebes denies it, to a man.

Creon.

And is Thebes about to tell me how to rule?

Haemon.

Now, you see? Who's talking like a child?

Creon.

Am I to rule this land for others—or myself?

Haemon.

It's no city at all, owned by one man alone.

Creon.

What? The city *is* the king's—that's the law!

Haemon.

What a splendid king you'd make of a desert island—
you and you alone.

Creon.
[*To the* CHORUS.]
                    This boy, I do believe,
   is fighting on her side, the woman's side.
Haemon.
   If you are a woman, yes;
   my concern is all for you.
Creon.
   Why, you degenerate—bandying accusations,
   threatening me with justice, your own father!
Haemon.
   I see my father offending justice—wrong.
Creon.
                                    Wrong?
   To protect my royal rights?
Haemon.
                         Protect your rights?
   When you trample down the honors of the gods?
Creon.
   You, you soul of corruption, rotten through—
   woman's accomplice!
Haemon.
                  That may be,
   but you'll never find me accomplice to a criminal.
Creon.
   That's what *she* is,
   and every word you say is a blatant appeal for her—
Haemon.
   And you, and me, and the gods beneath the earth.
Creon.
   You'll never marry her, not while she's alive.
Haemon.
   Then she'll die . . . but her death will kill another.
Creon.
   What, brazen threats? You go too far!
Haemon.
                              What threat?
   Combating your empty, mindless judgments with a word?
Creon.
   You'll suffer for your sermons, you and your empty wisdom!
Haemon.
   If you weren't my father, I'd say you were insane.

830

840

Creon.

Don't flatter me with Father—you woman's slave!

Haemon.

You really expect to fling abuse at me
and not receive the same?

Creon.

Is that so!

Now, by heaven, I promise you, you'll pay—
taunting, insulting me! Bring her out,
that hateful—she'll die now, here,
in front of his eyes, beside her groom!

Haemon.

No, no, she will never die beside me—
don't delude yourself. And you will never
see me, never set eyes on my face again.
Rage your heart out, rage with friends
who can stand the sight of you.

[*Rushing out.*]

Leader.

Gone, my king, in a burst of anger.
A temper young as his . . . hurt him once,
he may do something violent.

Creon.

Let him do—

dream up something desperate, past all human limit!
Good riddance. Rest assured,
he'll never save those two young girls from death.

Leader.

Both of them, you really intend to kill them both?

Creon.

No, not her, the one whose hands are clean;
you're quite right.

Leader.

But Antigone—

what sort of death do you have in mind for her?

Creon.

I'll take her down some wild, desolate path
never trod by men, and wall her up alive
in a rocky vault, and set out short rations,
just a gesture of piety

to keep the entire city free of defilement.
There let her pray to the one god she worships:
Death—who knows?—may just reprieve her from death.
Or she may learn at last, better late than never,
what a waste of breath it is to worship Death.

[*Exit to the palace.*]

Chorus.
Love, never conquered in battle
880 Love the plunderer laying waste the rich!
Love standing the night-watch
            guarding a girl's soft cheek,
you range the seas, the shepherds' steadings off in the wilds—
not even the deathless gods can flee your onset,
nothing human born for a day—
whoever feels your grip is driven mad.
                                    Love
you wrench the minds of the righteous into outrage,
swerve them to their ruin—you have ignited this,
this kindred strife, father and son at war
890   and Love alone the victor—
warm glance of the bride triumphant, burning with desire!
Throned in power, side-by-side with the mighty laws!
Irresistible Aphrodite,° never conquered—
Love, you mock us for your sport.

[ANTIGONE *is brought from the palace under guard.*]

But now, even I'd rebel against the king,
I'd break all bounds when I see this—
I fill with tears, can't hold them back,
not any more . . . I see Antigone make her way
to the bridal vault where all are laid to rest.

Antigone.
900 Look at me, men of my fatherland,
        setting out on the last road
looking into the last light of day
the last I'll ever see . . .
the god of death who puts us all to bed
takes me down to the banks of Acheron° alive—
        denied my part in the wedding-songs,

893. Aphrodite (af′rə·dīt′ē):
goddess of love and beauty.

905. Acheron (ak′ər·än′): one
of the rivers that dead souls
were ferried across to reach
Hades, the land of the dead.
(Hades is also the name of the
ruler of the Underworld.)

no wedding-song in the dusk has crowned my marriage—
I go to wed the lord of the dark waters.

Chorus.

910 Not crowned with glory, crowned with a dirge,
you leave for the deep pit of the dead.
No withering illness laid you low,
no strokes of the sword—a law to yourself,
alone, no mortal like you, ever, you go down
to the halls of Death alive and breathing.

Antigone.

But think of Niobe°—well I know her story—
think what a living death she died,
Tantalus'° daughter, stranger queen from the east:
there on the mountain heights, growing stone
binding as ivy, slowly walled her round
920 and the rains will never cease, the legends say
the snows will never leave her . . .

wasting away, under her brows the tears
showering down her breasting ridge and slopes—
a rocky death like hers puts me to sleep.

Chorus.

But she was a god, born of gods,
and we are only mortals born to die.
And yet, of course, it's a great thing
for a dying girl to hear, just hear
she shares a destiny equal to the gods,
during life and later, once she's dead.

Antigone.

930 O you mock me!

Why, in the name of all my fathers' gods
why can't you wait till I am gone—
must you abuse me to my face?
O my city, all your fine rich sons!
And you, you springs of the Dirce,
holy grove of Thebes where the chariots gather,
you at least, you'll bear me witness, look,
unmourned by friends and forced by such crude laws
I go to my rockbound prison, strange new tomb—
940 always a stranger, O dear god,
I have no home on earth and none below,
not with the living, not with the breathless dead.

915. Niobe (nī′ō·bē′): queen
of ancient Thebes who had
seven sons and seven daughters. Niobe boasted that she
was superior to Leto because
Leto had only two children,
the twins Apollo and Artemis.
Offended, Leto complained
to her children, who then
slaughtered all of Niobe's
children. Zeus turned the
weeping Niobe into a column
of stone; when she continued
to weep, her tears became a
stream.

917. Tantalus (tan′tə·ləs):
Tantalus was a king who
committed a crime against the
gods and was condemned to
suffer unending hunger and
thirst in the Underworld.
Though he stood in a lake, the
waters flowed away every time
he tried to drink. Though
branches of fruit hung over his
head, they always remained
just out of his reach.

Chorus.
>You went too far, the last limits of daring—
>smashing against the high throne of Justice!
>>Your life's in ruins, child—I wonder . . .
>do you pay for your father's terrible ordeal?

Antigone.
>There—at last you've touched it, the worst pain
>the worst anguish! Raking up the grief for father
>>three times over, for all the doom
950 >that's struck us down, the brilliant house of Laius.
>O mother, your marriage-bed
>the coiling horrors, the coupling there—
>>you with your own son, my father—doomstruck mother!
>Such, such were my parents, and I their wretched child.
>I go to them now, cursed, unwed, to share their home—
>>I am a stranger! O dear brother,° doomed
>>in your marriage—your marriage murders mine,
>>>your dying drags me down to death alive!

[*Enter* CREON.]

Chorus.
>>Reverence asks some reverence in return—
960 >>but attacks on power never go unchecked,
>>>not by the man who holds the reins of power.
>>Your own blind will, your passion has destroyed you.

Antigone.
>No one to weep for me, my friends,
>no wedding-song—they take me away
>in all my pain . . . the road lies open, waiting.
>Never again, the law forbids me to see
>the sacred eye of day. I am agony!
>No tears for the destiny that's mine,
>no loved one mourns my death.

Creon.
>>>>>Can't you see?
970 >If a man could wail his own dirge *before* he dies,
>he'd never finish.
>(*To the guards.*)
>>>Take her away, quickly!
>Wall her up in the tomb, you have your orders.
>Abandon her there, alone, and let her choose—

956. brother: Oedipus, having married his own mother, is both father and brother to Antigone.

death or a buried life with a good roof for shelter.
As for myself, my hands are clean. This young girl—
dead or alive, she will be stripped of her rights,
her stranger's rights, here in the world above.

Antigone.

O tomb, my bridal-bed—my house, my prison
cut in the hollow rock, my everlasting watch!

980   I'll soon be there, soon embrace my own,°
the great growing family of our dead
Persephone has received among her ghosts.

                                                    I,

the last of them all, the most reviled by far,
go down before my destined time's run out.
But still I go, cherishing one good hope:
my arrival may be dear to father,
dear to you, my mother,
dear to you, my loving brother, Eteocles—
When you died I washed you with my hands,

990   I dressed you all, I poured the cups
across your tombs. But now, Polynices,
because I laid your body out as well,
this, this is my reward. Nevertheless
I honored you—the decent will admit it—
well and wisely too.

                        Never, I tell you,
if I had been the mother of children
or if my husband died, exposed and rotting—
I'd never have taken this ordeal upon myself,
never defied our people's will. What law,

1000   you ask, do I satisfy with what I say?
A husband dead, there might have been another.
A child by another too, if I had lost the first.
But mother and father both lost in the halls of Death,
no brother could ever spring to light again.

For this law alone I held you first in honor.
For this, Creon, the king, judges me a criminal
guilty of dreadful outrage, my dear brother!
And now he leads me off, a captive in his hands,
with no part in the bridal-song, the bridal-bed,

1010   denied all joy of marriage, raising children—
deserted so by loved ones, struck by fate,

980. embrace my own: The Greeks thought of the Underworld as a place where the dead wandered as ghosts. Antigone is looking forward to being reunited there with her family.

I descend alive to the caverns of the dead.

What law of the mighty gods have I transgressed?
Why look to the heavens any more, tormented as I am?
Whom to call, what comrades now? Just think,
my reverence only brands me for irreverence!
Very well: if this is the pleasure of the gods,
once I suffer I will know that I was wrong.
But if these men are wrong, let them suffer
1020   nothing worse than they mete out to me—
these masters of injustice!

Leader.
Still the same rough winds, the wild passion
raging through the girl.

Creon.
(*To the guards.*)
                   Take her away.
You're wasting time—you'll pay for it too.

Antigone.
Oh god, the voice of death. It's come, it's here.

Creon.
True. Not a word of hope—your doom is sealed.

Antigone.
Land of Thebes, city of all my fathers—
O you gods, the first gods of the race!
They drag me away, now, no more delay.
1030   Look on me, you noble sons of Thebes—
the last of a great line of kings,
I alone, see what I suffer now
at the hands of what breed of men—
all for reverence, my reverence for the gods!

[*She leaves under guard; the* CHORUS *gathers.*]

Chorus.
       Danaë,° Danaë—
even she endured a fate like yours,
   in all her lovely strength she traded
the light of day for the bolted brazen vault—
buried within her tomb, her bridal-chamber,
1040   wed to the yoke and broken.
       But she was of glorious birth

1035. Danaë (dan′ā·ē′): When Danaë's father, the king of Argos, was told that his daughter would bear a son who would kill him, he shut his daughter up in a metal vault. But Zeus, the king of the gods, fell in love with Danaë and visited her in her prison as a shower of gold. Danaë thus bore a son by Zeus whom she named Perseus. Danaë's frightened father put his daughter and her newborn in a chest and set them adrift on the sea. They were saved by Zeus; when Perseus grew up, he did indeed kill his grandfather.

                    my child, my child
and treasured the seed of Zeus within her womb,
the cloudburst streaming gold!
          The power of fate is a wonder,
          dark, terrible wonder—
          neither wealth nor armies
          towered walls nor ships
          black hulls lashed by the salt
1050   can save us from that force.

The yoke tamed him too
          young Lycurgus° flaming in anger
king of Edonia, all for his mad taunts
Dionysus clamped him down, encased
in the chain-mail of rock
          and there his rage
                         his terrible flowering rage burst—
sobbing, dying away . . . at last that madman
came to know his god—
1060   the power he mocked, the power
          he taunted in all his frenzy
          trying to stamp out
          the women strong with the god—
          the torch, the raving sacred cries—
          enraging the Muses° who adore the flute.
And far north where the Black Rocks
          cut the sea in half
and murderous straits
split the coast of Thrace
1070   a forbidding city stands
where once, hard by the walls
the savage Ares thrilled to watch
a king's new queen, a Fury rearing in rage
          against his two royal sons—
               her bloody hands, her dagger-shuttle
stabbing out their eyes—cursed, blinding wounds—
their eyes blind sockets screaming for revenge!°

They wailed in agony, cries echoing cries
          the princes doomed at birth . . .
1080   and their mother doomed to chains,
walled off in a tomb of stone—

1052. Lycurgus (lī·kɐr′gəs):
Lycurgus, king of the
Edonians, disapproved of the
worship of Dionysus and
drove the god and his
followers into the sea. As
punishment, Dionysus drove
Lycurgus mad and imprisoned
him in a cave.

**1063–1065. the women . . . the
Muses:** Lycurgus also tried to
get rid of the women who
worshiped Dionysus with
ecstatic dancing and music;
this enraged the Muses,
goddesses of the arts
(including the music of the
flute).

**1066–1077. And far north . . .
revenge:** reference to the
horrible deeds done by a
queen, the second wife of King
Phineus of Thrace. Phineus
imprisoned his first wife, who
was the daughter of Boreas,
the North Wind. Then the new
queen, jealous of her stepsons,
gouged out the boys' eyes.

but she traced her own birth back
to a proud Athenian line and the high gods
and off in caverns half the world away,
born of the wild North Wind
    she sprang on her father's gales,
        racing stallions up the leaping cliffs—
child of the heavens. But even on her the Fates
the gray everlasting Fates rode hard
my child, my child.

[*Enter* TIRESIAS, *the blind prophet, led by a boy.*]

Tiresias.

1090   Lords of Thebes,
I and the boy have come together,
hand in hand. Two see with the eyes of one . . .
so the blind must go, with a guide to lead the way.
Creon.
What is it, old Tiresias? What news now?
Tiresias.
I will teach you. And you obey the seer.
Creon.
                              I will,
I've never wavered from your advice before.
Tiresias.
And so you kept the city straight on course.
Creon.
I owe you a great deal, I swear to that.°
Tiresias.
Then reflect, my son: you are poised,
1100   once more, on the razor-edge of fate.
Creon.
What is it? I shudder to hear you.
Tiresias.
                    You will learn
when you listen to the warnings of my craft.
As I sat on the ancient seat of augury,°
in the sanctuary where every bird I know
will hover at my hands—suddenly I heard it,
a strange voice in the wingbeats, unintelligible,
barbaric, a mad scream! Talons flashing, ripping,
they were killing each other—that much I knew—

1098. I owe . . . to that: Tiresias is indirectly responsible for Creon's being king of Thebes. Tiresias helped reveal to Oedipus, the former king of Thebes, the terrible truth—that Oedipus had unknowingly killed his father and married his own mother. As a result, Oedipus was exiled from Thebes. Since Oedipus's two sons were dead, Creon was next in line for the throne.

1103. augury (ô′gyo͞o·rē): skill of foretelling the future by examining certain signs, such as the flight of birds or the appearance of a comet.

the murderous fury whirring in those wings
made that much clear!

1110   I was afraid,
I turned quickly, tested the burnt-sacrifice,
ignited the altar at all points—but no fire,
the god in the fire never blazed.
Not from those offerings . . . over the embers
slid a heavy ooze from the long thighbones,
smoking, sputtering out, and the bladder
puffed and burst—spraying gall into the air—
and the fat wrapping the bones slithered off
and left them glistening white.° No fire!
1120   The rites failed that might have blazed the future
with a sign. So I learned from the boy here;
he is my guide, as I am guide to others.

                              And it's you—
your high resolve that sets this plague on Thebes.
The public altars and sacred hearths are fouled,
one and all, by the birds and dogs with carrion
torn from the corpse, the doomstruck son of Oedipus!
And so the gods are deaf to our prayers, they spurn
the offerings in our hands, the flame of holy flesh.
No birds cry out an omen clear and true—
1130   they're gorged with the murdered victim's blood and fat.
Take these things to heart, my son, I warn you.
All men make mistakes, it is only human.
But once the wrong is done, a man
can turn his back on folly, misfortune too,
if he tries to make amends, however low he's fallen,
and stops his bullnecked ways. Stubbornness
brands you for stupidity—pride is a crime.
No, yield to the dead!
Never stab the fighter when he's down.
1140   Where's the glory, killing the dead twice over?

I mean you well. I give you sound advice.
It's best to learn from a good adviser
when he speaks for your own good:
it's pure gain.
Creon.
                    Old man—all of you! So,
you shoot your arrows at my head like archers at the target—

**1114–1119. offerings . . .
white:** The ancient Greeks
wrapped the thighbones of
slaughtered animals in fat, set
other pieces of meat on top,
and offered it to the gods in
fire rituals. Seers like Tiresias
made omens based on the
burning of the offering.

I even have *him* loosed on me, this fortune-teller.
Oh his ilk has tried to sell me short
and ship me off for years. Well,
drive your bargains, traffic—much as you like—
1150   in the gold of India, silver-gold of Sardis.
You'll never bury that body in the grave,
not even if Zeus's eagles rip the corpse
and wing their rotten pickings off to the throne of god!
Never, not even in fear of such defilement
will I tolerate his burial, that traitor.
Well I know, we can't defile the gods—
no mortal has the power.
                     No,
reverend old Tiresias, all men fall,
it's only human, but the wisest fall obscenely
1160   when they glorify obscene advice with rhetoric—
all for their own gain.
Tiresias.
Oh god, is there a man alive
who knows, who actually believes . . .
Creon.
                               What now?
What earth-shattering truth are you about to utter?
Tiresias.
. . . just how much a sense of judgment, wisdom
is the greatest gift we have?
Creon.
                       Just as much, I'd say,
as a twisted mind is the worst affliction going.
Tiresias.
You are the one who's sick, Creon, sick to death.
Creon.
I am in no mood to trade insults with a seer.
Tiresias.
You have already, calling my prophecies a lie.
Creon.
1170   Why not?
You and the whole breed of seers are mad for money!
Tiresias.
And the whole race of tyrants lusts to rake it in.
Creon.
This slander of yours—

are you aware you're speaking to the king?
Tiresias.
Well aware. Who helped you save the city?
Creon.

                                     You—
you have your skills, old seer, but you lust for injustice!
Tiresias.
You will drive me to utter the dreadful secret in my heart.
Creon.
Spit it out! Just don't speak it out for profit.
Tiresias.
Profit? No, not a bit of profit, not for you.
Creon.
1180   Know full well, you'll never buy off my resolve.
Tiresias.
Then know this too, learn this by heart!
The chariot of the sun will not race through
so many circuits more, before you have surrendered
one born of your own loins, your own flesh and blood,
a corpse for corpses given in return, since you have thrust
to the world below a child sprung for the world above,
ruthlessly lodged a living soul within the grave—
then you've robbed the gods below the earth,
keeping a dead body here in the bright air,
1190   unburied, unsung, unhallowed by the rites.

You, you have no business with the dead,
nor do the gods above—this is violence
you have forced upon the heavens.
And so the avengers, the dark destroyers late
but true to the mark, now lie in wait for you,
the Furies° sent by the gods and the god of death
to strike you down with the pains that you perfected!

There. Reflect on that, tell me I've been bribed.
The day comes soon, no long test of time, not now,
1200   that wakes the wails for men and women in your halls.
Great hatred rises against you—
cities in tumult, all whose mutilated sons
the dogs have graced with burial, or the wild beasts,
some wheeling crow that wings the ungodly stench of carrion
back to each city, each warrior's hearth and home.

1196. the Furies: the three goddesses of vengeance who tormented wrongdoers who had gone unpunished. The Furies were repulsive, with snakes entwined in their hair and blood oozing from their eyes.

These arrows for your heart! Since you've raked me
I loose them like an archer in my anger,
arrows deadly true. You'll never escape
their burning, searing force.
(*Motioning to his escort.*)
1210   Come, boy, take me home.
So he can vent his rage on younger men,
and learn to keep a gentler tongue in his head
and better sense than what he carries now.

[*Exit to the side.*]

Leader.
The old man's gone, my king—
terrible prophecies. Well I know,
since the hair on this old head went gray,
he's never lied to Thebes.
Creon.
I know it myself—I'm shaken, torn.
It's a dreadful thing to yield . . . but resist now?
1220   Lay my pride bare to the blows of ruin?
That's dreadful too.
Leader.
                But good advice,
Creon, take it now, you must.
Creon.
What should I do? Tell me . . . I'll obey.
Leader.
Go! Free the girl from the rocky vault
and raise a mound for the body you exposed.
Creon.
That's your advice? You think I should give in?
Leader.
Yes, my king, quickly. Disasters sent by the gods
cut short our follies in a flash.
Creon.
                Oh it's hard,
giving up the heart's desire . . . but I will do it—
1230   no more fighting a losing battle with necessity.
Leader.
Do it now, go, don't leave it to others.

Creon.

>Now—I'm on my way! Come, each of you,
>take up axes, make for the high ground,
>over there, quickly! I and my better judgment
>have come round to this—I shackled her,
>I'll set her free myself. I am afraid . . .
>it's best to keep the established laws
>to the very day we die.

[*Rushing out, followed by his entourage.* THE CHORUS *clusters around the altar.*]

Chorus.

>God of a hundred names!
>   Great Dionysus—
1240 >   Son and glory of Semele! Pride of Thebes—
>Child of Zeus° whose thunder rocks the clouds—
>Lord of the famous lands of evening—
>King of the Mysteries!
>   King of Eleusis,° Demeter's plain
>her breasting hills that welcome in the world—
>Great Dionysus!
>   Bacchus, living in Thebes
>the mother-city of all your frenzied women°—
>   Bacchus
>   living along the Ismenus'° rippling waters
>standing over the field sown with the Dragon's teeth!°

>You—we have seen you through the flaring smoky fires,
1250 >   your torches blazing over the twin peaks
>where nymphs of the hallowed cave climb onward
>   fired with you, your sacred rage—
>we have seen you at Castalia's° running spring
>and down from the heights of Nysa crowned with ivy
>the greening shore rioting vines and grapes
>   down you come in your storm of wild women
>   ecstatic, mystic cries—
>   Dionysus—
>down to watch and ward the roads of Thebes!

>First of all cities, Thebes you honor first
1260 >you and your mother, bride of the lightning—

1240–1241. Semele (sem′ə·lē′) **. . . Zeus:** Semele, the mother of Dionysus, was the daughter of the founder of Thebes. Zeus, king of the gods and the father of Dionysus, was also often called the god of thunder.

1243–1247. King of Eleusis (e·loo′sis): Dionysus (also called Bacchus) had a major role in the Eleusian mysteries, secret rites performed at the city of Eleusis, northwest of Athens. The rites also honored the goddess Demeter and her daughter, Persephone. Demeter was goddess of the harvest; the original rites probably had to do with the fertility of the soil and the growth of crops. **frenzied women:** Dionysus's followers, mostly women, whipped themselves into a ritual frenzy to reach a state of inner peace. **Ismenus** (is·mē′nəs): river near Thebes.

1248. Dragon's teeth: This is a reference to the city of Thebes, where Dionysus's mother was born. In Greek mythology, Cadmus, searching for a place to found a city, stopped at a field guarded by a dragon. Cadmus killed the dragon and scattered its teeth in the field. From these teeth, warriors sprang up. The warriors fought one another until only five were left. With these five warriors, Cadmus established Thebes.

1253. Castalia (kas·tā′lē·ə): sacred spring named for the nymph who threw herself into it while fleeing Apollo.

come, Dionysus! now your people lie
in the iron grip of plague,
come in your racing, healing stride
        down Parnassus'° slopes
or across the moaning straits.
                Lord of the dancing—
dance, dance the constellations breathing fire!
Great master of the voices of the night!
Child of Zeus, God's offspring, come, come forth!
Lord, king, dance with your nymphs, swirling, raving
1270   arm-in-arm in frenzy through the night
        they dance you, Iacchus°—
                Dance, Dionysus
giver of all good things!

[*Enter a* MESSENGER *from the side.*]

Messenger.
                Neighbors,
friends of the house of Cadmus and the kings,
there's not a thing in this life of ours
I'd praise or blame as settled once for all.
Fortune lifts and Fortune fells the lucky
and unlucky every day. No prophet on earth
can tell a man his fate. Take Creon:
there was a man to rouse your envy once,
1280   as I see it. He saved the realm from enemies;
taking power, he alone, the lord of the fatherland,
he set us true on course—flourished like a tree
with the noble line of sons he bred and reared . . .
and now it's lost, all gone.
              Believe me,
when a man has squandered his true joys,
he's good as dead, I tell you, a living corpse.
Pile up riches in your house, as much as you like—
live like a king with a huge show of pomp,
but if real delight is missing from the lot,
1290   I wouldn't give you a wisp of smoke for it,
not compared with joy.
Leader.
            What now?
What new grief do you bring the house of kings?

1264. Parnassus (pär·nas′əs):
mountain in central Greece,
sacred to Apollo and Dionysus.
The sacred spring Castalia (see
note, line 1253) lies at its base.

1271. Iacchus (ē′ə·kəs):
another name for Dionysus.

Messenger.

Dead, dead—and the living are guilty of their death!

Leader.

Who's the murderer? Who is dead? Tell us.

Messenger.

Haemon's gone, his blood spilled by the very hand—

Leader.

His father's or his own?

Messenger.

His own . . .

raging mad with his father for the death—

Leader.

Oh great seer,

you saw it all, you brought your word to birth!

Messenger.

Those are the facts. Deal with them as you will.

[*As he turns to go,* EURYDICE *enters from the palace.*]

Leader.

1300   Look, Eurydice. Poor woman, Creon's wife,
so close at hand. By chance perhaps,
unless she's heard the news about her son.

Eurydice.

My countrymen,

all of you—I caught the sound of your words
as I was leaving to do my part,
to appeal to queen Athena with my prayers.
I was just loosing the bolts, opening the doors,
when a voice filled with sorrow, family sorrow,
struck my ears, and I fell back, terrified,
into the women's arms—everything went black.

1310   Tell me the news, again, whatever it is . . .
sorrow and I are hardly strangers;
I can bear the worst.

Messenger.

I—dear lady,

I'll speak as an eye-witness. I was there.
And I won't pass over one word of the truth.
Why should I try to soothe you with a story,
only to prove a liar in a moment?
Truth is always best.

So,
I escorted your lord, I guided him
to the edge of the plain where the body lay,
1320   Polynices, torn by the dogs and still unmourned.
And saying a prayer to Hecate of the Crossroads,
Pluto° too, to hold their anger and be kind,
we washed the dead in a bath of holy water
and plucking some fresh branches, gathering . . .
what was left of him, we burned them all together
and raised a high mound of native earth, and then
we turned and made for that rocky vault of hers,
the hollow, empty bed of the bride of Death.

And far off, one of us heard a voice,
1330   a long wail rising, echoing
out of that unhallowed wedding-chamber;
he ran to alert the master and Creon pressed on,
closer—the strange, inscrutable cry came sharper,
throbbing around him now, and he let loose
a cry of his own, enough to wrench the heart,
"Oh god, am I the prophet now? going down
the darkest road I've ever gone? My son—
it's *his* dear voice, he greets me! Go, men,
closer, quickly! Go through the gap,
1340   the rocks are dragged back—
right, to the tomb's very mouth—and look,
see if it's Haemon's voice I think I hear,
or the gods have robbed me of my senses."

The king was shattered. We took his orders,
went and searched, and there in the deepest,
dark recesses of the tomb we found her . . .
hanged by the neck in a fine linen noose,
strangled in her veils—and the boy,
his arms flung around her waist,
1350   clinging to her, wailing for his bride,
dead and down below, for his father's crimes
and the bed of his marriage blighted by misfortune.
When Creon saw him, he gave a deep sob,
he ran in, shouting, crying out to him,
"Oh my child—what have you done? what seized you,
what insanity? what disaster drove you mad?

1321–1322. Hecate (hek′ə·tē)
. . . **Pluto:** Hecate was the
goddess of sorcery and
witchcraft. Offerings to her
were left at crossroads, which
were believed to be the best
places for performing magic.
Pluto is another name for
Hades, king of the Underworld.

Come out, my son! I beg you on my knees!"
But the boy gave him a wild burning glance,
spat in his face, not a word in reply,
1360   he drew his sword—his father rushed out,
running as Haemon lunged and missed!—
and then, doomed, desperate with himself,
suddenly leaning his full weight on the blade,
he buried it in his body, halfway to the hilt.

And still in his senses, pouring his arms around her,
he embraced the girl and breathing hard,
released a quick rush of blood,
bright red on her cheek glistening white.
And there he lies, body enfolding body . . .
1370   he has won his bride at last, poor boy,
not here but in the houses of the dead.

Creon shows the world that of all the ills
afflicting men the worst is lack of judgment.

[EURYDICE *turns and reenters the palace.*]

Leader.
What do you make of that? The lady's gone,
without a word, good or bad.
Messenger.
                I'm alarmed too
but here's my hope—faced with her son's death,
she finds it unbecoming to mourn in public.
Inside, under her roof, she'll set her women
to the task and wail the sorrow of the house.
1380   She's too discreet. She won't do something rash.
Leader.
I'm not so sure. To me, at least,
a long heavy silence promises danger,
just as much as a lot of empty outcries.
Messenger.
We'll see if she's holding something back,
hiding some passion in her heart.
I'm going in. You may be right—who knows?
Even too much silence has its dangers.

[*Exit to the palace. Enter* CREON *from the side, escorted by attendants carrying* HAEMON's *body on a bier.*]

Leader.
The king himself! Coming toward us,
look, holding the boy's head in his hands.
1390   Clear, damning proof, if it's right to say so—
proof of his own madness, no one else's,
    no, his own blind wrongs.

Creon.
                    Ohhh,
so senseless, so insane . . . my crimes,
my stubborn, deadly—
Look at us, the killer, the killed,
father and son, the same blood—the misery!
My plans, my mad fanatic heart,
my son, cut off so young!
Ai, dead, lost to the world,
not through your stupidity, no, my own.

Leader.
1400   Too late,
too late, you see what justice means.

Creon.
                      Oh I've learned
through blood and tears! Then, it was then,
when the god came down and struck me—a great weight
shattering, driving me down that wild savage path,
ruining, trampling down my joy. Oh the agony,
    the heartbreaking agonies of our lives.

[*Enter the* MESSENGER *from the palace.*]

Messenger.
                    Master,
what a hoard of grief you have, and you'll have more.
The grief that lies to hand you've brought yourself—
(*Pointing to* HAEMON's *body.*)
the rest, in the house, you'll see it all too soon.

Creon.
What now? What's worse than this?

Messenger.
                    The queen is dead.
1410

The mother of this dead boy . . . mother to the end—
poor thing, her wounds are fresh.

Creon.
                                        No, no,
harbor of Death, so choked, so hard to cleanse!—
why me? why are you killing me?
Herald of pain, more words, more grief?
I died once, you kill me again and again!
What's the report, boy . . . some news for me?
My wife dead? O dear god!
Slaughter heaped on slaughter?

[*The doors open; the body of* EURYDICE *is brought out on her bier.*]

Messenger.
                                        See for yourself:
now they bring her body from the palace.

Creon.
1420   Oh no,
another, a second loss to break the heart.
What next, what fate still waits for me?
I just held my son in my arms and now,
look, a new corpse rising before my eyes—
        wretched, helpless mother—O my son!

Messenger.
She stabbed herself at the altar,
then her eyes went dark, after she'd raised
a cry for the noble fate of Megareus,° the hero
killed in the first assault, then for Haemon,
1430   then with her dying breath she called down
torments on your head—you killed her sons.

Creon.
                                                Oh the dread,
I shudder with dread! Why not kill me too?—
run me through with a good sharp sword?
Oh god, the misery, anguish—
I, I'm churning with it, going under.

Messenger.
Yes, and the dead, the woman lying there,
piles the guilt of all their deaths on you.

Creon.
How did she end her life, what bloody stroke?

1428. **Megareus** (mə·ga′rē·əs):
older son of Creon and
Eurydice. He was killed during
the Argive assault on Thebes.

Messenger.
> She drove home to the heart with her own hand,
> once she learned her son was dead . . . that agony.

1440

Creon.
> And the guilt is all mine—
> can never be fixed on another man,
> no escape for me. I killed you,
> I, god help me, I admit it all!
> (*To his attendants.*)
> Take me away, quickly, out of sight.
> I don't even exist—I'm no one. Nothing.

Leader.
> Good advice, if there's any good in suffering.
> Quickest is best when troubles block the way.

Creon.
> (*Kneeling in prayer.*)
> Come, let it come!—that best of fates for me
> that brings the final day, best fate of all.
> Oh quickly, now—
> so I never have to see another sunrise.

1450

Leader.
> That will come when it comes;
> we must deal with all that lies before us.
> The future rests with the ones who tend the future.

Creon.
> That prayer—I poured my heart into that prayer!

Leader.
> No more prayers now. For mortal men
> there is no escape from the doom we must endure.

Creon.
> Take me away, I beg you, out of sight.
> A rash, indiscriminate fool!
> I murdered you, my son, against my will—
> you too, my wife . . .
>   Wailing wreck of a man,
> whom to look to? where to lean for support?
> (*Desperately turning from* HAEMON *to* EURYDICE *on their biers.*)
> Whatever I touch goes wrong—once more
> a crushing fate's come down upon my head.

1460

[*The* MESSENGER *and attendants lead* CREON *into the palace.*]

Chorus.
    Wisdom is by far the greatest part of joy,
    and reverence toward the gods must be safeguarded.
    The mighty words of the proud are paid in full
    with mighty blows of fate, and at long last
1470   those blows will teach us wisdom.

[The old citizens exit to the side.]

Medea

Meet the Playwright

Euripides (484–406? B.C.)

Along with Sophocles and Aeschylus, Euripides (yoo·rip´ə·dēz´) was one of the great tragedians of ancient Greece. A prolific writer, he produced ninety-two plays during his lifetime, but only around nineteen have survived. Details about his life are in similarly short supply, and the few details that do exist are disputed by scholars. Most of what is known comes from characters based on Euripides that appeared in comic plays by his contemporary, Aristophanes. Most scholars agree that Euripides was born on the Greek island of Salamis. Ancient inscriptions suggest that the young Euripides rubbed shoulders with important members of society, and so scholars presume that his parents were well off. And although Aristophanes joked that Euripides' mother ran a grocery store, it is more likely that she was from a noble family. There are stories that suggest that Euripides studied as a boy with the great Greek philosopher Socrates, but most scholars believe that is only legend.

Second Fiddle to Sophocles

Euripides' public life is not clearly documented until 455 B.C., when he submitted his first entries to the annual drama contest in the Greek capital of Athens. These dramatic contests were to the Greeks what the World Series and the Super Bowl are to modern Americans: important competitions that drew thousands of spectators and guaranteed acclaim for the winners. Although Euripides submitted plays for more than twenty years, he rarely won first place. He received the coveted first prize only four times, including once after his death, while his competitor Sophocles won more than twenty times. Among the plays Euripides wrote were *Alcestis, Medea, Heracles, Trojan Women, Iphigenia among the Taurians, Helen*, and *Orestes*.

For reasons that are not clear, in 408 B.C. Euripides left his native Greece for neighboring Macedonia, to reside at the court of King Archelaus. Some believe that Euripides left because he was disgusted with the lack of attention given his work at home and that he entered a self-imposed exile. Others suspect that he was merely responding to an invitation to spend time abroad and build his reputation. He did not produce much work during his time away from home, however, because he died shortly after he left, in 407 or 406 B.C. Again, several different stories circulated about the cause of his death. Some say that hunting dogs attacked him or were set on him by enemies. Others suggest that a crowd of angry, violent women tore him apart. Perhaps these tales about his death arose from the fact that the characters in his plays are frequently either the victims or perpetrators of shockingly violent acts.

A Popularity That Eluded Him in Life

Ironically, Euripides' reputation as a playwright of significance took off only after his death. In the following century, he became the most popular of the Greek tragedians. His plays were revived onstage and collected in anthologies. Even after the decline of Greece in the fourth century B.C., his plays continued to be performed in the capital cities—Alexandria, Rome, Byzantium—of succeeding empires. As a result, the manuscripts of Euripides' plays were copied, preserved, and handed down over the centuries. Though Aristotle called Euripides' tragedies flawed, his work has captured the imagination of playgoers, readers, and writers throughout history. In medieval and Renaissance literature, there are more references to Euripedes' work than to the work of Sophocles or Aeschylus. Even today, his plays electrify audiences.

Background to *Medea*

When *Medea* was first presented in 431 B.C. along with the other dramas at the Dionysia, the Athenian festival celebrating the god Dionysus, it came in dead last in the popular vote. The unconventional drama, which turned the traditional ideal of the tragic hero on its head, apparently didn't sit well with audiences of the period. Over time, however, the paradox of raw emotion and cold calculation embodied in the drama's "hero" has tightened its grip on audiences' imaginations, and it has yet to let go.

Medea is based on myths that would have been familiar to Athenian audiences. The mythical Medea was the daughter of the king of Colchis (käl´kis), the niece of the sorceress Circe (sûr´sē), and the granddaughter of the sun god Helios (hē´lē·äs´). Although not a Greek, she was a powerful and passionate woman who entered Greek mythology through her association with Jason, one of ancient Greece's greatest heroes.

Prophecy and the Golden Fleece

In most versions of the Medea myth, divine intervention brings Jason to Medea. Jason is the rightful king of Iolcus, but his father's half-brother, Pelias, has usurped his throne. Though he had been sent away as a child, as a young man Jason returns to Iolcus with the help of Hera, queen of the gods, to reclaim his throne from Pelias. Pelias agrees to relinquish the throne if Jason can retrieve the Golden Fleece, the pelt of a divine ram that is protected by a dragon in the faraway kingdom of Colchis. Jason agrees to the challenge and joins the Argonauts, fifty of Greece's greatest heroes, in search of the fleece.

The adventures of Jason and the Argonauts lead them to the kingdom of Medea's father, who agrees to hand over the fleece if Jason can perform several seemingly impossible tasks. These tasks include harnessing two fire-breathing bulls and using them to plow a field and then planting teeth gathered from a dragon. Fortunately for Jason, Medea has fallen passionately in love with him. In exchange for his vow to marry her, she uses her magic to help him perform the feats. Medea also helps Jason and the Argonauts to make away with the fleece—she distracts her father's pursuit by chopping her brother into bits and casting the pieces into the ocean.

Grisly Revenge

Medea turns out to be an extraordinarily strong ally for Jason. Back in Iolcus, she takes revenge on Pelias, using her magic and her wiles. First, she restores youth to Jason's father. In one version of the myth, she accomplishes this by boiling him in a potion of magic herbs. Then she encourages Pelias's daughters to do the same for Pelias. This time, though, Medea substitutes ordinary herbs, and Pelias boils to death. Jason and Medea flee again, finding refuge in Corinth, where Euripides' play begins.

In this famous play, Medea is a woman driven by revenge to multiple murders: Enraged that Jason has decided to take a new wife, she murders first the young woman and then her own children.

In versions of the myth that predate Euripides' play, however, the events surrounding Medea in Corinth differ strikingly from those portrayed in Euripides' play. For example, in earlier versions of the myth, Medea is responsible for the murder of Glauce, Jason's new wife, but it is the citizens of Corinth who murder Medea's children (there were fourteen). The goddess Hera protects and honors Medea by making her children's souls immortal, and the people of Corinth annually pay penance for the child murders by sending fourteen of their own children to serve for a year in Hera's temple. By commissioning Euripides to revise the myth of Medea, the citizens of Corinth may have hoped to lift the cloud of dishonor from their city. His efforts on their behalf seem to have been a success. To this day, Euripides' version of the events in Corinth has become the one most identified with the mythical figure of Medea.

Medea

Euripides

Translated by **Alistair Elliot**

CHARACTERS

Medea (mə·dē′ə)

Chorus, women of Corinth

Nurse

Tutor

Children

Creon

Jason

Aegeus (ē′jē·əs)

Messenger

Scene: A palace near Corinth.

Enter NURSE.

Nurse.
　　I wish the Argo had never spread its wings
　　And flown to Colchis through the Clashing Rocks.
　　I wish the pine tree on the slopes of Pelion
　　Had not been felled; not split to feathery oars
　　To fledge° the arms of Argonauts. Oh why
　　Did Pelias send them for the Golden Fleece?
　　If they had never come, my mistress Medea
　　Would not have sailed back to Iolcos with them,
　　Dazed with passion for their leader, Jason.
10　Then she would not have made King Pelias' daughters
　　Kill their own father. And she'd not have come
　　To settle here in Corinth, but she has.

　　Here all went well at first: a blameless life
　　With husband and with children. Though an alien,
　　She did good service to the citizens
　　Of her new country, and she fitted in
　　As well with Jason's every wish. For women,
　　That's the best way to make yourself secure:
　　Never stand up and argue with a man.

20　But now the house is full of hate; and my dear girl
　　Is ill with it. For Jason has become
　　A traitor to his children and my mistress.
　　He abandons her, to lie in a royal bed:
　　He's marrying the king's daughter, Creon's child.
　　My poor Medea loses all her rights
　　And honors, everything. "He swore an oath,"
　　She cries, "He gave his word! I trusted him!"
　　She begs the gods to witness this reward
　　From Jason, after all she did for him.
30　She lies not eating, slumping into grief,
　　Melting the hours of life away in tears.
　　She never moves her head or lifts her eyes
　　From staring at the ground, deaf as a stone
　　Or wave of the sea to our advice and comfort—
　　Except, she sometimes turns that white white neck

5. fledge *v.*: to adorn with feathers.

To look away and mutter to herself
Mourning the father she betrayed, the home
And family she abandoned to come here
With a man who treats her now with such dishonor.
40 Poor thing, she's learnt at the ungentle hands
Of fortune, what it means to lose your country.
She hates to have her children near; she sees them
And does not smile. I fear she's plotting something,
And she is a woman to fear: if you arouse
The hatred of Medea, don't expect
An easy victory, and to go home singing.
    Here are the children, though. They're fresh from play,
Not thinking of their mother's misery
At all. The young mind runs away from pain.

[*Enter* MEDEA's *two small* BOYS, *followed by the* TUTOR
(*child-minder*).]

Tutor.
50 Old slave, old heirloom from my mistress' home,
What are you doing, standing here alone
Outside, and groaning to yourself? Medea
Usually wants you with her. Why not now?
Nurse.
Old slave yourself! Servant of Jason's children!
A good slave, when the mistress' luck runs out,
Feels the disaster falling on himself.
I felt such sympathy with what she suffered
I had to come out here and tell her troubles
To the witnesses of earth and air.
Tutor.
60 So our sad lady has no rest from weeping?
Nurse.
I wish I thought so. Her pain has hardly started.
Tutor.
Poor fool—if one may say such things of masters—
She doesn't know the latest news is worse.
Nurse.
What do you mean? Don't keep this to yourself.
Tutor.
It's nothing—I regret I mentioned it.
Nurse.
Old man, don't hide it from your fellow slave.

I can be silent if I have to be.
Tutor.
> I heard, when I was seeming not to listen,
> But standing where the old men sit and play

70
> At board games, by the sacred spring Pirene,°
> Somebody say the children are to be banished
> From Corinth, with their mother. It appears
> That is the king's intention. I don't know
> If this is true—I pray it turns out false.

Nurse.
> Jason won't let them treat his sons like that.
> He's quarreling with their mother, not with them.

Tutor.
> When new alliances are made, the old ones
> Are dropped behind. His love has left this house.

Nurse.
> We're sinking from the first of fortune's waves;

80
> We cannot take another; we shall drown.

Tutor.
> Anyway, this is not a time to tell the mistress
> What I have heard: for now, stay calm, and silent.

Nurse.
> Children, you hear what sort of father you have?
> I curse him—no, I must not—he's my master.
> But we have found him out: he's a bad friend
> To his own family, those he ought to love.

Tutor.
> What man on earth is different? Don't you know
> Everyone loves himself more than his neighbor?
> You're slow to learn, but now you see a father

90
> Can shed affection with a change of bed.

Nurse.
> Go in—all will be well—boys, go in.
> (*To* TUTOR) Keep them as isolated as you can.
> Don't let them near their mother: she's distraught.
> Already, I've seen her eyeing them, like a beast
> About to charge. I'm sure she'll never let
> Her anger rest until she's struck at someone—
> So long as it's her enemies, not her friends.

[*Before the* CHILDREN *and* TUTOR *can go off,* MEDEA *is heard offstage.*]

70. Pirene: fabled fountain in Corinth, named for the nymph whose tears were said to be the source of its water. She cried for the death of her son at the hands of the goddess Artemis.

Medea (*Scream*).

    The pain of misery! A world of trouble

    Is falling on me! I want to die!

Nurse.

100   I told you, children: that's your mother

    Raking the anger through her heart.

    Go in quickly, get inside—

    Don't go anywhere she can see you,

    Don't go up to her—just look out

    For her savage mood: she was always willful

        But now she's wild with hate.

    Go now, run inside; be quick.

[*The* CHILDREN *and* TUTOR *go into the palace.*]

    Clearly now the storm is rising;

    The cloud of pain will soon burst

110   Into greater fury. What will her proud

    Untameable spirit do

        Under the bite of suffering?

Medea (*Scream*).

    I have endured so much! I've earned

    The right to scream. O cursed children

    Of an unloved mother, may you die!

    Die with your father! May the whole

        Family of Jason perish!

Nurse.

    You poor unhappy woman.

    But why do you make your sons share

120   Their father's offense? Oh, why hate them?

    Poor children, I'm sick with fear for you.

    I know something is going to happen.

    (*She explains to the children*)

    Strange and terrible

        Are the minds of royal masters:

    Always commanding, never obeying,

    They have strong moods and cannot change them.

    Ordinary life where everyone's equal

    Is better, much better. I hope to grow old

    In a safe low place, not high and grand.

130   For man should live with limit and measure;

    That is a phrase we often use,

And it's proved true: Going beyond,
Going too far, brings no advantage.
It only means, when the gods are angry,
　　They extract a greater price.

[*Enter the* CHORUS, *who are Corinthian women.*]

Chorus.
I could hear the voice, I could hear the cries
From this unhappy woman of Colchis.
Is she still no calmer? Tell us, old woman.
Through the double doors of her inner room
140　　I could hear the lament—and I take no pleasure
In the sounds of sorrow that flow from this house:
The years have made us feel we are friends.

Nurse.
The house? The family? That is finished.
For he is held in a royal bed,
While she broods in her old rooms,
My mistress, wasting her hours away
With not one loving friend beside her
To warm and comfort her mind with words.

Medea *(Scream).*
O fire from heaven, pierce through my head!
150　　What use is living, now, to me?
Let me release myself in death
　　And leave this life I hate.

Chorus.
Gods of earth and light and sky,
Do you hear this painful cry,
　　The song of the unhappy wife?
Crazy wish, to lay your head
In death's abominable bed.
　　Oh never rush to finish life
　　　　Oh never pray for that.
160　　And if your husband turns from you
And starts to worship someone new,
Don't scratch your cheeks and pull your hair
　　　　Because he's leaving.
　　　　I know it hurts,
But Zeus will see that you get even;
Jason will get his just deserts.

So don't lose heart because you lose a man.

Medea.

Oh father, my city! My lost home!
What I left behind when I killed my brother,
When I killed my own brother, to get away!
Great goddess of Justice, look down and see
What I have to endure from my cursed husband,
And after I'd bound him with oaths of power!
How I'd love to tear the palace down
About the pair of them, crush and grind
Their bodies together in bloody rubble!
They started this—they dared to harm me.

Nurse.

You hear what she wants? She calls on the gods.
This is an anger worthy of heaven
    And nothing small will calm it.

Chorus.

How can we make her come out here
To see us face to face and hear
    The solemn words of good advice?
We might be able to assuage
The hunger of her heavy rage.
    I'll always be the sort who tries
        To be of use like that.
But you go fetch her out of there,
Out of the gloom into the air.
Tell her it's friends. We want to help.
        Be quick, before
        She does some wrong
To someone innocent inside,
Before her passion gets too strong.
I feel the violence gathering in the air.

Nurse.

I'll try again.
But I doubt if my mistress will listen to me.
Like a savage beast with newborn young,
She lowers,° she turns on any servant
Who moves towards her trying to speak.
If only we could charm her with music.
I sometimes think those clever men
Of the past were fools: it was stupid of them
To invent music only for festivals,

170

180

190

200

199. lowers (lou'ərz) *v.*: scowls.

Great banquets, and friendly dinners.
They made melodious news of life:
But no one made up a medicinal music,
A treatment of voices and instruments
That would ease the terrible pain of living—
210   The pangs of death and the downfall of families.
Couldn't they see there'd be profit in curing
Pain with song? But there at dinner,
At a lovely feast, why do they raise
Their voices and sing? The pleasure of food,
The present meal, is by itself
    Filling enough for mortals.

[*Exit* NURSE *into palace.*]

Chorus.
I hear the cry of discontent,
The still-continuing wail.
I hear the liquid voice lament
220   The evil husband, the betrayal.

Unjustly injured and abused,
She calls on Themis,° that goddess   **222. Themis** (thē′mis): the
Who stands at the right hand of Zeus   goddess of justice.
And guards our promises:

It was a promise and an oath
That brought her with the Golden Fleece° **226. Golden Fleece:** the wool
Away from Colchis in the night   of a golden, winged ram that
Across the sea to Greece,   carried the mythical characters
Through where the lock   of Helle and Phrixus away
230   And clashing key   from their evil stepmother,
Of salty Hellespont° still block   Ino. After the ram delivered
The impenetrable Euxine Sea.   Phrixus to safety (Helle had
                                          fallen to her death), it was
[*Enter* MEDEA.]   sacrificed to Zeus, king of the
                                          gods. The Golden Fleece was
Medea.   then guarded by a dragon in
Women of Corinth, I have come out to see you Colchis, the kingdom of
For fear you might reproach me. You mustn't think Medea's father.
I'm proud. I know some people hide themselves
From common sight, like gods, and that shows pride, **231. Hellespont** (hel′əs·pänt′):
                                          the strait, or narrow waterway,
                                          in which Helle fell to her
                                          death. The sea was named in
                                          her honor.

While others show it stalking down the street.
But some, who just walk quietly, get a name
For being haughty, distant and superior.
240 The eyes of men are not the fairest judges:
Sometimes, before they know a person's heart,
They hate on sight—when no one gave them cause.
Foreigners specially have to court a city—
But citizens should try to fit in too.
I think it can't be right for anyone
To stand aloof and simply please themselves—
They offend their fellow men; it's ignorant, it's wrong.

It's so with me: this unforeseen disaster
Has stunned my spirit. I am lost. The joy
250 Of life has gone. I even want to die.
You see, someone I should have known so well,
My husband, has turned out the worst of men.

Of all the creatures that have life and reason,
We women are the most unhappy kind:
First we must throw our money to the wind
To buy a husband; and what's worse, we have to
Accept him as the master of our body.
Then comes the question that decides our lives:
Is the master good or bad? It's possible
260 To change your spouse, but indecent for a woman;
And we can not refuse the man we're given.
We come to new conventions and new ways,
Innocent from home. You'd need to be clairvoyant
To please this stranger who is in your bed.
Suppose we manage all such duties well
And he can live in harness without fretting,
Then life's ideal; but if not, best die.
A man who's tired of what he gets at home
Goes out—and gives his heart a holiday.
270 But we are forced to look at one face always.
They tell us, "In this life you live at home
You run no risks, while we take arms and fight."
Not true, I say: I'd rather stand three times
In battle by my shield than once give birth.
Of course, the story's not so bad for you:
You have your city here, a father's house,

Pleasures in reach, and company of friends,
But I'm alone, a citizen of Nowhere,
Insulted by my husband, just a woman
280 He took as plunder from her barbarous country.
I have no mother, brother, any kin
To be my harbor in the storm of fortune.
Therefore I beg this single favor from you:
If I discover some device, some means
To make my husband pay for what I've suffered,
You will say nothing. A woman may be timid
In other ways, too weak to stand and fight
And almost fainting at the sight of weapons,
But when she finds her bed has been defiled,
290 No other creature has such deadly thoughts.
Chorus.
I promise. It's only fair to make him pay,
Medea. I don't wonder at your pain.

[*The other* CHORUS *members also say: "Promise."*]

But look, there's Creon. The king! He's here
Perhaps to announce some new decree.

[*Enter* CREON.]

Creon.
You sour-faced woman, squalling at your husband,
Medea, I give you notice: you are banished.
You must leave now. Now! Take your children with you.
Don't make me wait. I shall not leave
Until I've seen you off Corinthian land.
Medea (*A cry*).
300 This is the end of everything, my last moment.
My enemies speed me on with all sail set
Toward the rocks—and there's no place to land.
I have been much abused, but I still ask you,
Creon, why are you sending me away?
Creon.
I am afraid of you: no need to wrap
The fact in phrases: I'm afraid that you
Might do my daughter some irreparable harm.
And many things contribute to this fear:

You are clever; you have seen and known much evil;
310 You are wounded, and deprived of bed and man.
And now I hear that you've been making threats
Against me, for giving my daughter to your husband.
I hear you will do something. I must guard against it.
Better to draw your hatred now than soften
And later have to weep for being soft.

Medea *(Laughs bitterly).*

Oh Creon, this is not the first time: often before
My reputation has done me harm, much harm.
My father, if he'd been wise, would never have had me
Taught to be clever, out of the ordinary.
320 That only makes you envied and disliked.
Try teaching new ideas to stupid people—
They think you're stupid, certainly not clever;
As for the others, who aspire to wit,
You offend them, too, if you are reckoned wittier.
I've had my share of that experience.
I am clever, so the jealous hate me—or
They find me difficult; but I'm not that clever.
Still, you're afraid of me. What do you think
I'll do to you to spoil your harmony?
330 You need not be on edge, Creon: look, I'm hardly
In a state for crimes against the crown.
What harm have *you* done *me?* It's my husband I hate,
Not you. You gave your daughter as your heart commanded.
That is your right, and seems to me quite sensible.
I don't resent things going well for you:
Celebrate marriage; prosper—all of you.
But let me stay. In spite of being wronged,
I'll keep the peace. You're stronger, and I've lost.

Creon.

You seem to answer softly. But I shudder
340 To think what evil may be in your mind.
The softness makes me trust you even less.
For a hot-tempered woman—or man—is easier
To guard against than someone quiet and clever.
So you must leave. With no delay. No speeches.
The order's fixed. I know you are my enemy,
And you shall not contrive to stay among us.

Medea.

I beg you, in the name of your newly married daughter.

Creon.
> Your words are wasted: you shall not persuade me.

Medea.
> You'll banish me? There's nothing I can say?

Creon.
350 > Why should I care for you more than my flesh and blood?

Medea.
> My country! How much I think of home today!

Creon.
> It's what I care for most—except my children.

Medea.
> O Love, how great a curse you are to mortals!

Creon.
> Well, that depends upon the circumstance. . .

Medea.
> Zeus knows who caused all this: don't let him get off free.

Creon.
> Move, woman. Must I have you dragged away?

Medea.
> No, Creon, no—not that. I'm pleading now. . .

Creon.
> So are you going to give me trouble? Yes or no?

Medea.
> We'll go, we'll leave—that isn't what I'm asking.

Creon.
360 > Why argue then? Why not just quietly go?

Medea.
> One day. Let me stay on for just one day.
> Let me think out clearly where it is we'll go,
> Make provision for the children, since their father
> Puts rather low his duty to his sons.
> Take pity on them: you're a father too;
> It stands to reason you have kindness in you.
> For my part, exile doesn't worry me—
> I weep for them: they are so young to suffer.

Creon.
> I've never had the temper of a tyrant.
370 > Often, from honoring other people's wishes,
> I've spoiled things for myself—and even now
> I see I might be making a mistake.
> Still, you shall have your way. But in advance
> I warn you, if the eye of heaven tomorrow

Should see you and your children on my soil,
You die. That is my word. As true as prophecy.
Remain then, if you must, this one day more:
Too short a time for you to do us harm.

[*Exit* CREON.]

Chorus.
Poor suffering woman!
380 Poor, poor wretch, in a world of troubles
Where will you turn? What host, what refuge,
What house or country can you find
That's safe and welcoming? What a sea of pain
The god has set you to sail across,
    Medea, a trackless sea.
Medea (*To* CHORUS).
Everything's set in every way against me.
But don't imagine this is all—not yet.
There are still dangers for this bride and groom:
And more than a little *trouble* for her father.
390 Do you think that I'd have crawled and fawned on him
Without some hope of gain, some scheme in mind?
I'd not have spoken to him, not have touched him.
But he has reached the depths of folly now:
He could have banished me at once, and stopped
My plans—instead, he's given me this day:
I've time to turn three enemies to corpses—
The father and the daughter, and *my* husband.

There are so many paths to death for them—
I can't decide which route is best to take.
400 Shall I light up the bridal house with fire?
Take a sharp sword and drive it through their hearts?
I'd slip in silently and find their bed—
But there's the difficulty: if I'm caught
On the way in, still working out the plan,
I'm dead—instead of killing them, I make them laugh.
The best road is the most direct, the way
I have most skill: I'll take them with my poisons.
So be it.
Suppose they're dead: what city will receive me?
410 What host will offer me protection,

Asylum and a home that's safe? Not one,
At present. So I'll wait a little yet:
Either a place of refuge will appear,
And I can take them by deceit and stealth;
Or, if the inevitable hour of exile
Comes first to drive me out, I'll use the sword,
Though it may cost my life, and go to kill them
Along the path of bravery and strength.

420   I swear by all the gods, whom I adore
And whom I call to help me once again,
They shall not laugh at this tormented heart.
I'll make their marriage sour—and painful—to them,
Sour the alliance of their families,
And sour the day they chose to banish me.
Come then, Medea; use every means you know;
Move toward horror: this is the test of spirit.
Remember what they're doing. Don't accept
Their mockery, this marriage of a Jason
To a girl whose ancestor was Sisyphus!

430   A man who pushes stones uphill in Hades!
They laugh at me, granddaughter of the Sun°!
But I have knowledge to oppose them with:
And also, I'm a woman; so, although disbarred
By nature from the noble deeds of man,
I have mastered all the arts of cowardice.

Chorus.
The water in rivers is flowing uphill.
     From now, upstream means down.
The laws of nature, the laws of man
     Are all turned round:

440   It's men do the wiles and smiles, the cheating, now,
    It's men will not keep the vows they swore,
While women now find history reversing
The low esteem in which they lived before.
A woman soon will have both rights and honor;
She won't have gossip holding her in check
     And spitting insults on her.

Time-honored lyrics we used to sing
     Will have to be rewritten.
They can't keep saying, "Don't trust a woman,

430–431. A man . . . the Sun!:
Sisyphus (sis′ə·fəs), the
founder of the city of Corinth,
was a trickster who eluded
death several times; when he
finally died, his eternal
punishment was to roll a
heavy boulder up a hill every
day and watch it roll down
just before reaching the top.
Medea's grandfather was
Helios, the sun god.

450   You might get bitten."
  The trouble was, Apollo, god of song,
      Never passed on his poetic fire
  To one of us. He liked us dumb and dancing,
  And chose no woman poet to inspire.
  Otherwise, what an ode I'd sing on men!
  The ages can tell tales of us, but husbands
            Have been as bad again!

  Poor woman, you left the king your father's house,
  Insane with passion, and on Argo's° bows
460 Parted the double rocks of Hellespont.
      You came to live in a foreign land,
      You lost the husband from your bed
            And now you lose the bed,
  And even that last right, the right to stay:
      The king is sending you away.

  Now words of honor blow away like clouds.
  No shame is felt, for Shame has learned to fly—
  Shame has left Greece and taken to the sky.
      You have no home or parent near,
470   Poor wretch, to be an anchorage
            Out of this stormy age,
  And now a new king's daughter has taken over
      Your lover's household and your lover.

[*Enter* JASON.]

Jason.
  O this is not the first time; I have seen it
  Often before: a savage, bristling nature
  Can do such harm, impossible to deal with.
  You had, and could have kept, this land and house
  As home, for the small price of giving in
  Gracefully to the plans of your superiors;
480 Instead, you froth some nonsense and get banished.
  To me it doesn't matter: keep on saying
  How wicked Jason is: "the worst of men";
  But what you said against the royal house—
  Count yourself lucky to escape with exile.
  How often, after you'd enraged our rulers,

459. Argo: the ship on which Jason and Medea left her home country.

I had to placate them, wanting you to stay here.
But you could not give up your folly, and still
You curse the king. So naturally, you're banished.
But even so I won't disown my family—
490   I come here, woman, still thinking of your future,
So you shan't leave for exile with the children
In need or unprovided: banishment
Brings many hardships. And—though I know you hate me—
I can't imagine ever hating you.

Medea.
    Spineless man!—the only weapon I have
Is words, to attack your failure as a husband!
You come to us, where you're most hated, here?
Is this your courage and heroic boldness,
To wrong your friends, then look them in the face?
500   No: it's that worst disease of human minds,
A blank where shame should be. But I am glad you came:
It makes my heart a little easier
To spear you with my words, and watch you writhe.

I'll begin at the beginning.
I saved your life, as every Greek can witness
Who joined you in the voyage of the Argo;
I helped you catch the fire-breathing oxen
And harness them, and sow the fatal field;
I killed the dragon, the sleepless sentinel
510   That wound its coils around the Golden Fleece;
I held the light of safety over you.
I chose to desert my father and my home
To come with you to Iolcos: full of love,
Empty of thought, in those days. After that, I killed
King Pelias, using his own daughters' hands
For the unkindest death, to wipe his blood-line out.
I did all that for you, and now you drop me;
You take a new wife, seeming to forget
That we have children. If you were a childless man,
520   One might forgive your lusting for her bed . . .
But all your oaths and promises are broken:
I cannot trust you now. Nor can I understand
What you believe in—do you think the gods
That used to govern us no longer do?
You seem to imagine the moral law has changed—

But even you must realize you've not kept your word.
Look at this hand you took in yours so often,
These knees you clung to, begging me to help:
The meaningless embraces of a bad
530   Husband! The hopes I entertained and lost!

Come on! I shall confide in you, like some old friend—
There's nothing I can gain from you, I know that,
But still—I can expose your shame with questions:
Where can I turn to, now? Home to my father?
I betrayed my home and country to come with you.
To the grieving daughters of King Pelias?
A fine welcome they'd give me
              In the house where I killed their father.
It comes to this: the friends I had at home
540   Now hate me; and in other places too
Where I need not have harmed a soul, I did,
Because you asked me to. They hate me now as well.
So in return for that, you made me "happy"—
Greek women think so, anyway: "What a wonderful
And faithful man that lucky woman has!"
This husband who calmly lets me go, to exile,
Without a friend, alone with fatherless children—
A fine beginning for a newly married man,
That his children and the woman who saved his life
550   Must wander abroad in cringing beggary.

Oh Zeus, why did you give humanity
The clearest evidence when gold is false—
But set no markings on the skin of man
To single out the bad one from the good?

Chorus.
This is a terrible passion: there's no cure,
When those who met to love now join to fight.

Jason.
So now the bad man must be good at speaking,
And like the skillful captain of a boat
Brail up the canvas and with shortened sail
560   Run out from under your noisy squall of words.°

You greatly exaggerate your kind assistance.
You claim you saved the Argo expedition.

559–560. Brail up the canvas . . . squall of words: In an extended metaphor, Jason compares himself to the captain of a boat who shortens the sail to move quickly away from a storm.

I have to say I credit Aphrodite°
And only Aphrodite, no one else.
You have quick wits, so it's not necessary—
Indeed it would be indelicate and ungrateful
To list the many ways in which Desire
Drove you, helpless, on to save my life.
So I shan't press the point in any detail;
570   I grant you helped me, and I'm glad you did.
On the other hand, you got more than you gave.
The first thing is, you live in Greece, instead
Of somewhere barbarous; you have learned of justice,
To enjoy the rule of law—not the whim of despots.
Then, all the Greeks have heard of you, the wise one,
And you are famous; if you were still living
At the edge of the world, there'd be no talk of you.
For me, I wouldn't want a houseful of gold,
Or a finer singing voice than Orpheus°—
580   Unless mankind could hear and point me out.

I've said that much about the Labors of Jason°
Only because you put the subject forward.
You also reproach me for my royal marriage:
I'm going to show you that was well thought out,
Entirely prudent, not a mindless impulse:
I was acting as the greatest possible friend
For you, and for my children—just keep calm.

When I moved on from Iolcos and came here,
Drawing misfortune inescapably
590   Behind me, what better treasure-trove could I have found
Than marriage with the daughter of a king—I, an exile?
Now don't torment yourself: don't think I'm weary
Of your bed; or that I'm smitten with desire
For a fresh wife—or have some strange ambition
To rival others who have many children—
Those that I have suffice—I've no complaint—of them or you.
I acted solely to ensure that we live well
And never go without, because I know
People will shun a man who's lost his wealth.
600   Also, I hoped to bring my children up
In a manner worthy of my own descent;
I thought I'd breed some brothers for our sons,

563. Aphrodite (af′rə·dīt′ē): the goddess of love.

579. Orpheus (ôr′fē·əs): a musician and singer of legend; his singing helped the sailors of the Argo (the ship on which Medea fled her homeland) resist the sweet singing of the Sirens.

581. Labors of Jason: In order to regain his throne, Jason was challenged to complete several impossible tasks, or labors, including retrieving the Golden Fleece.

Make them all equal, bring our lines together.
That way our happiness and security lies.
You don't need children—you have had enough—
But I could make my sons to come be useful
To those that I have now—is that a bad ambition?

You would approve—except that the marriage irks you.
Isn't that like a woman? You believe
610   While bed is right that everything is right,
But if you're left alone between the sheets
You treat your nearest, dearest and best friend
As your worst enemy. We should make our children
Some other way—and have no breed of women.
Then we would live as happy as the gods.

Chorus.

Jason, your speech is jeweled. All the same
We disagree with you, perhaps unwisely:
We think deserting her can not be right.

Medea.

I seem to differ from so many people.
620   To me, a person who does wrong and then defends it
So plausibly, deserves the heaviest punishment.
He trusts his clever tongue to decorate
His crimes with pretty words, which makes him bold
Enough for anything—but he's not that clever.
That goes for you: don't dazzle me with words
And surface logic. One simple point will throw
Your argument and pin you to the ground.
If you'd been honest, you'd have talked it over:
Persuaded me first, and married her after—
630   Not kept it secret from those who loved you best.

Jason.

And fine support you'd have given me if I'd told you
About this possible marriage, when even now
You hug your anger and will not give it up.

Medea.

That wasn't what prevented you from speaking.
Wasn't it really the thought of being married
To a barbarian, and getting old—
And your great reputation in decline?

Jason.

Try understanding: it was not for lust

I climbed into my present royal bed.
640   I did it, as I said before, to keep
You safe—and for my children: to breed them brothers
Who would be kings, to comfort us and keep us.

Medea.
What painful comfort! I pray I never find it,
Or prosper in a way that blights the heart!

Jason.
Oh, pray for something wiser: pray instead,
"Help me: not to find pain in what is pleasant,
And not to feel unlucky, when I'm not."

Medea.
What arrogance, when you've got a safe retreat
And I'm alone and going into exile.

Jason.
650   You chose this course yourself; blame no one else.

Medea.
I chose it! How? Did I take a wife and leave you?

Jason.
You cursed the king, and cursed his royal house.

Medea.
Yes, and I'll be a curse to your house too.

Jason.
I'll not go on with this. There is no point.
But if you want some help from my estate
Towards your exile and the children's needs,
Say so: I'm ready to be generous,
And give you letters for my friends abroad
Who'll treat you well. Don't be so passionate, woman.
660   Listen to me, to refuse such help is mad.

Medea.
I'll make no use of any of your friends,
Nor will I take your bounty; give me nothing.
There is no profit in a bad man's gifts.

Jason.
Well then, I ask the gods to be my witness
I only wish to serve you and the children
In every way; but you do not like kindness;
You willfully push the help of friends away.
Because of this you are going to suffer more.

Medea.

670 Go, go: I see you've been so long away
From her, you're itching with desire
For your new-broken girl. Get on with being married,
While you still can. Because I prophecy:
Your marriage will be one of horror and regret.

[*Exit* JASON.]

Chorus.

Eros° at times comes over us too strong,
    Which wrecks our reputation
    And leads us into doing wrong.
But if she comes in moderation,
    No goddess can delight you
    As much as Aphrodite.
680   I beg you, heavenly mistress,
Don't draw your golden bow at me, to fire
Those arrows tipped with ointments of desire,
    Which never miss.

O Chastity, the gods' best gift, embrace me;
    Bring Self-control, instead
    Of letting Aphrodite chase me
Half-mad to someone else's bed,
    Loading my days and nights
    With quarrels, moods and fights.
690   I hope that she respects
The quiet of all peaceful marriage beds
And judges right whose bodies and whose heads
    To stir with sex.

    Dear country and dear home,
    O may I never lose my city
        And have to roam
Unhelped through life's impenetrable maze,
    A pain we all can pity.
    I'd rather die than live such days:
700 There is no fate so bad as being banned
        For ever
    From home, to see the world but never
        Your native land.

674. Eros (er′äs′): the god of love; the companion of Aphrodite.

I've seen, I did not learn
This tale from others, that no city
          Will shelter you;
No guest of yours remembers you and treats
          Your sufferings now with pity.
I curse the man who coldly meets
710   A fallen friend like that. Unlock your heart
          I say,
Give him the freedom of your house,
          Give him the key.

[*Enter* AEGEUS.]

Aegeus.
    Medea!
    I wish you happiness—how can anyone
    Better begin, when talking to his friend?
Medea.
    Aegeus! How do you come to be here in Corinth?
Aegeus.
    I've been at Apollo's ancient oracle.
Medea.
    Delphi, the middle of the world!° Why there?
Aegeus.
720   To ask for the blessing of a child of my own seed.
Medea.
    You've lived till now and still you have no children?
Aegeus.
    I have no heir; some god or fate prevents it.
Medea.
    And what words of advice did the oracle give?
Aegeus.
    Wise words, but too subtle for a man to grasp.
Medea.
    Am I allowed to hear them?
Aegeus.
    Certainly: it requires a clever mind.
Medea.
    Then tell me. What did it say?
Aegeus.
    I was told "not to unstop the wineskin's neck . . ."

718–719. Apollo's . . . middle of the world!: Delphi was a city in ancient Greece and home to the principal oracle, or shrine, of Apollo. (*Oracle* can also refer to the divine communication received at such a shrine or to the person who reveals the communication.) The oracle at Delphi was believed to contain the midpoint of the world.

Medea.

Till when? Till you do what? Till you go where?

Aegeus.

730   Until I returned "to my native land."

Medea.

All gods be with you. May you get what you desire.

Aegeus.

What's wrong? Why do you look so pale and strained?

Medea.

Aegeus, my husband is the worst man living.

Aegeus.

But why? What has he done?

Medea.

He's taken another wife to run his house.

Aegeus.

What? Jason dares do such a shameful thing!

Medea.

He does. And I, once loved, am now despised.

Aegeus.

Is he in love? Or, out of love with you?

Medea.

It's love. It's passion. He's betrayed his family.

Aegeus.

740   Forget him—if he's as bad as you say he is.

Medea.

He is in love with royalty and power.

Aegeus.

Tell me everything. Who is the father?

Medea.

Creon, who is the king of Corinth here.

Aegeus.

I see. Now I understand the reason for your despair.

Medea.

This is the end of everything. I'm to be banished.
Creon means to drive me out of Corinth.

Aegeus.

And Jason lets him? That is shameful.

Medea.

He does protest, he says—but happily
Endures the prospect of my banishment.

750   Aegeus, I beg you,
Take pity on me, pity my misfortune.

Don't stand by as they drive me out.
Receive me in your country, in your home.
And in return the gods will give you
The children you desire. You'll end a happy man.
You do not know how fate has favored you
In bringing us together: for I have
Such remedies. I can cure your childless state.

Aegeus.
There are many reasons, lady, why I would
760   Dearly like to help you: first, to please the gods,
Then for your promise of children—
For there I am completely powerless.
But I make this condition: you reach my country
And I shall do my best as your protector
To guard your rights. But that is all I promise.
I am unable to help your flight from Corinth;
If you arrive in Athens at my house
You shall be safe: I'll give you up to no one.
But you must travel out of here yourself:
770   I cannot abuse the kindness of my host.

Medea.
So be it. But you must confirm your promise
With an oath. Then I will rest content.

Aegeus.
Why, don't you trust me? What is troubling you?

Medea.
I trust you; but the house of Pelias
Is my enemy, and Creon too.
If you are bound by oaths, you cannot yield me
To any enemies.
With just your word, not sworn by any gods,
You might become their friend and yield perhaps
780   To their diplomacy. My state is weak,
They have the power of a royal house.

Aegeus.
Medea, you are looking far ahead!
But I'll not refuse to do as you think best.
In fact, the oath will be security for me—
A good excuse to give your enemies.
It makes your standing firmer too. Well then,
Begin: tell me the gods that I must swear by.

Medea.

    Swear by this dust of Earth, by Helios the Sun,
    My father's father; then, by all the gods together.

Aegeus.

790   What must I swear to do, or not do? Tell me.

Medea.

    That you will never banish me yourself,
    Nor will you, if my enemies want to take me,
    Release me to them willingly, while you live.

Aegeus.

    I swear by Earth, by the clear lamp of Helios,
    By all the gods, I shall abide by what you say.

Medea.

    I am content. But if you don't abide
    By this strong oath, what penalty should you suffer?

Aegeus.

    The fate of those who don't respect the gods.

Medea.

    Be happy in your journey. All's well now.
800   I shall come to your city very soon—
    When I have finished what I've got to do
    And hit the targets that I've set myself.

[*Exit* AEGEUS *as the* CHORUS *give the travel-blessing.* NURSE *appears
at door of palace.*]

Chorus.

    May Hermes° bring you safe to Athens,
        You noble man.
    And may you get the blessing you desire,
        A noble son.

Medea.

    O Zeus! O justice of Zeus! O Helios!

    Now we are winning; we shall stand in triumph
    Over my enemies. We have begun to move.
810   Just when we seemed caught helpless in the storm,
    This man appears, and offers me safe harbor.
    Now I shall tell you what I'm going to do.

    I'll send a servant who will ask for Jason
    To come and see me; and when Jason comes,

803. Hermes (hʉr′mēz′): the
god of roads, sleep, and luck;
also the messenger god who
accompanied dead souls to
Hades; a trickster, he was the
patron of merchants and
thieves as well as athletes,
herdsmen, and orators.

I'll lull him with soft words and calmly say,
"Yes, I agree with you, it's quite the best decision
To leave us, to make a royal marriage:
It's in all our interests, a clever move."
Then I shall ask him if our sons can stay—
820 I'll use them as messengers of death to Creon's child.
I'll send them to her with presents in their hands,
A long light veil and a wreath of beaten gold,
But I shall smear such ointments on each one
That when she takes these ornaments and puts them
Against her skin, she will die horribly—
And everyone who touches her will die.

All that is easy, but I weep
To think of what comes next, what must be done,
And done by me: I'm going to kill
830 My children. Nobody shall take them from me.
Then, with the house of Jason quite destroyed,
I shall escape from Corinth, and escape
The penalty of killing my dear sons,
The most unholy crime we can commit.
I cannot, will not tolerate the scorn
Of those I hate. So let it all come down.
What life have I to lose?
What a mistake I made, that day I left
My father's house, believing in the words
840 Of a Greek. But he shall pay the price:
He'll never see the sons he got on me
Alive again, nor will he father one
On his new-harnessed bride, because she's doomed.
Let no one think Medea mild and quiet
And meek: I am of another mold,
Gentle to friends, implacable to foes.
That is the way to be respected here.

Chorus.
You have made us share your plans. You have made us promise
To help you, but we have to take the side
850 Of human law. We therefore say: don't do this.

Medea.
No other way. Your words can be forgiven,
Because you have not suffered; but I have.

Chorus.

But woman, how can you bear to kill your children?

Medea.

It is the way to hurt my husband most.

Chorus.

And make yourself the most miserable of women.

Medea.

Let be—all words are vain from now till then.
(*To* NURSE)
Come on then; go; you, go and fetch me Jason:
It's always you when I need someone I can trust.
You will say nothing of what I plan to do,
860   If you care for your mistress, if you are a woman.

[*Exit* NURSE.]

Chorus.

The Athenians have been flourishing
      And happy ever since
    The gods first sowed them in that holy land—
It is a Holy Land, unravaged, where they feed
    On Wisdom, the ambrosia° of thought—
Filing so elegantly through that brilliant air
      Where once, the Athenians say,
      The virgin Muses came
And bore their fair-haired child, Harmonia.

870   That lovely stream of Cephisus°
      Is where the Queen of Love
    Draws her moist breath and breathes it out across
Their country, puffs of moderate breeze with her sweet scent.
    There all year round she decorates her hair
With a fresh crown of woven flowers, perfumed roses—
      And she controls her child;
      For Eros there is good:
She makes him work for virtue and the arts.

    So how will that city of holy rivers
880   That country hospitable to friends,
    Take in the murderess of her sons,
    Unclean among its citizens?
    Imagine doing a child harm.

865. ambrosia (am·brō′zhə):
the mythical food of the gods.

870. Cephisus: the main river
in the Athens area.

Imagine cutting and killing him.
We beg you every way we can:
     Do not kill your children.

Where in your heart will you find the daring,
How will you nerve the hand and breast
With the awful courage it must take
890   To maim the bodies you love best?
When you look down and raise your knife,
When they look up and beg for life,
The tears will stop you, you will not
     Stain your hands with children.

[*Enter* JASON *with* NURSE.]

Jason.
     I've come. I'm at your command. I know you hate me,
     But I could not refuse you: I shall listen.
     So, you want something new from me. What is it?
Medea.
     Jason, I'm asking you to be forgiving
     About the things I said. You should indulge
900   My anger, after all our acts of friendship.
     I have begun to take myself to task:
     "Obstinate, silly woman, you must be mad:
     Why are you so opposed to good advice?"
     Why make myself an enemy of the king
     And of my husband, who is acting only
     In our best interest, marrying a princess
     To give my children brothers? Will I never
     Curb my temper? What's wrong with me? The gods
     Provide so well for everything I need.
910   I've got children, haven't I? Have I forgotten
     That we're in exile here and have no friends?
     Thinking about it, I have seen how little
     I plan ahead, blinded by futile anger.
     So now I agree with everything you proposed.
     You made a sound and practical alliance
     On our behalf, while I was merely thoughtless:
     I should have helped you plan the match, perhaps
     As go-between. I could have stood beside
     Your bed, with pleasure tending your new wife.

920 But we are what we are. I am a woman.
Not wicked perhaps, but frail. But it was wrong of you
To imitate my frailty and reply
With childish answers to my childishness.
But that's all past. I admit that I was wrong,
Before. I am wiser now. I ask your pardon.

[*Enter* CHILDREN *and* TUTOR *from the palace.*]

Oh, children, here; children, don't stay inside.
Welcome your father, come and talk to him,
Give up your hatred as your mother has.
We have made peace; our anger's soothed away.
930 So take his hand, his right hand—O my dears!

[JASON *is startled. She covers up.*]

I thought of the pain the future hides from us.
O children! may you live long years like this
Holding out your arms . . . What a fool I am
To weep so easily, to be so frightened.
Here I am, ending the quarrel with your father
At last, and I blur the tender sight with tears.
Chorus.
Pale tears have started from my eyes too.
O may this evil go no further!
Jason.
This is much better, woman; this is good—
940 But I don't blame you for your other moods.
It's natural for a woman to be angry
With her husband embarking on a second marriage.
But now your mind has moved to better thoughts:
You've seen the winning strategy, in the end,
Which proves you can control yourself and think.
And you, my sons, your father's spent much thought
On you—I've made arrangements. You'll be safe,
With the gods' help. One day you will come back
And be the foremost here in Corinth, with your brothers.
950 What you must do is grow; leave all the rest
To your father—and the friendly gods.
I look to see you reaching, strong and well,
To the full mark of manhood, taller than my enemies!

But what are these fresh tears? Why are you crying
Instead of being glad at what I say?

Medea.

It's nothing. I was thinking of the children.

Jason.

Take heart then: I'm making good provision for them.

Medea.

I'll try—it's not that I distrust your words.
A woman's naturally soft and given to tears.

Jason *(Persists).*

960   You seem so mournful over them. Why's that?

Medea.

I bore them, Jason. When you talked of their great future,
Sadness came over me; life is so uncertain.

But now, you came so we could talk. I've said
Some of it, and I'll try to say the rest.
The king sees fit to send me out of Corinth,
And I agree—I understand—it's best
If I live somewhere else, not in your way
Or in the king's—because he thinks I hate him.
So I'll be exiled—I am going soon—
970   But the children—you should bring them up yourself:
Ask Creon not to banish them as well.

Jason.

I don't know I'd persuade him; one should try . . .

Medea.

In that case, get your wife to ask her father
This favor: not to banish them from Corinth.

Jason.

Certainly; her, I think I can persuade.

Medea.

If she's a woman like all other women . . .

This time I'll take a hand and do my share:
I'll send her presents, the most beautiful things,
By far, that any person living has—
980   Our sons shall carry them.
                    Go, children,
Bring the treasures to us right away.

            [*The* CHILDREN *go into the palace.*]

She shall have not one happiness, but many,
Not only catching a hero for a husband,
But also the adornments that the Sun,
My father's father, gave to his descendants.

Jason.
Why do you give away your greatest treasures?
Do you think the royal house is short of clothes?
Or needs more gold? Don't give your rich inheritance away.
Surely, if I'm worth anything to my bride,
990 She'll pay more heed to me than to these gifts.

Medea.
Don't be so sure. They tell us gifts can sway
Even the gods, and when it comes to mortals,
Bright gold is stronger than ten thousand words.
Fate's on her side, and makes her fortune grow,
She's young and she's in power.
But to save my sons from exile
I'd barter with my life, never mind gold.

[*The* CHILDREN *return with partly wrapped presents.*]

Take good care of these wedding presents, children,
Carry them properly
1000 To the princess, the lucky bride: she'll have
Presents from me that nobody could fault.

And listen now: when you reach the palace,
Find your father's new wife, my mistress now,
And ask her, beg her: not to have you banished;
Give her these fine things—this is most important—
Give them into her hands alone.
Go quickly now. May all go well.
And bring your mother the news she longs to hear.

[JASON *leaves with the* CHILDREN *and* TUTOR.]

Chorus.
Now there's no hope, not any more, for the children's lives.
1010 They are walking at this moment towards death.
The young wife will be taking in the golden bands,
She will be thanking them for her destruction,
As on her yellow hair she sets

Her finery for the underworld, with her own hands.

Persuaded by their beauty, their immortal glow,
    She will put on the veil, the golden crown,
Dressing the bride herself for those who wait below.
    She will be tripping in the snare and falling
        Into the trap of destiny
1020   And wretched death: it's closing and she won't get free.

You, wicked bridegroom, you shall suffer too:
    Marrying into power, you have brought,
        Not knowing what you do,
Disaster to your children, to your wife
        A horrible end.
How you have wandered from the hero's life!
And I must weep to see your painful doom,
    Unhappy mother, who will kill
        The children of your womb
1030   Because a treacherous husband left his place
        Between your arms
And broke the law, to kiss a different face.

[*Re-enter* TUTOR *with* CHILDREN. NURSE *still on through this scene.*]

Tutor.
    Mistress, your sons have been released from exile.
    The royal bride was pleased to take the presents
    In her own hands.
    The children have been spared. They have a truce.
    What's the matter? They and you are lucky.
Medea.
    How cruel.
Tutor.
    What have I said? I thought it was good news.
Medea.
1040   You told us what you told us: I don't blame you.
Tutor.
    Then why are you staring at the ground? Why are you weeping?
Medea.
    How can I help it?—when I think the gods
    And my own wicked thoughts have worked to make this happen.

Tutor.

    Take heart; some day the boys will come to Athens
    And bring you back from exile, down to Corinth.

Medea.

    Ah, before that, I shall bring others down.

Tutor.

    You're not the only woman to be separated
    From her children: we must learn to bear things lightly.

Medea.

    I'll try to do so. But go in. Get the children
1050   Whatever they need—like any other day.

[*The* TUTOR *goes in. The* CHILDREN *stay.*]

    Oh children, children—so you have a city:
    You'll have a home, to go and stay in always—
    Away from your mother, leaving me to grieve.
    For I am going somewhere else, to exile,
    Before I get the joy of you and see
    Your happiness, your weddings and your wives,
    Before I decorate your marriage beds
    Or hold the wedding torches over you.

    What misery I have chosen for myself!
1060   I suckled you, my children, but for nothing—
    My labor went for nothing, all the scratches
    Of fortune's claws, and crushing pangs of birth.
    Such hope, I had such hopes of you:
    That you would care for me when I was old;
    When I died, your hands would wrap me for the grave—
    The final wish of man. Those dreams were sweet
    But they have come to nothing: bereft of you,
    I shall drag out a life of pain and grief,
    While you will never see your mother again
1070   With those dear eyes, but change into another life.
    My children, why are you staring at me so?
    Why do you smile at me, that last of all your smiles?
    What am I going to do? My heart gives way,
    It betrays me, when I see their shining faces,
    My babies. I cannot do it. Forget all plans
    I made before. I'll take my boys with me.
    How can I harm them just to hurt their father,

When all his pain would be as nothing to mine?
I will not do it. No. Goodbye, my plans.

1080   What's happening to me? Do I really want
To leave my enemies mocking me—and unpunished?
I must be brave, and do it. Coward woman,
To let soft arguments invade my heart . . .
Go, children; in; go in.

[*The* CHILDREN *start to go but hesitate. She forgets them and speaks
the next line to the* CHORUS.]

       And anyone
Who has no right to attend the sacrifices
Of this household, keep away:
My hand's not going to weaken.
No! No!
No, raging heart, don't drive yourself to this.
1090   Not this! Not the children's lives: let them alone.
They'll live there with us—they will bring us joy.
No, by the vengeful spirits that live in Hades,°
I shall not leave my children, I cannot leave them
To suffer the violence of my enemies.

It's all done now, in any case: there's no escape.
Surely the crown is on her head by now,
And in her golden veil the bride lies dying.
It's done.
       And now I take the road of dreadful misery,
And set my children on a worse road yet
1100   I have to speak to them.
(*To the* CHILDREN.)
Oh, flesh of my flesh! Give me your hands,
And let your mother kiss your hands,
Your arms, your lips. O clear and noble face
And form of children! Now may you both be happy
But somewhere else—for here your father takes
All happiness to himself. O those sweet kisses,
And soft, soft skin—the gentle smell of childhood!
Go now, go, go.

[*The* CHILDREN *now enter the palace.*]

1092. Hades (hā′dēz): the
Underworld, where the spirits
of the dead were believed to
live.

I can not look at them
One moment longer: this evil is overwhelming.
1110 I know what I intend to do is wrong,
But the rage of my heart is stronger than my reason—
That is the cause of all man's foulest crimes.

[*She sits and waits, looking towards Corinth.*]

Chorus.
I have been thinking—for women too
Have a Muse° that visits our thoughtless days—
I have been asking, as men might ask,
What is this human desire for children?
Does it make sense? Perhaps it is better
To stay virgin, never to know
If sons and daughters bring in the end
1120 A taste of sweetness or bitter pain.

Look at the parents, look at their eyes,
The radiant lines of love and worry.
"Is there enough for us all to eat?
Are they warm and well? Will they lead good lives
Or grow up bad?" These are the thoughts
That carve the faces of those who engender
The new generation. For behind the thoughts
Is a terrible fear: We know that Fate
May suddenly come with casual hand
1130 And pick the children to die before us.

So what is the answer? Why do we persist
In the longing for children? Can't we see
They are only a target more for the marksmen
Who watch our lives from above?

Medea.
At last. At last—there's one of Jason's servants.
I've waited here so long for news from the palace.
He comes towards us. He fights for breath—
Perhaps that shows the kind of news he brings.

[*Enter* MESSENGER.]

Messenger.
Medea, you've done a terrible thing. Beyond

1114. Muse: one of the goddesses of literature, music, dance, and other intellectual pursuits.

1140   All laws of man. You must get away—escape
    By land, or sea, anything: go, at once.

Medea.
    What's so terrible that I must fly my home?

Messenger.
    She's dead, our newly married princess; Creon
    Her father, also; dying from your poisons.

Medea.
    Your message is beautiful; you shall count forever
    Among my benefactors and my friends.

Messenger.
    What are you saying? Woman, are you mad—
    Exulting at the pain you have inflicted
    Upon our royal house? You do not flinch
1150   To hear the terrible report of it?

Medea.
    I have an answer; I could counter that.
    But tell your story slowly. Take the time.
    My friend, how did they die? It will delight
    Me twice as much if they died horribly.

Messenger.
    When your two little boys, beside their father,
    Came hand in hand into the bridal house,
    We were so happy, we, the slaves, who shared
    With you your pain. The rumor spread from one
    To another: you and your husband had healed your quarrel.
1160   One kissed the hands, and one the small fair heads
    Of your children. Drawn by happiness, I followed
    Behind them to the princess's part of the house.
    The mistress—whom we honor now, as once
    We honored you—had only eyes for Jason.
    But when she saw your boys in the door together,
    She dropped her gaze and coldly turned
    Her pale young cheek away, as in disgust
    That they were in her room. Your husband tried
    To smooth away her anger and disdain
1170   By saying, "Don't be cross with them—they're children;
    Stop feeling angry, turn your head this way,
    Think of your husband's family as your own,
    Accept their gifts—and ask your father to release
    My children from their exile, for my sake."

She saw the gifts they bore—could not resist,
Agreed of all her new-made husband wanted.
Your children and their father had scarcely left
The room before she'd picked the lace-veil up,
And wrapped it round herself, and on her brow
1180   Settled the golden crown. She rearranged
Her hair with a bright mirror in one hand,
And smiled at the lifeless image of herself.
Then she stood up, delighted with her presents.
She paced around so elegantly, turning
To see the folds of finery at her ankles.
Then suddenly this pleasant scene turned to horror:
Her color changed, she paled, she staggered back
Into her chair, trembling in every limb.
One of her older women, thinking maybe
1190   Some god of frenzy was attacking her,
Started to intone a prayer, but saw her mouth
Ran with bright scum, her eyes were turning back
Into her skull, no blood was in her skin.
The chant of her prayer became a shriek.
The servants of the house ran off
To fetch the father, to fetch the husband,
To tell them the disaster. The whole palace
Resounded to the thud of running feet.

Long, long moments she lay, with close-shut eyes,
1200   In a speechless trance,
Then woke, poor girl, and gave a terrible cry.
A second torment opened its attack:
The golden garland clinging to her hair
Melted in a torrent of omnivorous° flame,
And the delicate gown, your children's gift to her,
Began devouring the poor girl's delicate flesh.
She rose out of her chair and ran, on fire
Shaking her hair, her head, this way and that
Trying to throw the crown off; but the gold
1210   Gripped strong and firm; and the flame blazed up
Still more, increasing when she shook her hair.
She fell to the floor, exhausted by the pain,
Past recognition now, even to her father—
The setting of her eyes, the lovely face
No longer showed, but blood, entwined with flame

1204. omnivorous
(ăm·niv′ə·rəs): taking
in everything.

Fell from the crown of her head in gouts° and spurts,
And from her bones dripped flesh like pinetree tears,°
The invisible teeth of poison pulping it,
A sight so horrible we were all afraid
1220 To touch the corpse: the terror had taught us caution.
But her poor father, not knowing how she'd died,
Coming in suddenly, fell upon the body
Folding his arms about the corpse
And crying aloud, "My child, my child,
What god has destroyed you in this abominable way?
Who robs an old man close to the grave of an only child?
May I die—let me die beside my daughter."
His tears and laments stilled at last,
He tried to lift his aged body up,
1230 But the delicate gown clung fast like tangling ivy
On a laurel branch: a dreadful wrestling match.
He struggled to his knees, the sparkling dress
Holding him down, and as he used his strength
He tore the age-worn flesh from off his bones.
Fainting at last, no longer able to resist,
He gave to his unhappy soul release.
So they lie dead, the daughter and the father,
Together—a relief that gave us tears.
(*Directly to* MEDEA)
What happens to you I do not wish to think of—
1240 You will know some way to escape their vengeance.
But I must think, as I have thought before,
That human life is nothing but a shadow,
Nor would I hesitate to say that clever men,
Or those reputed clever, who play with words,
Are wrong—they should be called the greatest fools:
No mortal man is happy—safe from god.
Oh, if wealth pours down, one human might become
More prosperous than another—but happy, no.
Chorus.
The gods came down today and heaped on Jason
1250 A terrible punishment, but it was deserved.

[*Exit* MESSENGER *towards Corinth.*]

Medea.
Well then, it is decided: I must do it

1216. **gouts:** large spouts or
gushes.

1217. **like pinetree tears:** like
the thick, sticky sap from pine
trees.

And quickly: kill the children, leave the country;
No time, not a moment's delay lest I surrender
My sons for some unkinder hand to kill.
They'll have to die in any case: and therefore
I'll kill them—I'm the one who gave them life.
Come heart, fasten your armor. Why delay
The awful but inevitable crime?
Come wretched hand, my hand, pick up the sword,
1260   And creep towards the starting-line of pain.
No cowardice! No memories of the children
Being lovely, being born—for this short day
Forget your boys—weep for them afterwards:
For though you're going to kill them, they were loved—
While I was born unlucky and a woman.

[*Exit* NURSE *and* MEDEA.]

Chorus.
O Earth, O Helios shining everywhere
      Look down your rays and see
This deadly woman now before she kills
And reddens her white hands with children's gore.
1270   It's her own blood she spills
But also yours: they are your golden seed.
      A fearful thing, to pour
      A god's blood on the ground,
A god's blood dripping from a human hand.
O light of heaven, prevent her, intercede
Against Medea, the Fury of this house,
Unhappy, murderous, driven to revenge.

Your work of having children goes to waste,
      Your labor and your love,
1280   All wasted, all since you became a wife,
Since you came down the cruel passage, through
      The clashing rocks of life.
Poor wretch, why did this weight of anger fall
      So heavily on you?
      And why did murder find
A place among the answers in your mind?
The stain of family blood is hard to bear
For us on earth: when someone kills his kin,

The gods themselves come down to take revenge.

[*A child screams offstage.*]

Chorus.
1290   Do you hear the cries? Do you hear the children?
     Unhappy woman, woman of misery.
Boys (*Offstage cries*).
     What can I do to escape from mother's hands?
     —I don't know, brother. We are going to die.
Chorus.
     Dare we go in? We ought, we ought.
     To protect the children.
Boys (*Offstage cries*).
     Protect us! Yes, we need your help. Come quick.
     —We are nearly in the net: the sword will catch us.
Chorus.
     Wretched woman, you must be made
     Of stone or iron, to cut your crop
1300   Of children down, making your hand
     The hand of Fate.
     One woman only before our time
     Has ever laid hands on her own children.

     But that was Ino, who was driven mad
     By jealous Hera.° Medea is not mad.

     When Ino killed her little boys,
     She jumped into the sea. But Medea is not mad.

     She wandered to the edge of a sea cliff
     And fell and drowned. But Medea is not mad.

1310   What further horror is left to happen?
     O women, marriage, bed of pain,
     How much evil you have brought to mankind!

[*Enter* JASON, *in haste.*]

Jason.
     You, women—
     Is she—I cannot say the name; she's done

1304–1305. Ino. . . Hera: When Zeus fathered Dionysus with Semele (daughter of Cadmus), Zeus's wife Hera tricked him into killing Semele. Zeus then entrusted Dionysus into the care of Semele's sister Ino. The still-jealous Hera then punished Ino by driving her mad, causing her to leap into the sea with her own son.

Such terrible things—is she still here?—Medea?
Has she hidden away? She'd have to cower
Under the earth or else grow wings and rise
To the deepest layer of heaven, to escape
Being punished for the royal house of Corinth.
1320 Did she think to kill the rulers of the country,
Then leave this house and get away scot-free?
But it's my sons I'm anxious for, not her:
The family she has harmed will see to her,
But I have come to save my children's lives:
I fear the royal clan may take revenge
On me and mine for their mother's bloody deed.

Chorus.
Poor Jason! Poor man! You still don't seem to know
How bad it is—how far your misery goes.

Jason.
What deeper misery? Will she kill me too?

Chorus.
1330 Your sons are dead, and by their mother's hand.

Jason.
What, dead? Who, dead? Woman, you're killing me.

Chorus.
Your children are no longer living.

Jason.
She killed them? Where? In the house? Where?

Chorus.
Open the doors: you'll see them, slaughtered.

Jason.
Unbar the doors. Let me see.
Let me see my murdered sons.
Let me see them dead, and let me take revenge.

[*As* JASON *pounds on the doors,* MEDEA *appears high up in the house. Near her lie the children's corpses, ready to be displayed.*]

Medea.
What are you doing breaking down the doors?
Searching for corpses and the woman who made them?
1340 Stay there. If you have need of me, then say so:
Say what you like; you can never touch me, now.
Not in this chariot which my father's father,
The Sun, has given me for my protection.

Jason.

> You hateful woman, abominable thing,
> Loathed by the gods and me and all mankind!
> You could pick up a sword and hack the bodies
> Of children you had borne, to leave me childless.
> You have done this and dare to face the Sun
> And Earth! Oh harsh and sacrilegious° heart!

1350
> I curse you—now, in my right mind at last,
> Not senseless as I was when from your home,
> That barbarous place, I brought you back with me
> To a civilized land, already evil then.
> The avenging demon who was meant for you
> The gods have turned on me—you killed your brother,
> The boy who shared your childhood: foul with blood
> You stepped aboard my lovely boat, the Argo.
> So you began; and after lying as a wife
> Beside me, after bearing sons to me,

1360
> From jealousy and lust you kill them too.
> No woman born in Greece could bring herself
> To such an act, and yet in preference to them
> I chose to marry you, I chose the hand
> Of the enemy who was going to destroy me,
> A tiger, a savage, not a woman.
> Ah, but a million insults could not bite
> Into your heart, it is so brazen hard.
> Go, monstrous spirit, stained with children's blood.
> Out of my sight. Leave me to weep, and rail

1370
> Upon the god who minds my destiny:
> That I shall never enjoy my new-found bride,
> Never hold my sons again in my arms.
> All, all; all is lost; I lost them all

Medea.

> I could reply to everything you've said.
> But Zeus, father of gods and men, has witnessed all
> I did for you and all you did to me.
> You were not fated to insult my bed
> And live on pleasantly, laughing in my face,
> Nor was your princess. Nor was the father Creon—

1380
> Who gave her to you—allowed to banish me
> Without retaliation. Call me savage,
> Call me a tigress, call me what you like.
> But I have reached you. I have struck your heart.

1349. sacrilegious
(sak'rə·lij'əs) *adj.*: involving the disrespectful behavior toward God, or in this case, the gods.

Jason.
And hurt yourself: you share the loss and pain.
Medea.
The cry of your pain is music. It eases mine.
Jason.
My sons, what an unnatural mother you were given!
Medea.
Children,
Your father was ill with love: you died of it.
Jason.
It was not my hand that has brought them death.
Medea.
1390   No, just the insult of your other marriage.
Jason.
You thought it right to kill them for a marriage!
Medea.
You think that pain was little, to a woman?
Jason.
To a sane one, yes. But you find pain in everything.
Medea.
Look: they are dead. That thought stings even you.
Jason.
They live, as Furies to curse your blood.
Medea.
The gods know who began this agony.
Jason.
Because they see the horrors of your mind.
Medea.
Hate on. How I detest your snarling voice.
Jason.
And I loathe yours; parting from that is easy.
Medea.
1400   Well, what is left? I want it over too.
Jason.
To bury and mourn them—let me have the bodies.
Medea.
No. I shall bury them. These hands shall do it
When I have carried them to Hera's temple
Where they'll be safe from insults of their enemies,
Who might dig up their graves; and in this land
Where Sisyphus was king, we'll institute
A holy festival and sacrifice

For ever, to expiate their sinful murder.
Then I shall go to the city of Athena,°

1410 To Aegeus' house, and live in peace with him.
But you shall have no hero's death, no glory
You shall be crushed by a rotting timber of your Argo—
A bitter end to your marriage to Medea.

Jason.
Then I call down the Fury of vengeance
For little children: Swoop and destroy her.

Medea.
What kind of god do you think will listen
To a breaker of oaths, a deceiver of strangers?

Jason.
Unclean, abhorrent, killer of children.

Medea.
Go home. You can bury your wife.

Jason.
1420 I am going, bereft of my two sons.

Medea.
These tears are nothing. Wait till you're old.

Jason.
Oh my children, dear sons.

Medea.
To their mother, not you.

Jason.
So dear that you killed them?

Medea.
To give you pain.

Jason.
I long to kiss the gentle lips
Of my poor children.

Medea.
Now you talk to them, now you cling to them—
Then you rejected them.

Jason.
By the gods, allow me
1430 To hold my sons' poor bodies one last time.

Medea.
Nevermore. Your words are thrown away,
Mouthfuls of rubbish.

Jason.
Zeus, do you hear? She refuses me that!

1409. Athena: the goddess of wisdom and war, who was worshiped particularly in the city-state of Athens.

Even that! You see what she's done to me!
Look at this beast, fouled with blood.
It is the blood of her own young.
Nothing is left me, nothing to do
But stand and cry like a woman to heaven.
You killed my sons and now you deny me
1440 My right to touch them, to cradle, to bury them.
Oh gods, I wish
I had never bred these sons.
Oh gods, I wish I had never lain
In their mother's murderous arms.

[*Pause*]

Chorus.
And that is how it happened here.

Atsumori

Meet the Playwright

Seami Motokiyo (c. 1363–1443)

Seami Motokiyo (zā·ä′mē mō·tō·kē′yō) is one of the most enduring figures of the classical Japanese dramatic form called Noh, developed during Japan's medieval period, probably in the fourteenth century. Although Seami is remembered today as a playwright, he was born with acting in his blood: His father was one of the finest performers of his day. At the time of Seami's birth around 1363, Noh was still an unrefined art. Under the patronage of the shogun Ashikaga Yoshimitsu (äsh·ē·kā′gä yō·shē·mē′tsōō), this began to change. Ashikaga, a passionate devotee of the arts, brought various performers, including Seami's father, to live at his palace in Kyoto. He was particularly fond of young Seami and personally supervised the boy's education.

Seami's training in Noh began very early, probably around the time he was seven years old. At the age of twenty, not long after his father's death, he took over his father's acting school and began to write plays. At least two dozen of the best Noh dramas in the classical Japanese repertory are attributed to Seami.

Honor, Then Exile

We know very little of Seami's personal life. After Ashikaga's death in 1408, Seami lost favor at court and was eventually exiled for a period of time in 1434. According to legend, this brilliant and versatile figure of Noh drama died alone in 1443, at the age of eighty-one, in a Buddhist temple near Kyoto.

By all accounts, Seami, like his father, was a brilliant actor. His performances were said to have been graceful, restrained, and mysterious. He strove to invest his students with the same qualities, encouraging them to act purely for the fun of it in the beginning of their training at the age of six or seven and then work hard for the next fifteen or twenty years to achieve mastery of basic roles found in most Noh dramas: the warrior, the woman, and the old man. Like Zen Buddhism, the meditative practice that heavily influenced Noh drama, mastery of Noh was and is a lifelong task requiring immense discipline and dedication.

Background to *Atsumori*

Noh is a dramatic art form of medieval Japan that incorporates music, mime, dance, and verse. Just as Western drama is thought to have begun in religious ritual, so did Noh develop from songs and dances performed at religious festivals. Noh is influenced by Shintoism—the ancient religion of Japan—as well as by the principles of Zen Buddhism.

In Japanese, Noh is written with the Chinese character signifying "talent," and, indeed, the actors who perform Noh plays must be talented mimes and dancers as well as skilled interpreters of character. They must be able to convey a mood or feeling in a single word or gesture. The power of Noh, with its twin emphases on spirituality and artistry, lies in its ability to produce feelings of both peacefulness and ecstasy.

A Highly Stylized Dramatic Form

Noh plays are formal and stylized, following strict traditional patterns. Like haiku poetry, they are deceptively simple, evoking emotional responses through a kind of subtle poetry. Noh plays are performed on a small stage bare of all scenery except for a symbolic pine tree and pillars. The actors are few, and they are always male. Most of them wear hand-painted wooden masks that represent a particular character or emotion: a vengeful ghost, a holy man, a beautiful girl, a warrior, a wrathful serpent-woman. A chorus consisting of eight or ten singers echoes a principal actor's words or speaks for him as he mimes an action.

Each Noh drama involves two principal actors. The first is a ghost or a spirit called the *shite* (shtā), who wanders restlessly in the form of an ordinary person. The second actor is a bystander, or *waki* (wä´kē´)—often a wandering priest. One of the most common themes in Noh drama involves the *shite*'s release from suffering and restlessness. The characters in Noh drama are flat and one-dimensional, and time and space are treated in an unrealistic way. A span of several years may be distilled into one motion of a fan, or a single moment of joy or pain may be expressed in a lengthy dance.

The Legend Behind *Atsumori*

Atsumori (ä·tso͞o·mō´rē) is one of Seami's most famous plays. It is drawn from an episode of *The Tale of the Heike* (hä´kə), a medieval Japanese epic based on historical fact that tells the story of the rise and fall of the Taira family, otherwise known as the Heike.

The Heike suffered one of their most terrible defeats at a place by the sea called Ichi no tani. *Atsumori* takes place many years after this battle. A priest named Rensei, who was once a warrior with the rival Genji clan, has decided to return to the scene of the battle to pray for a sixteen-year-old named Atsumori, whom he killed on the beach that day. Rensei had taken pity on Atsumori and had almost refrained from killing him. He had realized, though, that if he did not kill the boy, his fellow warriors would. On that fateful day, Rensei had explained to Atsumori that he must kill him, but he promised to pray for Atsumori's soul.

Years later, Rensei returns to Ichi no tani. There he meets a peasant who is not what he seems. It is this meeting that Seami dramatizes in *Atsumori*.

Atsumori

Seami Motokiyo

Translated by **Arthur Waley**

CHARACTERS

The Priest Rensei (ren'sā), formerly the warrior Kumagai of the Genji clan

A Young Reaper, who turns out to be the ghost of Atsumori (ä·tsōō·mo'rē), a young warrior of the (Taira) Heike clan

His Companion

Chorus

Priest.

> Life is a lying dream, he only wakes
> Who casts the world aside.
> I am Kumagai no Naozane, a man of the country
> of Musashi. I have left my home and call
> myself the priest Rensei; this I have done
> because of my grief at the death of Atsumori,
> who fell in battle by my hand. Hence it comes
> that I am dressed in priestly guise.
> And now I am going down to Ichi no tani° to pray
> for the salvation of Atsumori's soul.

[He walks slowly across the stage, singing a song descriptive of his journey.]

> I have come so fast that here I am already
> at Ichi no tani, in the country of Tsu.
> Truly the past returns to my mind as though it
> were a thing of today.
> But listen! I hear the sound of a flute coming
> from a knoll of rising ground. I will wait
> here till the flute-player passes, and ask him
> to tell me the story of this place.

Reapers *(together).*

> To the music of the reaper's flute
> No song is sung
> But the sighing of wind in the fields.

Young Reaper.

> They that were reaping,
> Reaping on that hill,
> Walk now through the fields
> Homeward, for it is dusk.

Reapers *(together).*

> Short is the way that leads
> From the sea of Suma back to my home.
> This little journey, up to the hill
> And down to the shore again, and up to the hill—
> This is my life, and the sum of hateful tasks.
> If one should ask me
> I too would answer
> That on the shore of Suma
> I live in sadness.
> Yet if any guessed my name,

9. Ichi no tani (ē′chē nō tä′nē): location of a battle lost by the (Taira) Heike clan, of which Atsumori was a member.

Then might I too have friends.
But now from my deep misery
Even those that were dearest
Are grown estranged. Here must I dwell
    abandoned
40   To one thought's anguish:
That I must dwell here.°

Priest.
    Hey, you reapers! I have a question to ask you.

Young Reaper.
    Is it to us you are speaking? What do you wish
      to know?

Priest.
    Was it one of you who was playing on the flute
      just now?

Young Reaper.
    Yes, it was we who were playing.

Priest.
    It was a pleasant sound, and all the pleasanter
50   because one does not look for such music from
      men of your condition.

Young Reaper.
    Unlooked for from men of our condition, you
      say!
    Have you not read:
    "Do not envy what is above you
    Nor despise what is below you"?
    Moreover the songs of woodmen and the flute-
      playing of herdsmen,
    Flute-playing even of reapers and songs of
60   wood-fellers
    Through poets' verses are known to all the
      world.
    Wonder not to hear among us
    The sound of a bamboo flute.

Priest.
    You are right. Indeed it is as you have told me.
    Songs of woodmen and flute-playing of
      herdsmen . . .

Reaper.
    Flute-playing of reapers . . .

26–42. The reapers are speaking as one person. It is common in Noh theater for a chorus to speak a leading character's lines, often while the lead character is dancing.

Priest.

Songs of wood-fellers . . .

Reapers.

70   Guide us on our passage through this sad world.

Priest.

Song . . .

Reaper.

And dance . . .

Priest.

And the flute . . .

Reaper.

And music of many instruments . . .

Chorus.

These are the pastimes that each chooses to his
    taste.
Of floating bamboo wood
Many are the famous flutes that have been
    made;
80   Little Branch and Cicada Cage,
And as for the reaper's flute,
Its name is Green Leaf;
On the shore of Sumiyoshi
The Korean flute they play.
And here on the shore of Suma
On Stick of the Salt-kilns°
The fishers blow their tune.

Priest.

How strange it is! The other reapers have all
    gone home, but you alone stay loitering here.
90   How is that?

Reaper.

How is it, you ask? I am seeking for a prayer
    in the voice of the evening waves. Perhaps
    you will pray the Ten Prayers for me?

Priest.

I can easily pray the Ten Prayers for you, if
    you will tell me who you are.

Reaper.

To tell you the truth—I am one of the family of
    Lord Atsumori.

Priest.

One of Atsumori's family? How glad I am!

80–86. Little Branch, Cicada Cage, Green Leaf, and **Stick of the Salt-kilns** are all names of flutes; a cicada is a type of insect.

Then the priest joined his hands *(he kneels down)* and prayed:

Namu Amidabu.°

Praise to Amida Buddha!°
"If I attain to Buddhahood,
In the whole world and its ten spheres
Of all that dwell here none shall call on my
    name
And be rejected or cast aside."
Chorus.
"Oh, reject me not!
One cry suffices for salvation,
Yet day and night
Your prayers will rise for me.
Happy am I, for though you know not my name,
Yet for my soul's deliverance
At dawn and dusk henceforward I know that you
    will pray."
So he spoke. Then vanished and was seen no
    more.

[*Here follows the Interlude between the two Acts, in which a recitation concerning* ATSUMORI's *death takes place. These interludes are subject to variation and are not considered part of the literary text of the play.*]

Priest.
Since this is so, I will perform all night the
    rites of prayer for the dead, and calling upon
    Amida's name will pray again for the
    salvation of Atsumori.

[*The ghost of* ATSUMORI *appears, dressed as a young warrior.*]

Atsumori.
Would you know who I am
That like the watchmen at Suma Pass
Have wakened at the cry of sea birds roaming
Upon Awaji shore?
Listen, Rensei. I am Atsumori.

100

110

120

101. *Namu Amidabu* (nä′mōō ä′mə·dä′bōō): prayer by which followers of the Amida Buddha obtained salvation.

102. Amida Buddha (ä′mē′dä bōō′də): an enlightened being worshiped by followers of a Buddhist sect in medieval Japan.

Priest.

How strange! All this while I have never
stopped beating my gong and performing the
rites of the Law.° I cannot for a moment have

130   dozed, yet I thought that Atsumori was
standing before me. Surely it was a dream.

Atsumori.

Why need it be a dream? It is to clear the
karma° of my waking life that I am come here
in visible form before you.

Priest.

Is it not written that one prayer will wipe
away ten thousand sins? Ceaselessly I have
performed the ritual of the Holy Name° that
clears all sin away. After such prayers, what
evil can be left? Though you should be sunk

140   in sin as deep . . .

Atsumori.

As the sea by a rocky shore,
Yet should I be saved by prayer.

Priest.

And that my prayers should save you . . .

Atsumori.

This too must spring
From kindness of a former life.°

Priest.

Once enemies . . .

Atsumori.

But now . . .

Priest.

In truth may we be named . . .

Atsumori.

Friends in Buddha's Law.

Chorus.

150   There is a saying, "Put away from you a wicked
friend; summon to your side a virtuous
enemy." For you it was said, and you have
proven it true.
And now come tell with us the tale of your confession,
while the night is still dark.

Chorus.

He° bids the flowers of spring

128–129. **the rites of the Law:**
doctrines of Buddhism, or of a
Buddhist sect.

133. **karma** (kär′mə): a
person's actions, which
Buddhists believe
influence the fate of a person
in this and future lives.

137. **the ritual of the Holy
Name:** recitation of the prayer
"Namu Amidabu."

145. **From kindness of a
former life:** Atsumori must
have done Rensei some
kindness in a former
incarnation. This would
account for Rensei's remorse.

156. **He:** Buddha.

Mount the treetop that men may raise their
    eyes
And walk on upward paths;
160   He bids the moon in autumn waves be drowned
In token that he visits laggard men
And leads them out from valleys of despair.

Atsumori.
Now the clan of Taira,° building wall to wall,
Spread over the earth like the leafy branches of
    a great tree:

Chorus.
Yet their prosperity lasted but for a day;
It was like the flower of the convolvulus.°
There was none to tell them
That glory flashes like sparks from flint-
170   stone,
And after—darkness.
Oh wretched, the life of men!

Atsumori.
When they were on high they afflicted the
    humble;
When they were rich they were reckless in
    pride.
And so for twenty years and more
They ruled this land.
But truly a generation passes like the space of a
180   dream.
The leaves of the autumn of Juyei°
Were tossed by the four winds;
Scattered, scattered (like leaves too) floated
    their ships.
And they, asleep on the heaving sea, not even in
    dreams
Went back to home.
Caged birds longing for the clouds—
Wild geese were they rather, whose ranks are
190   broken
As they fly to southward on their doubtful
    journey.
So days and months went by; spring came again
And for a little while
Here dwelt they on the shore of Suma

163. Taira (tä·ē′rä): clan of the Heike.

167. convolvulus (kən·väl′vyōō·ləs): flower of the morning-glory family.

181. Juyei (jōō·yā′): The Taira evacuated the capital in the second year of Juyei, 1188.

At the first valley.°
From the mountain behind us the winds blew
 down
Till the fields grew wintry again.
200 Our ships lay by the shore, where night and day
The sea gulls cried and salt waves washed on
 our sleeves.
We slept with fishers in their huts
On pillows of sand.
We knew none but the people of Suma.
And when among the pine trees
The evening smoke was rising,
Brushwood, as they called it,
Brushwood we gathered
210 And spread for carpet.
Sorrowful we lived
On the wild shore of Suma,
Till the clan Taira and all its princes
Were but villagers of Suma.

Atsumori.
But on the night of the sixth day of the second
 month
My father Tsunemori° gathered us together.
"Tomorrow," he said, "we shall fight our last
 fight.
220 Tonight is all that is left us."
We sang songs together, and danced.

Priest.
Yes, I remember; we in our siege-camp
Heard the sound of music
Echoing from your tents that night;
There was the music of a flute . . .

Atsumori.
The bamboo flute! I wore it when I died.

Priest.
We heard the singing . . .

Atsumori.
Songs and ballads . . .

Priest.
Many voices

Atsumori.
230 Singing to one measure.

[ATSUMORI *dances.*]

First comes the royal boat.

Chorus.

The whole clan has put its boats to sea.
He° will not be left behind;
He runs to the shore.
But the royal boat and the soldiers' boats
Have sailed far away.

Atsumori.

What can he do?
He spurs his horse into the waves.
He is full of perplexity.

240 And then

Chorus.

He looks behind him and sees
That Kumagai pursues him;
He cannot escape.
Then Atsumori turns his horse
Knee-deep in the lashing waves,
And draws his sword.
Twice, three times he strikes; then, still
    saddled,
In close fight they twine; roll headlong together

250 Among the surf of the shore.
So Atsumori fell and was slain, but now the
    Wheel of Fate
Has turned and brought him back.

[ATSUMORI *rises from the ground and advances toward the Priest
with uplifted sword.*]

"There is my enemy," he cries, and would
    strike.
But the other is grown gentle
And calling on Buddha's name
Has obtained salvation for his foe;
So that they shall be reborn together

260 On one lotus° seat.
"No, Rensei is not my enemy.
Pray for me again, oh pray for me again."

233. He: Atsumori; the passage is mimed throughout.

260. lotus (lōt′əs): waterlily sacred to Buddhists.

The Flying Doctor

Meet the Playwright

Molière (1622–1673)

In explaining the importance of Molière (mōl·yer´) to non-French audiences, critics and teachers have often called him the French Shakespeare. Although Molière was not as wide-ranging in his writing as Shakespeare (who wrote tragedies and histories as well as comedies), he successfully transformed comedy into a sophisticated form of drama.

Molière, whose real name was Jean Baptiste Poquelin, was born in Paris about six years after Shakespeare's death. He was the eldest son of a man who served in the court of the French king Louis XIII. Jean Baptiste's father had gained respectability through his career as the upholsterer of the king's furniture, and he had lofty ambitions for his son. He made sure that his son completed his education, studied law, and eventually took a position in court.

Unfortunately for the father, the son's love for the theater, as well as for an actress named Madeleine Béjart, brought Jean Baptiste's royal career to an end. In 1643, Jean Baptiste abandoned the luxury of life at court, changed his name to Molière, and pursued a career in the rough-and-tumble world of theater. He acted and stage-managed a struggling troupe. His inexperience (and poorly received acting) led quickly to the troupe's bankruptcy and, for Molière, time in jail for unpaid debts. After prison, Molière left Paris for the countryside, where, for the next thirteen years, he learned to write and perform popular comedies based on an old Italian theatrical form called **commedia dell'arte** ("comedy of art"), a stylized form of comic theater involving stock situations and masked characters with names like Harlequin, Scaramouch, and Pierrot.

A Victorious Return

In 1658, Molière and his players returned to Paris to perform his comedy *The Amorous Quarrel*, which was an instant success. King Louis XIV, a great patron of French culture and the arts, agreed to support Molière's players and granted them free theater space in which to perform. For the next fifteen years, Molière wrote sophisticated, often controversial comedies that provoked his enemies and delighted his fans. One play in particular,

Tartuffe (1664), so scandalized the authorities with its treatment of religious hypocrisy that it was banned twice.

By the time of Molière's sudden death from a blood clot in his lung in 1673, his plays were so popular that they were often plagiarized or stolen outright. By the eighteenth century, though, audiences had tired of Molière; his style and plots were so overexposed that his works fell out of circulation in France. In the nineteenth century, however, his plays were rediscovered and championed by critics and performers alike. His plays *The School for Wives, Tartuffe, The Misanthrope,* and *The Imaginary Invalid* delight audiences to this day.

Background to *The Flying Doctor*

Molière's *The Flying Doctor* is a one-act play written around 1645, during his long years of touring in the French countryside. Molière had not yet come into his own as a playwright and social commentator, yet the basic elements of his more mature works—some of the first examples of the **comedy of manners**—are here. Like the comedy of manners, the play features a love plot in which two young people conquer all obstacles to their union. While the true comedy of manners would focus more on the customs, costumes, and gestures of its middle- and upper-class characters, *The Flying Doctor* gives us a sample of the witty dialogue that is Molière's trademark.

The Flying Doctor is at heart a gentle, frivolous comedy, but the seeds of satire—which Molière would push to the limit in his later plays—are planted in this short play. Molière always walked a fine line between pleasing and teasing his audiences. He poked fun at courtiers (attendants in the king's court), priests, doctors, lawyers, and the middle class, and most of the targets of his satire loved his plays. But some did not, and so Molière made enemies—at court, in the church, and on the street. Through his irreverent drama, Molière expressed a new spirit that was just beginning to take hold in Europe in the seventeenth century. It was the spirit of a new intellectual movement called the Enlightenment.

The Age of Reason

The Enlightenment was the period between about 1650 and 1800 in which significant social and political change overtook Europe. Frustrated with the dominance of the Roman Catholic Church and inspired by advances in science, seventeenth-century Europeans turned to rationalism, a school of thought that stressed reason over faith and reliance on human achievements rather than on God. Rationalists began to question the influence of the church and the absolute right of kings who claimed their power came directly from God. Movement toward modern, representational government started during this time, as the power of court and the church began to wane and the middle class became more educated and wealthy. Scientific discoveries, international commerce, and a new consciousness of human rights also helped Europeans see the world and their place in it in a completely new way. It was a time of great confidence in human potential. Europeans thought they could create a perfect world by applying reason to any problem.

Molière's plays reflect the spirit of the early Enlightenment. He satirizes the aristocracy, the church, and the merchant class alike. More importantly, he makes his characters seem human. By making his characters flawed and vulnerable, Molière inspires audiences' affection and empathy for them. Although the situations in Molière's works may seem quaint and dated to modern audiences, his characters and his humor do not, and that is why his plays have endured.

The Flying Doctor

Molière

Translated by **Albert Bermel**

CHARACTERS

Gorgibus (gôr′ʒhē·bo͞os), a respectable, comfortable, credulous citizen

Lucile (lo͞o·sēl′), his daughter

Sabine (sa·bēn′), his niece

Valère (va·lār′), young man in love with Lucile

Sganarelle (zga·na·rel′), valet to Valère

Gros-René (grō·rə·nā′), valet to Gorgibus

A Lawyer

Scene: A street in a small French town.

VALÈRE, *a young man, is talking to* SABINE, *a young woman, in front of the house of* GORGIBUS, *her uncle.*

Valère. Sabine, what do you advise me to do?

Sabine. We'll have to work fast. My uncle is determined to make Lucile marry this rich man, Villebrequin,[1] and he's pushed the preparations so far that the marriage would have taken place today if my cousin were not in love with you. But she is—she has told me—and since my greedy uncle is forcing our hand, we've come up with a device for putting off the wedding. Lucile is pretending to be ill, and the old man, who'll believe almost anything, has sent me for a doctor. If you have a friend we can trust, I'll take him to my uncle and he can suggest that Lucile is not getting nearly enough fresh air. The old boy will then let her live in the pavilion at the end of our garden, and you can meet her secretly, marry her, and leave my uncle to take out his anger on Villebrequin.

Valère. But where can I find a doctor who will be sympathetic to me and risk his reputation? Frankly, I can't think of a single one.

Sabine. I was wondering if you could disguise your valet? It'll be easy for him to fool the old man.

Valère. If you knew my valet as I do—He's so dense he'll ruin everything. Still, I can't think of anybody else. I'll try to find him.

[SABINE *leaves.*]

Where can I start to look for the half-wit?

[SGANARELLE *comes in, playing intently with a yo-yo.*]

Sganarelle, my dear boy, I'm delighted to see you. I need you for an important assignment. But I don't know what you can do——

Sganarelle. Don't worry, Master, I can do anything. I can handle any assignment, especially important ones. Give me a difficult job. Ask me to find out what time it is. Or to check on the price of butter at the market. Or to water your horse. You'll soon see what I can do.

Valère. This is more complicated. I want you to impersonate a doctor.

Sganarelle. A doctor! You know I'll do anything you want, Master, but when it comes to impersonating a doctor, I couldn't do it if I tried—wouldn't know how to start. I think you're making fun of me.

Valère. If you care to try, I'll give you one hundred francs.[2]

Sganarelle. One hundred whole francs, just for pretending to be a doctor? No, Master, it's impossible. You see I don't have the brains for it. I'm not subtle enough; I'm not even bright. So that's settled. I impersonate a doctor. Where?

Valère. You know Gorgibus? His daughter is lying in there ill—No, it's no use; you'll only confuse matters.

Sganarelle. I bet I can confuse matters as well as all the doctors in this town put together. Or kill patients as easily. You know the old saying, "After you're dead, the doctor comes." When I take a hand there'll be a new saying: "After the doctor comes, you're dead." Now I think it over, though, it's not that easy to play a doctor. What if something goes wrong?

Valère. What can go wrong? Gorgibus is a simple man, not to say stupid, and you can dazzle him by talking about Hippocrates and Galen.[3] Put on a bold front.

---

1. **Villebrequin** (vēl·brə·ka*n*ʹ).

2. **francs:** plural of *franc* (frä*n*), the traditional monetary unit of France.

3. **Hippocrates** (hi·päkʹrə·tēzʹ) **and Galen** (gāʹlən): The Greek physicians Hippocrates (460?–377? B.C.) and Galen (A.D. 130?–200?) laid down major principles of medical science.

Sganarelle. In other words, talk about philosophy and mathematics and the like. Leave it to me, Master; if he's a fool, as you say, I think I can swing it. All I need is a doctor's cloak and a few instructions. And also my license to practice, or to put it another way, those hundred francs.

[*They go out together.* GORGIBUS *enters with his fat valet,* GROS-RENÉ.]

Gorgibus. Hurry away and find a doctor. My daughter's sick. Hurry.

Gros-René. The trouble is you're trying to marry her off to an old man when she wants a young man; that's the only thing making her sick. Don't you see any connection between the appetite and the illness?

Gorgibus. I can see that the illness will delay the wedding. Get a move on.

Gros-René. All this running about and my stomach's crying out for a new inner lining of food and now I have to wait for it. I need the doctor for myself as much as for your daughter. I'm in a desperate state.

[*He lumbers off.* SABINE *comes in with* SGANARELLE *behind her.*]

Sabine. Uncle, I have good news. I've brought a remarkably skilled doctor with me, a man who has traveled across the world and knows the medical secrets of Asia and Africa. He'll certainly be able to cure Lucile. As luck would have it, somebody pointed him out to me and I knew you'd want to meet him. He's so clever that I wish I were ill myself so that he could cure me.

Gorgibus. Where is he?

Sabine. Standing right behind me. (*She moves away.*) There he is.

Gorgibus. Thank you so much for coming, Doctor. I'll take you straight to my daughter, who is unwell. I'm putting all my trust in you.

Sganarelle. Hippocrates has said—and Galen has confirmed it with many persuasive arguments—that when a girl is not in good health she must be sick. You are right to put your trust in me, for I am the greatest, the most brilliant, the most doctoral physician in the vegetable, mineral, and animal kingdoms.

Gorgibus. I'm overjoyed to hear it.

Sganarelle. No ordinary physician am I, no common medico. In my opinion, all others are quacks. I have peculiar talents. I have secrets. *Salamalec and shalom aleichem. Nil nisi bonum? Si, Signor. Nein, mein Herr. Para siempre.*[4] But let us begin.

[*He takes* GORGIBUS's *pulse.*]

Sabine. He's not the patient. His daughter is.

Sganarelle. That is of no consequence. The blood of the parent and the blood of the child are the same. *Si? Nein. Per quanto? Nada.* . . .

Sabine. She may be up by now. I'll bring her out.

[*She goes into the house and brings* LUCILE *back with her.*]

Sganarelle. How do you do, Mademoiselle?[5] So you are sick?

Lucile. Yes, Doctor.

Sganarelle. That is a striking sign that you are not well. Do you feel pains in your head, in your kidneys?

Lucile. Yes, Doctor.

Sganarelle. Very good. As one great physician has said in regard to the nature of animal life—well—he said many things. We must attribute

---

4. *Salamalec . . . siempre:* This passage and Sganarelle's next one contain a nonsensical mixture of phrases from several different languages.
5. **Mademoiselle** (mad′ə·mə·zel′): French for the courtesy title *Miss.*

this to the interconnections between the humors and the vapors.[6] For example, since melancholy is the natural enemy of joy, and since the bile that spreads through the body makes us turn yellow, and since there is nothing more inimical to good health than sickness, we may conclude with that great man that your daughter is indisposed. Let me write you a prescription.

Gorgibus. Quick! A table, paper, some ink——

Sganarelle. Is there anybody here who knows how to write?

Gorgibus. Don't you?

Sganarelle. I have so many things to think of I forget half of them. Now it's obvious to me that your daughter needs fresh air and open prospects.

Gorgibus. We have a very beautiful garden and a pavilion with some rooms that look out on it. If you agree, I can have her stay there.

Sganarelle. Let us examine this dwelling.

[*They start to go out. The* LAWYER *appears.*]

Lawyer. Monsieur[7] Gorgibus—

Gorgibus. Your servant, Monsieur.

Lawyer. I hear that your daughter is sick. May I offer my services, as a friend of the family?

Gorgibus. I have the most scholarly doctor you ever met looking into this.

Lawyer. Really? I wonder if I might be able to meet him, however briefly?

[GORGIBUS *beckons to* SGANARELLE. LUCILE *and* SABINE *have moved offstage.*]

Gorgibus. Doctor, I would like you to meet one of my dear friends, who is a lawyer and would like the privilege of conversing with you.

Sganarelle. I wish I could spare the time, Monsieur, but I dare not neglect my patients. Please forgive me.

[*He tries to go. The* LAWYER *holds his sleeve.*]

Lawyer. My friend Gorgibus has intimated, Monsieur, that your learning and abilities are formidable, and I am honored to make your acquaintance. I therefore take the liberty of saluting you in your noble work, and trust that it may resolve itself well. Those who excel in any branch of knowledge are worthy of all praise, but particularly those who practice medicine, not only because of its utility, but because it contains within itself other branches of knowledge, all of which render a perfect familiarity with it almost impossible to achieve. As Hippocrates so well observes in his first aphorism, "Life is short, art is long, opportunity fleeting, experiment perilous, judgment difficult: *Vita brevis, ars vero longa, occasio autem praeceps, experimentum periculosum, judicium difficile.*"

Sganarelle (*confidentially to* GORGIBUS). Ficile, bicile, uptus, downtus, inandaboutus, wrigglo, gigolo.

Lawyer. You are not one of those doctors who apply themselves to so-called rational or dog-matic medicine, and I am sure that you conduct your work with unusual success. Experience is the great teacher: *experientia magistra rerum.* The first men who practiced medicine were so esteemed that their daily cures earned them the status of gods on earth. One must not condemn a doctor who does not restore his patients to health, for healing may not be effected by his remedies and wisdom alone. Ovid[8] remarks,

---

6. **humors ... vapors:** Before modern medical science, four types of body fluids, called humors, were thought to influence moods and health. The vapors were believed to be harmful exhalations from the stomach and were sometimes associated with hypochondria or depression.

7. **Monsieur** (mə·syö′): French for *Mr.* or *Sir.*

8. **Ovid:** Roman poet (43 B.C.–A.D. 17?).

"Sometimes the ill is stronger than art and learning combined." Monsieur, I will not detain you longer. I have enjoyed this dialogue and am more impressed than before with your percipience and breadth of knowledge. I take my leave, hoping that I may have the pleasure of conversing with you further at your leisure. I am sure that your time is precious, and . . . .

[*He goes off, walking backwards, still talking, waving good-bye.*]

Gorgibus. How did he strike you?
Sganarelle. He's moderately well informed. If I had more time I could engage him in a spirited discussion on some sublime and elevated topic. However, I must go. What is this?

[GORGIBUS *is tucking some money into his hand.*]

Gorgibus. Believe me, Doctor, I know how much I owe you.
Sganarelle. You must be joking, Monsieur Gorgibus. I am no mercenary. (*He takes the money.*) Thank you very much.

[GORGIBUS *goes off, and* SGANARELLE *drops his doctor's cloak and hat at the edge of the stage, just as* VALÈRE *reappears.*]

Valère. Sganarelle, how did it go? I've been worried. I was looking for you. Did you ruin the plan?
Sganarelle. Marvel of marvels. I played the part so well that Gorgibus thought I knew what I was talking about—and paid me. I looked at his home and told him that his daughter needed air, and he's moved her into the little house at the far end of his garden. You can visit her at your pleasure.
Valère. You've made me very happy, Sganarelle. I'm going to her now. (*He rushes away.*)

Sganarelle. That Gorgibus is a bigger dimwit than I am to let me get away with a trick like that. Save me—here he comes again. I'll have to talk fast.

[GORGIBUS *returns.*]

Gorgibus. Good morning, Monsieur.
Sganarelle. Monsieur, you see before you a poor lad in despair. Have you come across a doctor who arrived in town a short while ago and cures people miraculously?
Gorgibus. Yes, I've met him. He just left my house.
Sganarelle. I am his brother. We are identical twins and people sometimes take one of us for the other.
Gorgibus. Heaven help me if I didn't nearly make the same mistake. What is your name?
Sganarelle. Narcissus,[9] Monsieur, at your service. I should explain that once, when I was in his study, I accidentally knocked over two containers perched on the edge of his table. He flew into such a rage that he threw me out and swore he never wanted to see me again. So here I am now, a poor boy without means or connections.
Gorgibus. Don't worry; I'll put in a good word for you. I'm a friend of his; I promise to bring you together again. As soon as I see him, I'll speak to him about it.
Sganarelle. I am very much obliged to you, Monsieur. (*He goes out and reappears in the cloak and hat, playing the doctor again and talking to himself.*) When patients refuse to follow their doctor's advice and abandon themselves to debauchery[10] and——
Gorgibus. Doctor, your humble servant. May I ask a favor of you?

---

9. **Narcissus** (när·sis′əs): The original Narcissus, a young man in Greek myth, was fascinated by his reflection in the water. Molière's Narcissus is supposed to be the twin, or reflection, of Sganarelle.
10. **debauchery** (dē·bôch′ər·ē): immoral behavior.

Sganarelle. What can I do for you, Monsieur Gorgibus?

Gorgibus. I just happened to meet your brother, who is quite distressed——

Sganarelle. He's a rascal, Monsieur Gorgibus.

Gorgibus. But he truly regrets that he made you so angry, and——

Sganarelle. He's a drunkard, Monsieur Gorgibus.

Gorgibus. But surely, Doctor, you're not going to give the poor boy up?

Sganarelle. Not another word about him. The impudence of the rogue, seeking you out to intercede for him! I implore you not to mention him to me.

Gorgibus. In God's name, Doctor, and out of respect for me, too, have pity on him. I'll do anything for you in return. I promised——

Sganarelle. You plead so insistently that, even though I swore a violent oath never to forgive him—well, I'll shake your hand on it; I forgive him. You can be assured that I am doing myself a great injury and that I would not have consented to this for any other man. Good-bye, Monsieur Gorgibus.

Gorgibus. Thank you, Doctor, thank you. I'll go off and look for the boy to tell him the glad news.

[*He walks off.* SGANARELLE *takes off the doctor's cloak and hat.* VALÈRE *appears.*]

Valère. I never thought Sganarelle would do his duty so magnificently. Ah, my dear boy, I don't know how to repay you. I'm so happy I——

Sganarelle. It's easy for you to talk. Gorgibus just ran into me without my doctor's outfit, and if I hadn't come up with a quick story we'd have been sunk. Here he comes again. Disappear.

[VALÈRE *runs away.* GORGIBUS *returns.*]

Gorgibus. Narcissus, I've been looking every-where for you. I spoke to your brother and he forgives you. But to be safe, I want to see the two of you patch up your quarrel in front of me. Wait here in my house, and I'll find him.

Sganarelle. I don't think you'll find him, Monsieur. Anyhow, I wouldn't dare to wait; I'm terrified of him.

Gorgibus (*pushing* SGANARELLE *inside*). Yes, you will stay. I'm locking you in. Don't be afraid of your brother. I promise you that he's not angry now.

[*He slams the door and locks it, then goes off to look for the doctor.*]

Sganarelle (*at the upstairs window*). Serves me right; I trapped myself and there's no way out. The weather in my future looks threatening, and if there's a storm I'm afraid I'll feel a rain of blows on my back. Or else they'll brand me across the shoulders with a whip—not exactly the brand of medicine any doctor ever prescribed. Yes, I'm in trouble. But why give up when we've come this far? Let's go the limit. I can still make a bid for freedom and prove that Sganarelle is the king of swindlers.

[*He holds his nose, closes his eyes, and jumps to the ground, just as* GROS-RENÉ *comes back. Then he darts away, picking up the cloak and hat.* GROS-RENÉ *stands staring.*]

Gros-René. A flying man! What a laugh! I'll wait around and see if there's another one.

[GORGIBUS *reenters with* SGANARELLE *following him in the doctor's outfit.*]

Gorgibus. Can't find that doctor. Where the devil has he hidden himself?

[*He turns and* SGANARELLE *walks into him.*]

There you are. Now, Doctor, I know you said

you forgive your brother, but that's not enough. I won't be satisfied until I see you embrace him. He's waiting here in my house.

Sganarelle. You are joking, Monsieur Gorgibus. Have I not extended myself enough already? I wish never to see him again.

Gorgibus. Please, Doctor, for me.

Sganarelle. I cannot refuse when you ask me like that. Tell him to come down.

[*As* GORGIBUS *goes into the house,* SGANARELLE *drops the clothes, clambers swiftly up to the window again, and scrambles inside.*]

Gorgibus (*at the window*). Your brother is waiting for you downstairs, Narcissus. He said he'd do what I asked.

Sganarelle (*at the window*). Couldn't you please make him come up here? I beg of you—let me see him in private to ask his forgiveness, because if I go down there he'll show me up and say nasty things to me in front of everybody.

Gorgibus. All right. Let me tell him.

[*He leaves the window, and* SGANARELLE *leaps out, swiftly puts on his outfit again, and stands waiting for* GORGIBUS *outside the door.*]

Doctor, he's so ashamed of himself he wants to beg your forgiveness in private, upstairs. Here's the key. Please don't refuse me.

Sganarelle. There is nothing I would not do for you, Monsieur Gorgibus. You will hear how I deal with him.

[*He walks into the house and soon appears at the window.* GORGIBUS *has his ear cocked at the door below.* SGANARELLE *alternates his voice, playing the characters one at a time.*]

Sganarelle. So there you are, you scoundrel!
—Brother, listen to me, please. I'm sorry I

knocked those containers over——
—You clumsy ox!
—It wasn't my fault, I swear it.
—Not your fault, you bumpkin? I'll teach you to destroy my work.
—Brother, no, please——
—I'll teach you to trade on Monsieur Gorgibus' good nature. How dare you ask him to ask me to forgive you!
—Brother, I'm sorry, but——
—Silence, you dog!
—I never wanted to hurt you or——
—Silence, I say——

Gros-René. What exactly do you think is going on up there?

Gorgibus. It's the doctor and his brother, Narcissus. They had a little disagreement, but now they're making it up.

Gros-René. Doctor and his brother? But there's only one man.

Sganarelle (*at the window*). Yes, you drunkard, I'll thump some good behavior into you. (*Pretends to strike a blow.*) Ah, he's lowering his eyes; he knows what he's done wrong, the jailbird. And now this hypocrite wants to play the good apostle——

Gros-René. Just for fun, tell him to let his brother appear at the window.

Gorgibus. I will. (*To* SGANARELLE) Doctor, let me see your brother for a moment.

Sganarelle. He is not fit to be seen by an honest gentleman like yourself. Besides, I cannot bear to have him next to me.

Gorgibus. Please don't say no, after all you've done for me.

Sganarelle. Monsieur Gorgibus, you have such power over me that I must grant whatever you wish. Show yourself, beast! (*He appears at the window as* NARCISSUS.) Monsieur Gorgibus, I thank you for your kindness. (*He reappears as the doctor.*) Well, Monsieur, did you take a good look at that image of impurity?

Gros-René. There's only one man there, Monsieur. We can prove it. Tell them to stand by the window together.

Gorgibus. Doctor, I want to see you at the window embracing your brother, and then I'll be satisfied.

Sganarelle. To any other man in the world I would return a swift and negative answer, but to you, Monsieur Gorgibus, I will yield, although not without much pain to myself. But first I want this knave to beg your pardon for all the trouble he has caused you. (*He comes back as* NARCISSUS.) Yes, Monsieur Gorgibus, I beg your pardon for having bothered you, and I promise you, brother, in front of Monsieur Gorgibus there, that I'll be so good from now on that you'll never be angry with me again. Please let bygones be bygones. (*He embraces the cloak and hat.*)

Gorgibus. There they are, the two of them together.

Gros-René. The man's a magician.

[*He hides;* SGANARELLE *comes out of the house, dressed as the doctor.*]

Sganarelle. Here is your key, Monsieur. I have left my brother inside because I am ashamed of him. One does not wish to be seen in his company now that one has some reputation in this town. You may release him whenever you think fit. Goodbye, Monsieur.

[*He strides off, then as* GORGIBUS *goes into the house, he wheels, dropping the cloak and hat, and climbs back through the window.*]

Gorgibus (*upstairs*). There you are, my boy, you're free. I am pleased that your brother forgave you, although I think he was rather hard on you.

Sganarelle. Monsieur, I cannot thank you enough. A brother's blessing on you. I will remember you all my life.

[*While they are upstairs,* GROS-RENÉ *has picked up the cloak and hat, and stands waiting for them. They come out of the door.*]

Gros-René. Well, where do you think your doctor is now?

Gorgibus. Gone, of course.

Gros-René. He's right here, under my arm. And by the way, while this fellow was getting in and out of the cloak, the hat, and the window, Valère ran off with your daughter and married her.

Gorgibus. I'm ruined! I'll have you strung up, you dog, you knave! Yes, you deserve every name your brother called you—What am I saying?

Sganarelle. You don't really want to string me up, do you, Monsieur? Please listen for one second. It's true that I was having a game with you while my master was with Mademoiselle Lucile. But in serving him I haven't done you any harm. He's a most suitable partner for her, by rank and by income, by God. Believe me, if you make a row about this you'll only bring more confusion on your head. As for that porker there, let him get lost and take Villebrequin with him. Here come our loving couple.

[VALÈRE *enters contritely with* LUCILE. *They kneel to* GORGIBUS.]

Valère. We apologize to you.

Gorgibus. Well, perhaps it's lucky that I was tricked by Sganarelle; he's brought me a fine son-in-law. Let's go out to celebrate the marriage and drink a toast to the health of all the company.

[*They dance off in couples:* VALÈRE *with* LUCILE, GORGIBUS *with* GROS-RENÉ, *and* SGANARELLE *with* SABINE.]

CURTAIN

A Doll's House

Meet the Playwright

Henrik Ibsen (1828–1906)

Henrik Ibsen was born in Skien, Norway, the oldest child in a large, well-to-do family. When he was seven, his father suddenly went bankrupt and the family had to move to a farm, where they lived in much-reduced circumstances. A loner, Ibsen read avidly and lived mostly in the world of his imagination.

Unable to attend medical school, Ibsen worked for a time as a pharmacist's apprentice. Then, as his interests shifted from science to literature, Ibsen began to read widely and write verse plays. At twenty-three, with some university theatrical experience behind him, he became stage manager and resident playwright for a new theater in Bergen, Norway. There, and later at Christiania (now Oslo), Ibsen became an expert in all aspects of stage technique.

Ibsen then married and wrote verse comedies. During this period, he was extremely poor, and he was discouraged by the negative response most of his plays received.

Success and Controversy

In his late thirties Ibsen finally achieved commercial success with the verse plays *Brand* (1866) and *Peer Gynt* (1867). But, dissatisfied with the quality of his work, Ibsen gave up verse and began to write realistic dramas in prose. Finally, in 1879, came *A Doll's House*. This portrayal of a woman who frees herself from a stifling marriage created a stir throughout northern Europe. The dramatization of marital conflict in the play was considered so scandalous that the producers of the German version changed the last act. Ibsen himself, under considerable pressure, wrote an alternate ending. He later regretted this, commenting that the entire play was written for the sake of the final scene and its famous "slamming door."

Drama as Social Commentary

Ibsen used new dramatic techniques to expose the social and economic problems of the day. His next play, *Ghosts* (1881), dealt with the controversial subject of syphilis; the play was violently attacked by critics and rejected by all theaters and bookstores. Ibsen's response to his critics was his next masterpiece, *An Enemy of the People* (1882), in which an honest doctor is vilified by his townspeople for speaking the truth about the polluted water of the town.

These plays and others that streamed from Ibsen's imagination in his fifties and sixties were unlike any that had been written before. Starting with *A Doll's House*, Ibsen's plays formed the foundation of modern realistic drama.

Background to *A Doll's House*

Although nineteenth-century realist novels and short stories held up a mirror to society as it really was, it was not until Ibsen that drama began to reflect the world in a similar way. Before Ibsen, nineteenth-century audiences went to the theater to see spectacle and romance, not realistic or truthful depictions of everyday life. Ibsen (and later playwrights such as Anton Chekhov and George Bernard Shaw) dramatically altered the theater experience by making the stage an extension of real life. In his plays, Ibsen concentrated on the kinds of situations experienced by real people—such as a married woman in a financial bind.

During the nineteenth century, most middle-class European and American women were economically and legally dependent on their husbands. Realist writers such as Leo Tolstoy, Guy de Maupassant, and Thomas Hardy wrote works sympathizing with defiant, unconventional women, but their rebellious female characters usually came to ruin. In *A Doll's House*, Ibsen creates a modern tragic heroine and allows her to achieve self-knowledge and independence.

Ibsen's Innovations: The Fourth Wall

In *A Doll's House*, Ibsen imitates some of the techniques first developed by Sophocles in ancient Greece (see page 9). For example, the major events affecting the characters have already occurred before the curtain is raised; the action of the play serves to expose these events. The techniques that Ibsen borrowed, however, are not as remarkable as those he innovated.

Ibsen was one of the first playwrights to make an audience forget that what it was watching was imaginary, not real. He treated the stage as if it were a room in which real events were actually taking place. For the audience, it was as though the "fourth wall" of the room had been removed. In order to create a realistic "room," the whole look of the stage changed. Suddenly, every detail was important: The set had to look like an actual place, such as a sitting room or a front porch; lighting was used to indicate different times of day or to create special effects. The way actors moved onstage was intended to look real, not affected or posed.

Other Pioneering Techniques

Ibsen used various techniques to create a feeling of intimacy—to make audiences feel they were watching real life unfold onstage. First, he changed the language of the stage, developing a style of dialogue that revealed the inner conflicts of his characters. His dialogue sounds like everyday speech, and offhand statements reveal depths of characterization. Ibsen was also one of the first playwrights to incorporate elaborate stage directions. To enhance the illusion of reality onstage, he wrote detailed descriptions of the settings and added directions to the script ("a little embarrassed," "laughing," and so on) indicating how actors should move and deliver their lines. Stage directions of this kind were virtually nonexistent in earlier drama, but they have since become standard in contemporary Western plays. All of these techniques are in full effect in *A Doll's House*, the play that inaugurated the age of modern Western drama.

A Doll's House

Henrik Ibsen

Translated by **Michael Meyer**

CHARACTERS

Torvald Helmer, a lawyer

Nora, his wife

Dr. Rank

Mrs. Linde

Nils Krogstad, also a lawyer

The Helmers' Three Small Children

Anne-Marie, their nurse

Helen, the maid

A Porter

The action takes place in the Helmers' apartment.

ACT 1

A comfortably and tastefully, but not expensively, furnished room. Backstage right a door leads to the hall; backstage left, another door to HELMER'*s study. Between these two doors stands a piano. In the middle of the left-hand wall is a door, with a window downstage of it. Near the window, a round table with armchairs and a small sofa. In the right-hand wall, slightly upstage, is a door; downstage of this, against the same wall, a stove lined with porcelain tiles, with a couple of armchairs and a rocking chair in front of it. Between the stove and the side door is a small table. Engravings on the wall. A whatnot with china and other bric-a-brac; a small bookcase with leather-bound books. A carpet on the floor; a fire in the stove. A winter day.*

[*A bell rings in the hall outside. After a moment we hear the front door being opened.* NORA *enters the room, humming contentedly to herself. She is wearing outdoor clothes and carrying a lot of parcels, which she puts down on the table right. She leaves the door to the hall open; through it, we can see a* PORTER *carrying a Christmas tree and a basket. He gives these to the* MAID, *who has opened the door for them.*]

Nora. Hide that Christmas tree away, Helen. The children mustn't see it before I've decorated it this evening. (*to the* PORTER, *taking out her purse*) How much?
Porter. A shilling.[1]
Nora. Here's ten shillings. No, keep it.

[*The* PORTER *touches his cap and goes.* NORA *closes the door. She continues to laugh happily to herself*

as she removes her coat, etc. She takes from her pocket a bag containing macaroons and eats a couple. Then she tiptoes across and listens at her husband's door.*]

Nora. Yes, he's here. (*starts humming again as she goes over to the table, right.*)
Helmer (*from his room*). Is that my skylark twittering out there?
Nora (*opening some of the parcels*). It is!
Helmer. Is that my squirrel rustling?
Nora. Yes!
Helmer. When did my squirrel come home?
Nora. Just now. (*pops the bag of macaroons in her pocket and wipes her mouth*) Come out here, Torvald, and see what I've bought.
Helmer. You mustn't disturb me!

[*Short pause; then he opens the door and looks in, his pen in his hand.*]

Helmer. Bought, did you say? All that? Has my little squanderbird been overspending again?
Nora. Oh, Torvald, surely we can let ourselves go a little this year! It's the first Christmas we don't have to scrape.
Helmer. Well, you know, we can't afford to be extravagant.
Nora. Oh yes, Torvald, we can be a little extravagant now. Can't we? Just a tiny bit? You've got a big salary now, and you're going to make lots and lots of money.
Helmer. Next year, yes. But my new salary doesn't start till April.
Nora. Pooh; we can borrow till then.
Helmer. Nora! (*goes over to her and takes her playfully by the ear*) What a little spendthrift[2] you are! Suppose I were to borrow fifty pounds today, and you spent it all over Christmas, and

---

1. **shilling:** a coin of little value.

2. **spendthrift:** someone who spends money carelessly or wastefully.

then on New Year's Eve a tile fell off a roof onto my head—

Nora (*puts her hand over his mouth*). Oh, Torvald! Don't say such dreadful things!

Helmer. Yes, but suppose something like that did happen? What then?

Nora. If anything as frightful as that happened, it wouldn't make much difference whether I was in debt or not.

Helmer. But what about the people I'd borrowed from?

Nora. Them? Who cares about them? They're strangers.

Helmer. Oh, Nora, Nora, how like a woman! No, but seriously, Nora, you know how I feel about this. No debts! Never borrow! A home that is founded on debts and borrowing can never be a place of freedom and beauty. We two have stuck it out bravely up to now; and we shall continue to do so for the few weeks that remain.

Nora (*goes over towards the stove*). Very well, Torvald. As you say.

Helmer (*follows her*). Now, now! My little songbird mustn't droop her wings. What's this? Is little squirrel sulking? (*takes out his purse*) Nora; guess what I've got here!

Nora (*turns quickly*). Money!

Helmer. Look. (*hands her some bank notes*) I know how these small expenses crop up at Christmas.

Nora (*counts them*). One—two—three—four. Oh, thank you, Torvald, thank you! I should be able to manage with this.

Helmer. You'll have to.

Nora. Yes, yes, of course I will. But come over here, I want to show you everything I've bought. And so cheap! Look, here are new clothes for Ivar—and a sword. And a horse and a trumpet for Bob. And a doll and a cradle for Emmy—they're nothing much, but she'll pull them apart in a few days. And some bits of material and handkerchiefs for the maids. Old Annie-Marie

ought to have had something better, really.

Helmer. And what's in that parcel?

Nora (*cries*). No, Torvald, you mustn't see that before this evening!

Helmer. Very well. But now, tell me, my little spendthrift, what do you want for Christmas?

Nora. Me? Oh, pooh, I don't want anything.

Helmer. Oh yes, you do. Now tell me, what within reason would you most like?

Nora. No, I really don't know. Oh, yes—Torvald—!

Helmer. Well?

Nora (*plays with his coat buttons; not looking at him*). If you really want to give me something, you could—you could—

Helmer. Come on, out with it.

Nora (*quickly*). You could give me money, Torvald. Only as much as you feel you can afford; then later I'll buy something with it.

Helmer. But, Nora—

Nora. Oh yes, Torvald dear, please! Please! Then I'll wrap up the notes in pretty gold paper and hang them on the Christmas tree. Wouldn't that be fun?

Helmer. What's the name of that little bird that can never keep any money?

Nora. Yes, yes, squanderbird; I know. But let's do as I say, Torvald; then I'll have time to think about what I need most. Isn't that the best way? Mm?

Helmer (*smiles*). To be sure it would be, if you could keep what I give you and really buy yourself something with it. But you'll spend it on all sorts of useless things for the house, and then I'll have to put my hand in my pocket again.

Nora. Oh, but Torvald—

Helmer. You can't deny it, Nora dear. (*puts his arm around her waist*) The squanderbird's a pretty little creature, but she gets through an awful lot of money. It's incredible what an expensive pet she is for a man to keep.

Nora. For shame! How can you say such a thing? I save every penny I can.

Helmer (*laughs*). That's quite true. Every penny you can. But you can't.

Nora (*hums and smiles, quietly gleeful*). Hm. If you only knew how many expenses we larks and squirrels have, Torvald.

Helmer. You're a funny little creature. Just like your father used to be. Always on the lookout for some way to get money, but as soon as you have any it just runs through your fingers and you never know where it's gone. Well, I suppose I must take you as you are. It's in your blood. Yes, yes, yes, these things are hereditary, Nora.

Nora. Oh, I wish I'd inherited more of Papa's qualities.

Helmer. And I wouldn't wish my darling little songbird to be any different from what she is. By the way, that reminds me. You look awfully—how shall I put it?—awfully guilty today.

Nora. Do I?

Helmer. Yes, you do. Look me in the eyes.

Nora (*looks at him*). Well?

Helmer (*wags his finger*). Has my little sweet tooth been indulging herself in town today, by any chance?

Nora. No, how can you think such a thing?

Helmer. Not a tiny little digression into a pastry shop?

Nora. No, Torvald, I promise—

Helmer. Not just a wee jam tart?

Nora. Certainly not.

Helmer. Not a little nibble at a macaroon?

Nora. No, Torvald—I promise you, honestly—!

Helmer. There, there. I was only joking.

Nora (*goes over to the table, right*). You know I could never act against your wishes.

Helmer. Of course not. And you've given me your word—(*goes over to her*) Well, my beloved Nora, you keep your little Christmas secrets to yourself. They'll be revealed this evening, I've no doubt, once the Christmas tree has been lit.

Nora. Have you remembered to invite Dr. Rank?

Helmer. No. But there's no need; he knows he'll be dining with us. Anyway, I'll ask him when he comes this morning. I've ordered some good wine. Oh, Nora, you can't imagine how I'm looking forward to this evening.

Nora. So am I. And, Torvald, how the children will love it!

Helmer. Yes, it's a wonderful thing to know that one's position is assured and that one has an ample income. Don't you agree? It's good to know that, isn't it?

Nora. Yes, it's almost like a miracle.

Helmer. Do you remember last Christmas? For three whole weeks you shut yourself away every evening to make flowers for the Christmas tree, and all those other things you were going to surprise us with. Ugh, it was the most boring time I've ever had in my life.

Nora. I didn't find it boring.

Helmer (*smiles*). But it all came to nothing in the end, didn't it?

Nora. Oh, are you going to bring that up again? How could I help the cat getting in and tearing everything to bits?

Helmer. No, my poor little Nora, of course you couldn't. You simply wanted to make us happy, and that's all that matters. But it's good that those hard times are past.

Nora. Yes, it's wonderful.

Helmer. I don't have to sit by myself and be bored. And you don't have to tire your pretty eyes and your delicate little hands—

Nora (*claps her hands*). No, Torvald, that's true, isn't it? I don't have to any longer! Oh, it's really all just like a miracle. (*takes his arm*) Now I'm going to tell you what I thought we might do, Torvald. As soon as Christmas is over—

[*A bell rings in the hall.*]

Oh, there's the doorbell. (*tidies up one or two*

things in the room) Someone's coming. What a bore.

Helmer. I'm not at home to any visitors. Remember!

Maid (*in the doorway*). A lady's called, madam. A stranger.

Nora. Well, ask her to come in.

Maid. And the doctor's here too, sir.

Helmer. Has he gone to my room?

Maid. Yes, sir.

[HELMER *goes into his room. The* MAID *shows in* MRS. LINDE, *who is dressed in traveling clothes; then closes the door.*]

Mrs. Linde (*shyly and a little hesitantly*). Good morning, Nora.

Nora (*uncertainly*). Good morning—

Mrs. Linde. I don't suppose you recognize me.

Nora. No, I'm afraid I—Yes, wait a minute—surely—I—(*exclaims*) Why, Christine! Is it really you?

Mrs. Linde. Yes, it's me.

Nora. Christine! And I didn't recognize you! But how could I—? (*more quietly*) How you've changed, Christine!

Mrs. Linde. Yes, I know. It's been nine years—nearly ten—

Nora. Is it so long? Yes, it must be. Oh, these last eight years have been such a happy time for me! So you've come to town? All that way in winter! How brave of you!

Mrs. Linde. I arrived by the steamer this morning.

Nora. Yes, of course, to enjoy yourself over Christmas. Oh, how splendid! We'll have to celebrate! But take off your coat. You're not cold, are you? (*helps her off with it*) There! Now let's sit down here by the stove and be comfortable. No, you take the armchair. I'll sit here in the rocking chair. (*clasps* MRS. LINDE'*s hands*) Yes, now you look like your old self. Just at first I—you've got a little paler, though, Christine. And perhaps a bit thinner.

Mrs. Linde. And older, Nora. Much, much older.

Nora. Yes, perhaps a little older. Just a tiny bit. Not much. (*checks herself suddenly and says earnestly*) Oh, but how thoughtless of me to sit here and chatter away like this! Dear, sweet Christine, can you forgive me?

Mrs. Linde. What do you mean, Nora?

Nora (*quietly*). Poor Christine, you've become a widow.

Mrs. Linde. Yes. Three years ago.

Nora. I know, I know—I read it in the papers. Oh, Christine, I meant to write to you so often, honestly. But I always put it off, and something else always cropped up.

Mrs. Linde. I understand, Nora dear.

Nora. No, Christine, it was beastly of me. Oh, my poor darling, what you've gone through! And he didn't leave you anything?

Mrs. Linde. No.

Nora. No children, either?

Mrs. Linde. No.

Nora. Nothing at all, then?

Mrs. Linde. Not even a feeling of loss or sorrow.

Nora (*looks incredulously at her*). But, Christine, how is that possible?

Mrs. Linde (*smiles sadly and strokes* NORA'*s hair*). Oh, these things happen, Nora.

Nora. All alone. How dreadful that must be for you. I've three lovely children. I'm afraid you can't see them now, because they're out with Nanny. But you must tell me everything—

Mrs. Linde. No, no, no. I want to hear about you.

Nora. No, you start. I'm not going to be selfish today, I'm just going to think about you. Oh, but there's one thing I *must* tell you. Have you heard of the wonderful luck we've just had?

Mrs. Linde. No. What?

Nora. Would you believe it—my husband's just been made vice-president of the bank!

Mrs. Linde. Your husband? Oh, how lucky—!

Nora. Yes, isn't it? Being a lawyer is so uncertain, you know, especially if one isn't prepared to touch any case that isn't—well—quite nice. And of course Torvald's been very firm about that—and I'm absolutely with him. Oh, you can imagine how happy we are! He's joining the bank in the new year, and he'll be getting a big salary, and lots of percentages too. From now on we'll be able to live quite differently—we'll be able to do whatever we want. Oh, Christine, it's such a relief! I feel so happy! Well, I mean, it's lovely to have heaps of money and not to have to worry about anything. Don't you think?

Mrs. Linde. It must be lovely to have enough to cover one's needs, anyway.

Nora. Not just our needs! We're going to have heaps and heaps of money!

Mrs. Linde (*smiles*). Nora, Nora, haven't you grown up yet? When we were at school you were a terrible little spendthrift.

Nora (*laughs quietly*). Yes, Torvald still says that. (*wags her finger*) But "Nora, Nora" isn't as silly as you think. Oh, we've been in no position for me to waste money. We've both had to work.

Mrs. Linde. You too?

Nora. Yes, little things—fancywork, crocheting, embroidery and so forth. (*casually*) And other things, too. I suppose you know Torvald left the Ministry when we got married? There were no prospects of promotion in his department, and of course he needed more money. But the first year he overworked himself dreadfully. He had to take on all sorts of extra jobs, and worked day and night. But it was too much for him, and he became frightfully ill. The doctors said he'd have to go to a warmer climate.

Mrs. Linde. Yes, you spent a whole year in Italy, didn't you?

Nora. Yes. It wasn't easy for me to get away, you know, I'd just had Ivar. But, of course, we had to do it. Oh, it was a marvelous trip! And it saved Torvald's life. But it cost an awful lot of money, Christine.

Mrs. Linde. I can imagine.

Nora. Two hundred and fifty pounds. That's a lot of money, you know.

Mrs. Linde. How lucky you had it.

Nora. Well, actually, we got it from my father.

Mrs. Linde. Oh, I see. Didn't he die just about that time?

Nora. Yes, Christine, just about then. Wasn't it dreadful, I couldn't go and look after him. I was expecting little Ivar any day. And then I had my poor Torvald to care for—we really didn't think he'd live. Dear, kind Papa! I never saw him again, Christine. Oh, it's the saddest thing that's happened to me since I got married.

Mrs. Linde. I know you were very fond of him. But you went to Italy—?

Nora. Yes. Well, we had the money, you see, and the doctors said we mustn't delay. So we went the month after Papa died.

Mrs. Linde. And your husband came back completely cured?

Nora. Fit as a fiddle!

Mrs. Linde. But—the doctor?

Nora. How do you mean?

Mrs. Linde. I thought the maid said that the gentleman who arrived with me was the doctor.

Nora. Oh yes, that's Dr. Rank, but he doesn't come because anyone's ill. He's our best friend, and he looks us up at least once every day. No, Torvald hasn't had a moment's illness since we went away. And the children are fit and healthy and so am I. (*jumps up and claps her hands*) Oh, God, oh God, Christine, isn't it a wonderful thing to be alive and happy! Oh, but how beastly of me! I'm only talking about myself. (*sits on a footstool and rests her arms on* MRS. LINDE's *knee*) Oh, please don't be angry with me! Tell me, is it really true you didn't love your husband? Why did you marry him, then?

Mrs. Linde. Well, my mother was still alive; and she was helpless and bedridden. And I had my two little brothers to take care of. I didn't feel I could say no.

Nora. Yes, well, perhaps you're right. He was rich then, was he?

Mrs. Linde. Quite comfortably off, I believe. But his business was unsound, you see, Nora. When he died it went bankrupt and there was nothing left.

Nora. What did you do?

Mrs. Linde. Well, I had to try to make ends meet somehow, so I started a little shop, and a little school, and anything else I could turn my hand to. These last three years have been just one endless slog for me, without a moment's rest. But now it's over, Nora. My poor dead mother doesn't need me any more; she's passed away. And the boys don't need me either; they've got jobs now and can look after themselves.

Nora. How relieved you must feel—

Mrs. Linde. No, Nora. Just unspeakably empty. No one to live for any more. (*gets up restlessly*) That's why I couldn't bear to stay out there any longer, cut off from the world. I thought it'd be easier to find some work here that will exercise and occupy my mind. If only I could get a regular job—office work of some kind—

Nora. Oh but, Christine, that's dreadfully exhausting; and you look practically finished already. It'd be much better for you if you could go away somewhere.

Mrs. Linde (*goes over to the window*). I have no papa to pay for my holidays, Nora.

Nora (*gets up*). Oh, please don't be angry with me.

Mrs. Linde. My dear Nora, it's I who should ask you not to be angry. That's the worst thing about this kind of situation—it makes one so bitter. One has no one to work for; and yet one has to be continually sponging for jobs. One has to live; and so one becomes completely egocentric. When you told me about this luck you've just had with Torvald's new job—can you imagine?—I was happy not so much on your account, as on my own.

Nora. How do you mean? Oh, I understand. You mean Torvald might be able to do something for you?

Mrs. Linde. Yes, I was thinking that.

Nora. He will too, Christine. Just you leave it to me. I'll lead up to it so delicately, so delicately; I'll get him in the right mood. Oh, Christine, I do so want to help you.

Mrs. Linde. It's sweet of you to bother so much about me, Nora. Especially since you know so little of the worries and hardships of life.

Nora. I? You say *I* know little of—?

Mrs. Linde (*smiles*). Well, good heavens—those bits of fancywork of yours—well, really! You're a child, Nora.

Nora (*tosses her head and walks across the room*). You shouldn't say that so patronizingly.

Mrs. Linde. Oh?

Nora. You're like the rest. You all think I'm incapable of getting down to anything serious—

Mrs. Linde. My dear—

Nora. You think I've never had any worries like the rest of you.

Mrs. Linde. Nora dear, you've just told me about all your difficulties—

Nora. Pooh—that! (*quietly*) I haven't told you about the big thing.

Mrs. Linde. What big thing? What do you mean?

Nora. You patronize me, Christine; but you shouldn't. You're proud that you've worked so long and so hard for your mother.

Mrs. Linde. I don't patronize anyone, Nora. But you're right—I am both proud and happy that I was able to make my mother's last months on earth comparatively easy.

Nora. And you're also proud at what you've done for your brothers.

Mrs. Linde. I think I have a right to be.

Nora. I think so, too. But let me tell you something, Christine. I, too, have done something to be proud and happy about.

Mrs. Linde. I don't doubt it. But—how do you mean?

Nora. Speak quietly! Suppose Torvald should hear! He mustn't, at any price—no one must know, Christine—no one but you.

Mrs. Linde. But what is this?

Nora. Come over here. (*pulls her down onto the sofa beside her*) Yes, Christine—I, too, have done something to be happy and proud about. It was I who saved Torvald's life.

Mrs. Linde. Saved his—? How did you save it?

Nora. I told you about our trip to Italy. Torvald couldn't have lived if he hadn't managed to get down there—

Mrs. Linde. Yes, well—your father provided the money—

Nora (*smiles*). So Torvald and everyone else thinks. But—

Mrs. Linde. Yes?

Nora. Papa didn't give us a penny. It was I who found the money.

Mrs. Linde. You? All of it?

Nora. Two hundred and fifty pounds. What do you say to that?

Mrs. Linde. But, Nora, how could you? Did you win a lottery or something?

Nora (*scornfully*). Lottery? (*sniffs*) What would there be to be proud of in that?

Mrs. Linde. But where did you get it from, then?

Nora (*hums and smiles secretively*). Hm; tra-la-la-la!

Mrs. Linde. You couldn't have borrowed it.

Nora. Oh? Why not?

Mrs. Linde. Well, a wife can't borrow money without her husband's consent.

Nora (*tosses her head*). Ah, but when a wife has a little business sense, and knows how to be clever—

Mrs. Linde. But Nora, I simply don't understand—

Nora. You don't have to. No one has said I borrowed the money. I could have got it in some other way. (*throws herself back on the sofa*) I could have got it from an admirer. When a girl's as pretty as I am—

Mrs. Linde. Nora, you're crazy!

Nora. You're dying of curiosity now, aren't you, Christine?

Mrs. Linde. Nora dear, you haven't done anything foolish?

Nora (*sits up again*). Is it foolish to save one's husband's life?

Mrs. Linde. I think it's foolish if without his knowledge you—

Nora. But the whole point was that he mustn't know! Great heavens, don't you see? He hadn't to know how dangerously ill he was. It was me they told that his life was in danger and that only going to a warm climate could save him. Do you suppose I didn't try to think of other ways of getting him down there? I told him how wonderful it would be for me to go abroad like other young wives; I cried and prayed; I asked him to remember my condition, and said he ought to be nice and tender to me; and then I suggested he might quite easily borrow the money. But then he got almost angry with me, Christine. He said I was frivolous, and that it was his duty as a husband not to pander to my moods and caprices—I think that's what he called them. Well, well, I thought, you've got to be saved somehow. And then I thought of a way—

Mrs. Linde. But didn't your husband find out from your father that the money hadn't come from him?

Nora. No, never. Papa died just then. I'd thought of letting him into the plot and asking him not to tell. But since he was so ill—! And as things turned out, it didn't become necessary.

Mrs. Linde. And you've never told your husband about this?

Nora. For heaven's sake, no! What an idea! He's

frightfully strict about such matters. And besides—he's so proud of being a man—it'd be so painful and humiliating for him to know that he owed anything to me. It'd completely wreck our relationship. This life we have built together would no longer exist.

Mrs. Linde. Will you never tell him?

Nora (*thoughtfully, half-smiling*). Yes—sometime, perhaps. Years from now, when I'm no longer pretty. You mustn't laugh! I mean, of course, when Torvald no longer loves me as he does now; when it no longer amuses him to see me dance and dress up and play the fool for him. Then it might be useful to have something up my sleeve. (*breaks off*) Stupid, stupid, stupid! That time will never come. Well, what do you think of my big secret, Christine? I'm not completely useless, am I? Mind you, all this has caused me a frightful lot of worry. It hasn't been easy for me to meet my obligations punctually. In case you don't know, in the world of business there are things called quarterly installments and interest, and they're a terrible problem to cope with. So I've had to scrape a little here and save a little there, as best I can. I haven't been able to save much on the housekeeping money, because Torvald likes to live well; and I couldn't let the children go short of clothes—I couldn't take anything out of what he gives me for them. The poor little angels!

Mrs. Linde. So you've had to stint yourself, my poor Nora?

Nora. Of course. Well, after all, it was my problem. Whenever Torvald gave me money to buy myself new clothes, I never used more than half of it; and I always bought what was cheapest and plainest. Thank heaven anything suits me, so that Torvald's never noticed. But it made me a bit sad sometimes, because it's lovely to wear pretty clothes. Don't you think?

Mrs. Linde. Indeed it is.

Nora. And then I've found one or two other sources of income. Last winter I managed to get a lot of copying to do. So I shut myself away and wrote every evening, late into the night. Oh, I often got so tired, so tired. But it was great fun, though, sitting there working and earning money. It was almost like being a man.

Mrs. Linde. But how much have you managed to pay off like this?

Nora. Well, I can't say exactly. It's awfully difficult to keep an exact check on these kind of transactions. I only know I've paid everything I've managed to scrape together. Sometimes I really didn't know where to turn. (*smiles*) Then I'd sit here and imagine some rich old gentleman had fallen in love with me—

Mrs. Linde. What! What gentleman?

Nora. Silly! And that now he'd died and when they opened his will it said in big letters: "Everything I possess is to be paid forthwith to my beloved Mrs. Nora Helmer in cash."

Mrs. Linde. But, Nora dear, who was this gentleman?

Nora. Great heavens, don't you understand? There wasn't any old gentleman; he was just something I used to dream up as I sat here evening after evening wondering how on earth I could raise some money. But what does it matter? The old bore can stay imaginary as far as I'm concerned, because now I don't have to worry any longer! (*jumps up*) Oh, Christine, isn't it wonderful? I don't have to worry any more! No more troubles! I can play all day with the children, I can fill the house with pretty things, just the way Torvald likes. And, Christine, it'll soon be spring, and the air'll be fresh and the skies blue—and then perhaps we'll be able to take a little trip somewhere. I shall be able to see the sea again. Oh, yes, yes, it's a wonderful thing to be alive and happy!

[*The bell rings in the hall.*]

Mrs. Linde (*gets up*). You've a visitor. Perhaps I'd better go.

Nora. No, stay. It won't be for me. It's someone for Torvald—

Maid (*in the doorway*). Excuse me, madam, a gentleman's called who says he wants to speak to the master. But I didn't know—seeing as the doctor's with him—

Nora. Who is this gentleman?

Krogstad (*in the doorway*). It's me, Mrs. Helmer.

[MRS. LINDE *starts, composes herself and turns away to the window.*]

Nora (*takes a step towards him and whispers tensely*). You? What is it? What do you want to talk to my husband about?

Krogstad. Business—you might call it. I hold a minor post in the bank, and I hear your husband is to become our new chief—

Nora. Oh—then it isn't—?

Krogstad. Pure business, Mrs. Helmer. Nothing more.

Nora. Well, you'll find him in his study.

[*Nods indifferently as she closes the hall door behind him. Then she walks across the room and sees to the stove.*]

Mrs. Linde. Nora, who was that man?

Nora. A lawyer called Krogstad.

Mrs. Linde. It was him, then.

Nora. Do you know that man?

Mrs. Linde. I used to know him—some years ago. He was a solicitor's[3] clerk in our town, for a while.

Nora. Yes, of course, so he was.

Mrs. Linde. How he's changed!

Nora. He was very unhappily married, I believe.

Mrs. Linde. Is he a widower now?

Nora. Yes, with a lot of children. Ah, now it's alight.

[*She closes the door of the stove and moves the rocking chair a little to one side.*]

Mrs. Linde. He does—various things now, I hear?

Nora. Does he? It's quite possible—I really don't know. But don't let's talk about business. It's so boring.

[DR. RANK *enters from* HELMER's *study.*]

Dr. Rank (*still in the doorway*). No, no, my dear chap, don't see me out. I'll go and have a word with your wife. (*closes the door and notices* MRS. LINDE) Oh, I beg your pardon. I seem to be *de trop*[4] here, too.

Nora. Not in the least. (*introduces them*) Dr. Rank. Mrs. Linde.

Rank. Ah! A name I have often heard in this house. I believe I passed you on the stairs as I came up.

Mrs. Linde. Yes. Stairs tire me. I have to take them slowly.

Rank. Oh, have you hurt yourself?

Mrs. Linde. No, I'm just a little run down.

Rank. Ah, is that all? Then I take it you've come to town to cure yourself by a round of parties?

Mrs. Linde. I have come here to find work.

Rank. Is that an approved remedy for being run down?

Mrs. Linde. One has to live, Doctor.

Rank. Yes, people do seem to regard it as a necessity.

Nora. Oh, really, Dr. Rank. I bet you want to stay alive.

Rank. You bet I do. However wretched I sometimes feel, I still want to go on being tortured for

---

3. **solicitor:** lawyer.

---

4. *de trop* (də trō'): French for "in the way."

as long as possible. It's the same with all my patients; and with people who are morally sick, too. There's a moral cripple in with Helmer at this very moment—

Mrs. Linde (*softly*). Oh!

Nora. Whom do you mean?

Rank. Oh, a lawyer fellow called Krogstad—you wouldn't know him. He's crippled all right, morally twisted. But even he started off by announcing, as though it were a matter of enormous importance, that he had to live.

Nora. Oh? What did he want to talk to Torvald about?

Rank. I haven't the faintest idea. All I heard was something about the bank.

Nora. I didn't know that Krog—that this man Krogstad had any connection with the bank.

Rank. Yes, he's got some kind of job down there. (*to* MRS. LINDE) I wonder if in your part of the world you too have a species of creature that spends its time fussing around trying to smell out moral corruption? And when they find a case they give him some nice, comfortable position so that they can keep a good watch on him. The healthy ones just have to lump it.

Mrs. Linde. But surely it's the sick who need care most?

Rank (*shrugs his shoulders*). Well, there we have it. It's that attitude that's turning human society into a hospital.

[NORA, *lost in her own thoughts, laughs half to herself and claps her hands.*]

Rank. Why are you laughing? Do you really know what society is?

Nora. What do I care about society? I think it's a bore. I was laughing at something else—something frightfully funny. Tell me, Dr. Rank—will everyone who works at the bank come under Torvald now?

Rank. Do you find that particularly funny?

Nora (*smiles and hums*). Never you mind! Never you mind! (*walks around the room*) Yes, I find it very amusing to think that we—I mean, Torvald—has obtained so much influence over so many people. (*takes the paper bag from her pocket*) Dr. Rank, would you like a small macaroon?

Rank. Macaroons! I say! I thought they were forbidden here.

Nora. Yes, well, these are some Christine gave me.

Mrs. Linde. What? I—?

Nora. All right, all right, don't get frightened. You weren't to know Torvald had forbidden them. He's afraid they'll ruin my teeth. But, dash it—for once—! Don't you agree, Dr. Rank? Here! (*pops a macaroon into his mouth*) You, too, Christine. And I'll have one, too. Just a little one. Two at the most. (*begins to walk round again*) Yes, now I feel really, really happy. Now there's just one thing in the world I'd really love to do.

Rank. Oh? And what is that?

Nora. Just something I'd love to say to Torvald.

Rank. Well, why don't you say it?

Nora. No, I daren't. It's too dreadful.

Mrs. Linde. Dreadful?

Rank. Well then, you'd better not. But you can say it to us. What is it you'd so love to say to Torvald?

Nora. I've the most extraordinary longing to say: "Bloody hell!"

Rank. Are you mad?

Mrs. Linde. My dear Nora—!

Rank. Say it. Here he is.

Nora (*hiding the bag of macaroons*). Ssh! Ssh!

[HELMER, *with his overcoat on his arm and his hat in his hand, enters from his study.*]

Nora (*goes to meet him*). Well, Torvald dear, did you get rid of him?

Helmer. Yes, he's just gone.

Nora. May I introduce you—? This is Christine. She's just arrived in town.

Helmer. Christine—? Forgive me, but I don't think—

Nora. Mrs. Linde, Torvald dear. Christine Linde.

Helmer. Ah. A childhood friend of my wife's, I presume?

Mrs. Linde. Yes, we knew each other in earlier days.

Nora. And imagine, now she's traveled all this way to talk to you.

Helmer. Oh?

Mrs. Linde. Well, I didn't really—

Nora. You see, Christine's frightfully good at office work, and she's mad to come under some really clever man who can teach her even more than she knows already—

Helmer. Very sensible, madam.

Nora. So when she heard you'd become head of the bank—it was in her local paper—she came here as quickly as she could and—Torvald, you will, won't you? Do a little something to help Christine? For my sake?

Helmer. Well, that shouldn't be impossible. You are a widow, I take it, Mrs. Linde?

Mrs. Linde. Yes.

Helmer. And you have experience of office work?

Mrs. Linde. Yes, quite a bit.

Helmer. Well, then, it's quite likely I may be able to find some job for you—

Nora (*claps her hands*). You see, you see!

Helmer. You've come at a lucky moment, Mrs. Linde.

Mrs. Linde. Oh, how can I ever thank you—?

Helmer. There's absolutely no need. (*puts on his overcoat*) But now I'm afraid I must ask you to excuse me—

Rank. Wait. I'll come with you.

[*He gets his fur coat from the hall and warms it at the stove.*]

Nora. Don't be long, Torvald dear.

Helmer. I'll only be an hour.

Nora. Are you going, too, Christine?

Mrs. Linde (*puts on her outdoor clothes*). Yes, I must start to look round for a room.

Helmer. Then perhaps we can walk part of the way together.

Nora (*helps her*). It's such a nuisance we're so cramped here—I'm afraid we can't offer to—

Mrs. Linde. Oh, I wouldn't dream of it. Goodbye, Nora dear, and thanks for everything.

Nora. *Au revoir.*[5] You'll be coming back this evening, of course. And you too, Dr. Rank. What? If you're well enough? Of course you'll be well enough. Wrap up warmly, though.

[*They go out, talking, into the hall.* CHILDREN*'s voices are heard from the stairs.*]

Nora. Here they are! Here they are!

[*She runs out and opens the door. The* NURSE, ANNE-MARIE, *enters with the* CHILDREN.]

Nora. Come in, come in! (*stoops down and kisses them*) Oh, my sweet darlings—! Look at them, Christine! Aren't they beautiful?

Rank. Don't stand here chattering in this draft!

Helmer. Come, Mrs. Linde. This is for mothers only.

[DR. RANK, HELMER, *and* MRS. LINDE *go down the stairs. The* NURSE *brings the* CHILDREN *into the room.* NORA *follows, and closes the door to the hall.*]

Nora. How well you look! What red cheeks you've got! Like apples and roses!

[*The* CHILDREN *answer her inaudibly as she talks to them.*]

Nora. Have you had fun? That's splendid. You

---

5. *Au revoir* (ō′ rə·vwär′): French for "goodbye."

gave Emmy and Bob a ride on the sledge? What, both together? I say! What a clever boy you are, Ivar! Oh, let me hold her for a moment, Anne-Marie! My sweet little baby doll! (*takes the* SMALLEST CHILD *from the* NURSE *and dances with her*) Yes, yes, mummy will dance with Bob, too. What? Have you been throwing snowballs? Oh, I wish I'd been there! No, don't—I'll undress them myself, Anne-Marie. No, please let me; it's such fun. Go inside and warm yourself; you look frozen. There's some hot coffee on the stove.

[*The* NURSE *goes into the room on the left.* NORA *takes off the* CHILDREN*'s outdoor clothes and throws them anywhere while they all chatter simultaneously.*]

Nora. What? A big dog ran after you? But he didn't bite you? No, dogs don't bite lovely little baby dolls. Leave those parcels alone, Ivar. What's in them? Ah, wouldn't you like to know! No, no; it's nothing nice. Come on, let's play a game. What shall we play? Hide-and-seek? Yes, let's play hide-and-seek. Bob shall hide first. You want me to? All right, let me hide first.

[NORA *and the* CHILDREN *play around the room, and in the adjacent room to the right, laughing and shouting. At length* NORA *hides under the table. The* CHILDREN *rush in, look, but cannot find her. Then they hear her half-stifled laughter, run to the table, lift up the cloth and see her. Great excitement. She crawls out as though to frighten them. Further excitement. Meanwhile, there has been a knock on the door leading from the hall, but no one has noticed it. Now the door is half opened and* KROGSTAD *enters. He waits for a moment; the game continues.*]

Krogstad. Excuse me, Mrs. Helmer—
Nora (*turns with a stifled cry and half jumps up*). Oh! What do you want?

Krogstad. I beg your pardon—the front door was ajar. Someone must have forgotten to close it.
Nora (*gets up*). My husband is not at home, Mr. Krogstad.
Krogstad. I know.
Nora. Well, what do you want here, then?
Krogstad. A word with you.
Nora. With—? (*to the* CHILDREN, *quietly*) Go inside to Anne-Marie. What? No, the strange gentleman won't do anything to hurt mummy. When he's gone we'll start playing again.

[*She takes the* CHILDREN *into the room on the left and closes the door behind them.*]

Nora (*uneasy, tense*). You want to speak to me?
Krogstad. Yes.
Nora. Today? But it's not the first of the month yet.
Krogstad. No, it is Christmas Eve. Whether or not you have a merry Christmas depends on you.
Nora. What do you want? I can't give you anything today—
Krogstad. We won't talk about that for the present. There's something else. You have a moment to spare?
Nora. Oh, yes. Yes, I suppose so—though—
Krogstad. Good. I was sitting in the café down below and I saw your husband cross the street—
Nora. Yes.
Krogstad. With a lady.
Nora. Well?
Krogstad. Might I be so bold as to ask; was not that lady a Mrs. Linde?
Nora. Yes.
Krogstad. Recently arrived in town?
Nora. Yes, today.
Krogstad. She is a good friend of yours, is she not?
Nora. Yes, she is. But I don't see—
Krogstad. I used to know her, too, once.

Nora. I know.

Krogstad. Oh? You've discovered that. Yes, I thought you would. Well then, may I ask you a straight question: is Mrs. Linde to be employed at the bank?

Nora. How dare you presume to cross-examine me, Mr. Krogstad? You, one of my husband's employees? But since you ask, you shall have an answer. Yes, Mrs. Linde is to be employed by the bank. And I arranged it, Mr. Krogstad. Now you know.

Krogstad. I guessed right, then.

Nora (*walks up and down the room*). Oh, one has a little influence, you know. Just because one's a woman it doesn't necessarily mean that—When one is in a humble position, Mr. Krogstad, one should think twice before offending someone who—hm—!

Krogstad. —who has influence?

Nora. Precisely.

Krogstad (*changes his tone*). Mrs. Helmer, will you have the kindness to use your influence on my behalf?

Nora. What? What do you mean?

Krogstad. Will you be so good as to see that I keep my humble position at the bank?

Nora. What do you mean? Who is thinking of removing you from your position?

Krogstad. Oh, you don't need to play the innocent with me. I realize it can't be very pleasant for your friend to risk bumping into me. And now I also realize whom I have to thank for being hounded out like this.

Nora. But I assure you—

Krogstad. Look, let's not beat about the bush. There's still time, and I'd advise you to use your influence to stop it.

Nora. But, Mr. Krogstad, I have no influence!

Krogstad. Oh? I thought you just said—

Nora. But I didn't mean it like that! I? How on earth could you imagine that I would have any influence over my husband?

Krogstad. Oh, I've known your husband since we were students together. I imagine he has his weaknesses like other married men.

Nora. If you speak impertinently[6] of my husband, I shall show you the door.

Krogstad. You're a bold woman, Mrs. Helmer.

Nora. I'm not afraid of you any longer. Once the new year is in, I'll soon be rid of you.

Krogstad (*more controlled*). Now listen to me, Mrs. Helmer. If I'm forced to, I shall fight for my little job at the bank as I would fight for my life.

Nora. So it sounds.

Krogstad. It isn't just the money—that's the last thing I care about. There's something else. Well, you might as well know. It's like this, you see. You know of course, as everyone else does, that some years ago I committed an indiscretion.

Nora. I think I did hear something—

Krogstad. It never came into court; but from that day, every opening was barred to me. So I turned my hand to the kind of business you know about. I had to do something; and I don't think I was one of the worst. But now I want to give up all that. My sons are growing up: for their sake, I must try to regain what respectability I can. This job in the bank was the first step on the ladder. And now your husband wants to kick me off that ladder back into the dirt.

Nora. But, my dear Mr. Krogstad, it simply isn't in my power to help you.

Krogstad. You say that because you don't want to help me. But I have the means to make you.

Nora. You don't mean you'd tell my husband that I owe you money?

Krogstad. And if I did?

Nora. That'd be a filthy trick! (*almost in tears*) This secret that is my pride and my joy—that he

---

6. **impertinently:** insolently; without the proper respect or manners.

should hear about it in such a filthy, beastly way—hear about it from you! It'd involve me in the most dreadful unpleasantness—

Krogstad. Only—unpleasantness?

Nora (*vehemently*). All right, do it! You'll be the one who'll suffer. It'll show my husband the kind of man you are, and then you'll never keep your job.

Krogstad. I asked you whether it was merely domestic unpleasantness you were afraid of.

Nora. If my husband hears about it, he will of course immediately pay you whatever is owing. And then we shall have nothing more to do with you.

Krogstad (*takes a step closer*). Listen, Mrs. Helmer. Either you've a bad memory or else you know very little about financial transactions. I had better enlighten you.

Nora. What do you mean?

Krogstad. When your husband was ill, you came to me to borrow two hundred and fifty pounds.

Nora. I didn't know anyone else.

Krogstad. I promised to find that sum for you—

Nora. And you did find it.

Krogstad. I promised to find that sum for you on certain conditions. You were so worried about your husband's illness and so keen to get the money to take him abroad that I don't think you bothered much about the details. So it won't be out of place if I refresh your memory. Well—I promised to get you the money in exchange for an I.O.U., which I drew up.

Nora. Yes, and which I signed.

Krogstad. Exactly, But then I added a few lines naming your father as security for the debt. This paragraph was to be signed by your father.

Nora. Was to be? He did sign it.

Krogstad. I left the date blank for your father to fill in when he signed this paper. You remember, Mrs. Helmer?

Nora. Yes, I think so—

Krogstad. Then I gave you back this I.O.U. for you to post to your father. Is that not correct?

Nora. Yes.

Krogstad. And of course you posted it at once; for within five or six days you brought it along to me with your father's signature on it. Whereupon I handed you the money.

Nora. Yes, well. Haven't I repaid the installments as agreed?

Krogstad. Mm—yes, more or less. But to return to what we are speaking about—that was a difficult time for you just then, wasn't it, Mrs. Helmer?

Nora. Yes, it was.

Krogstad. Your father was very ill, if I am not mistaken.

Nora. He was dying.

Krogstad. He did in fact die shortly afterwards?

Nora. Yes.

Krogstad. Tell me, Mrs. Helmer, do you by any chance remember the date of your father's death? The day of the month, I mean.

Nora. Papa died on the twenty-ninth of September.

Krogstad. Quite correct; I took the trouble to confirm it. And that leaves me with a curious little problem—(*takes out a paper*)—which I simply cannot solve.

Nora. Problem? I don't see—

Krogstad. The problem, Mrs. Helmer, is that your father signed this paper three days after his death.

Nora. What? I don't understand—

Krogstad. Your father died on the twenty-ninth of September. But look at this. Here your father has dated his signature the second of October. Isn't that a curious little problem, Mrs. Helmer?

[NORA *is silent*.]

Krogstad. Can you suggest any explanation?

[*She remains silent.*]

Krogstad. And there's another curious thing. The words "second of October" and the year are written in a hand which is not your father's, but which I seem to know. Well, there's a simple explanation to that. Your father could have forgotten to write in the date when he signed, and someone else could have added it before the news came of his death. There's nothing criminal about that. It's the signature itself I'm wondering about. It *is* genuine, I suppose, Mrs. Helmer? It was your father who wrote his name here?

Nora (*after a short silence, throws back her head and looks defiantly at him*). No, it was not. It was I who wrote Papa's name there.

Krogstad. Look, Mrs. Helmer, do you realize this is a dangerous admission?

Nora. Why? You'll get your money.

Krogstad. May I ask you a question? Why didn't you send this paper to your father?

Nora. I couldn't. Papa was very ill. If I'd asked him to sign this, I'd have had to tell him what the money was for. But I couldn't have told him in his condition that my husband's life was in danger. I couldn't have done that!

Krogstad. Then you would have been wiser to have given up your idea of a holiday.

Nora. But I couldn't! It was to save my husband's life. I couldn't put it off.

Krogstad. But didn't it occur to you that you were being dishonest towards me?

Nora. I couldn't bother about that. I didn't care about you. I hated you because of all the beastly difficulties you'd put in my way when you knew how dangerously ill my husband was.

Krogstad. Mrs. Helmer, you evidently don't appreciate exactly what you have done. But I can assure you that it is no bigger nor worse a crime than the one I once committed and thereby ruined my whole social position.

Nora. You? Do you expect me to believe that you would have taken a risk like that to save your wife's life?

Krogstad. The law does not concern itself with motives.

Nora. Then the law must be very stupid.

Krogstad. Stupid or not, if I show this paper to the police, you will be judged according to it.

Nora. I don't believe that. Hasn't a daughter the right to shield her father from worry and anxiety when he's old and dying? Hasn't a wife the right to save her husband's life? I don't know much about the law, but there must be something somewhere that says that such things are allowed. You ought to know that, you're meant to be a lawyer, aren't you? You can't be a very good lawyer, Mr. Krogstad.

Krogstad. Possibly not. But business, the kind of business we two have been transacting—I think you'll admit I understand something about that? Good. Do as you please. But I tell you this. If I get thrown into the gutter for a second time, I shall take you with me.

[*He bows and goes out through the hall.*]

Nora (*stands for a moment in thought, then tosses her head*). What nonsense! He's trying to frighten me! I'm not that stupid. (*busies herself gathering together the children's clothes; then she suddenly stops.*) But—? No, it's impossible. I did it for love, didn't I?

Children (*in the doorway, left*). Mummy, the strange gentleman has gone out into the street.

Nora. Yes, yes, I know. But don't talk to anyone about the strange gentleman. You hear? Not even to Daddy.

Children. No, Mummy. Will you play with us again now?

Nora. No, no. Not now.

Children. Oh but, Mummy, you promised!

Nora. I know, but I can't just now. Go back to the nursery. I've a lot to do. Go away, my darlings, go away.

[*She pushes them gently into the other room, and closes the door behind them. She sits on the sofa, takes up her embroidery, stitches for a few moments, but soon stops.*]

Nora. No! (*throws the embroidery aside, gets up, goes to the door leading to the hall and calls*) Helen! Bring in the Christmas tree! (*She goes to the table on the left and opens the drawer in it; then pauses again.*) No, but it's utterly impossible!

Maid (*enters with the tree*). Where shall I put it, madam?

Nora. There, in the middle of the room.

Maid. Will you be wanting anything else?

Nora. No, thank you. I have everything I need.

[*The* MAID *puts down the tree and goes out.*]

Nora (*busy decorating the tree*). Now—candles here—and flowers here. That loathsome man! Nonsense, nonsense, there's nothing to be frightened about. The Christmas tree must be beautiful. I'll do everything that you like, Torvald. I'll sing for you, dance for you—

[HELMER, *with a bundle of papers under his arm, enters.*]

Nora. Oh—are you back already?

Helmer. Yes. Has anyone been here?

Nora. Here? No.

Helmer. That's strange. I saw Krogstad come out of the front door.

Nora. Did you? Oh yes, that's quite right— Krogstad was here for a few minutes.

Helmer. Nora, I can tell from your face, he has been here and asked you to put in a good word for him.

Nora. Yes.

Helmer. And you were to pretend you were doing it of your own accord? You weren't going to tell me he'd been here? He asked you to do that too, didn't he?

Nora. Yes, Torvald. But—

Helmer. Nora, Nora! And you were ready to enter into such a conspiracy? Talking to a man like that, and making him promises—and then, on top of it all, to tell me an untruth!

Nora. An untruth?

Helmer. Didn't you say no one had been here? (*wags his finger*) My little songbird must never do that again. A songbird must have a clean beak to sing with. Otherwise she'll start twittering out of tune. (*puts his arm around her waist*) Isn't that the way we want things? Yes, of course it is. (*lets go of her*) So let's hear no more about that. (*sits down in front of the stove*) Ah, how cosy and peaceful it is here! (*glances for a few moments at his papers*)

Nora (*busy with the tree; after a short silence*). Torvald.

Helmer. Yes.

Nora. I'm terribly looking forward to that fancy-dress ball at the Stenborgs on Boxing Day.[7]

Helmer. And I'm terribly curious to see what you're going to surprise me with.

Nora. Oh, it's so maddening.

Helmer. What is?

Nora. I can't think of anything to wear. It all seems so stupid and meaningless.

Helmer. So my little Nora has come to that

---

7. **Boxing Day:** the first weekday after Christmas.

conclusion, has she?

Nora (*behind his chair, resting her arms on its back*). Are you very busy, Torvald?

Helmer. Oh—

Nora. What are those papers?

Helmer. Just something to do with the bank.

Nora. Already?

Helmer. I persuaded the trustees to give me authority to make certain immediate changes in the staff and organization. I want to have everything straight by the new year.

Nora. Then that's why this poor man Krogstad—

Helmer. Hm.

Nora (*still leaning over his chair, slowly strokes the back of his head*). If you hadn't been so busy, I was going to ask you an enormous favor, Torvald.

Helmer. Well, tell me. What was it to be?

Nora. You know I trust your taste more than anyone's. I'm so anxious to look really beautiful at the fancy-dress ball. Torvald, couldn't you help me to decide what I shall go as, and what kind of costume I ought to wear?

Helmer. Aha! So little Miss Independent's in trouble and needs a man to rescue her, does she?

Nora. Yes, Torvald, I can't get anywhere without your help.

Helmer. Well, well, I'll give the matter thought. We'll find something.

Nora. Oh, how kind of you! (*goes back to the tree; pauses*) How pretty these red flowers look! But, tell me, is it so dreadful, this thing that Krogstad's done?

Helmer. He forged someone else's name. Have you any idea what that means?

Nora. Mightn't he have been forced to do it by some emergency?

Helmer. He probably just didn't think—that's what usually happens. I'm not so heartless as to condemn a man for an isolated action.

Nora. No, Torvald, of course not!

Helmer. Men often succeed in reestablishing themselves if they admit their crime and take their punishment.

Nora. Punishment?

Helmer. But Krogstad didn't do that. He chose to try and trick his way out of it. And that's what has morally destroyed him.

Nora. You think that would—?

Helmer. Just think how a man with that load on his conscience must always be lying and cheating and dissembling—how he must wear a mask even in the presence of those who are dearest to him, even his own wife and children! Yes, the children. That's the worst danger, Nora.

Nora. Why?

Helmer. Because an atmosphere of lies contaminates and poisons every corner of the home. Every breath that the children draw in such a house contains the germs of evil.

Nora. (*comes closer behind him*). Do you really believe that?

Helmer. Oh, my dear, I've come across it so often in my work at the bar. Nearly all young criminals are the children of mothers who are constitutional liars.

Nora. Why do you say mothers?

Helmer. It's usually the mother—though of course the father can have the same influence. Every lawyer knows that only too well. And yet this fellow Krogstad has been sitting at home all these years poisoning his children with his lies and pretenses. That's why I say that, morally speaking, he is dead. (*stretches out his hand towards her*) So my pretty little Nora must promise me not to plead his case. Your hand on it. Come, come, what's this? Give me your hand. There. That's settled, now. I assure you it'd be quite impossible for me to work in the same building as him. I literally feel physically ill in the presence of a man like that.

Nora (*draws her hand from his and goes over to the other side of the Christmas tree*). How hot it is in here! And I've so much to do.

Helmer (*gets up and gathers his papers*). Yes, and I must try to get some of this read before dinner. I'll think about your costume, too. And I may even have something up my sleeve to hang in gold paper on the Christmas tree. (*lays his hand on her head*) My precious little songbird!

[*He goes into his study and closes the door.*]

Nora (*softly, after a pause*). It's nonsense. It must be. It's impossible. It *must* be impossible!

Nurse (*in the doorway, left*). The children are asking if they can come in to Mummy.

Nora. No, no, no—don't let them in. You stay with them, Anne-Marie.

Nurse. Very good, madam. (*closes the door*)

Nora (*pale with fear*). Corrupt my little children—! Poison my home! (*short pause; she throws back her head*) It isn't true! It *couldn't* be true!

ACT 2

The same room. In the corner by the piano the Christmas tree stands, stripped and disheveled, its candles burned to their sockets. NORA's *outdoor clothes lie on the sofa. She is alone in the room, walking restlessly to-and-fro. At length she stops by the sofa and picks up her coat.*

Nora (*drops the coat again*). There's someone coming! (*goes to the door and listens*) No, it's no one. Of course—no one'll come today, it's Christmas Day. Nor tomorrow. But perhaps—! (*opens the door and looks out*) No. Nothing in the letter box. Quite empty. (*walks across the room*) Silly, silly. Of course he won't do anything. It couldn't happen. It isn't possible. Why, I've three small children.

[*The* NURSE, *carrying a large cardboard box, enters from the room on the left.*]

Nurse. I found those fancy dress clothes at last, madam.
Nora. Thank you. Put them on the table.
Nurse (*does so*). They're all rumpled up.
Nora. Oh, I wish I could tear them into a million pieces!
Nurse. Why, madam! They'll be all right. Just a little patience.
Nora. Yes, of course. I'll go and get Mrs. Linde to help me.
Nurse. What, out again? In this dreadful weather? You'll catch a chill, madam.
Nora. Well, that wouldn't be the worst. How are the children?
Nurse. Playing with their Christmas presents, poor little dears. But—
Nora. Are they still asking to see me?
Nurse. They're so used to having their mummy with them.
Nora. Yes, but, Anne-Marie, from now on I

shan't be able to spend so much time with them.
Nurse. Well, children get used to anything in time.
Nora. Do you think so? Do you think they'd forget their mother if she went away from them—forever?
Nurse. Mercy's sake, madam! Forever!
Nora. Tell me, Anne-Marie—I've so often wondered. How could you bear to give your child away—to strangers?
Nurse. But I had to when I came to nurse my little Miss Nora.
Nora. Do you mean you wanted to?
Nurse. When I had the chance of such a good job? A poor girl what's got into trouble can't afford to pick and choose. That good-for-nothing didn't lift a finger.
Nora. But your daughter must have completely forgotten you.
Nurse. Oh no, indeed she hasn't. She's written to me twice, once when she got confirmed and then again when she got married.
Nora (*hugs her*). Dear old Anne-Marie, you were a good mother to me.
Nurse. Poor little Miss Nora, you never had any mother but me.
Nora. And if my little ones had no one else, I know you would—no, silly, silly, silly! (*opens the cardboard box*) Go back to them, Anne-Marie. Now I must—! Tomorrow you'll see how pretty I shall look.
Nurse. Why, there'll be no one at the ball as beautiful as my Miss Nora.

[*She goes into the room, left.*]

Nora (*begins to unpack the clothes from the box, but soon throws them down again*). Oh, if only I dared go out! If I could be sure no one would come and nothing would happen while I was away! Stupid, stupid! No one will come. I just mustn't think about it. Brush this muff. Pretty gloves, pretty gloves! Don't think about it, don't think about it! One, two, three, four, five, six— (*cries*) Ah—they're coming—!

[*She begins to run towards the door, but stops uncertainly.* MRS. LINDE *enters from the hall, where she has been taking off her outdoor clothes.*]

Nora. Oh, it's you, Christine. There's no one else outside, is there? Oh, I'm so glad you've come.

Mrs. Linde. I hear you were at my room asking for me.

Nora. Yes, I just happened to be passing. I want to ask you to help me with something. Let's sit down here on the sofa. Look at this. There's going to be a fancy-dress ball tomorrow night upstairs at Consul Stenborg's, and Torvald wants me to go as a Neapolitan fisher-girl and dance the tarantella. I learned it in Capri.

Mrs. Linde. I say, are you going to give a performance?

Nora. Yes, Torvald says I should. Look, here's the dress. Torvald had it made for me in Italy—but now it's all so torn, I don't know—

Mrs. Linde. Oh, we'll soon put that right—the stitching's just come away. Needle and thread? Ah, here we are.

Nora. You're being awfully sweet.

Mrs. Linde (*sews*). So you're going to dress up tomorrow, Nora? I must pop over for a moment to see how you look. Oh, but I've completely forgotten to thank you for that nice evening yesterday.

Nora (*gets up and walks across the room*). Oh, I didn't think it was as nice as usual. You ought to have come to town a little earlier, Christine. . . . Yes, Torvald understands how to make a home look attractive.

Mrs. Linde. I'm sure you do, too. You're not your father's daughter for nothing. But, tell me—is Dr. Rank always in such low spirits as he was yesterday?

Nora. No, last night it was very noticeable. But he's got a terrible disease—he's got spinal tuberculosis, poor man. His father was a frightful creature who kept mistresses and so on. As a result Dr. Rank has been sickly ever since he was a child—you understand—

Mrs. Linde (*puts down her sewing*). But, my dear Nora, how on earth did you get to know about such things?

Nora (*walks about the room*). Oh, don't be silly, Christine—when one has three children, one comes into contact with women who—well, who know about medical matters, and they tell one a thing or two.

Mrs. Linde (*sews again; a short silence*). Does Dr. Rank visit you every day?

Nora. Yes, every day. He's Torvald's oldest friend, and a good friend to me too. Dr. Rank's almost one of the family.

Mrs. Linde. But, tell me—is he quite sincere? I mean, doesn't he rather say the sort of thing he thinks people want to hear?

Nora. No, quite the contrary. What gave you that idea?

Mrs. Linde. When you introduced me to him yesterday, he said he'd often heard my name mentioned here. But later I noticed your husband had no idea who I was. So how could Dr. Rank—

Nora. Yes, that's quite right, Christine. You see, Torvald's so hopelessly in love with me that he wants to have me all to himself—those were his very words. When we were first married, he got quite jealous if I as much as mentioned any of my old friends back home. So naturally, I stopped talking about them. But I often chat with Dr. Rank about that kind of thing. He enjoys it, you see.

Mrs. Linde. Now listen, Nora. In many ways you're still a child; I'm a bit older than you and have a little more experience of the world.

There's something I want to say to you. You ought to give up this business with Dr. Rank.
Nora. What business?
Mrs. Linde. Well, everything. Last night you were speaking about this rich admirer of yours who was going to give you money—
Nora. Yes, and who doesn't exist—unfortunately. But what's that got to do with—?
Mrs. Linde. Is Dr. Rank rich?
Nora. Yes.
Mrs. Linde. And he has no dependants?
Nora. No, no one. But—
Mrs. Linde. And he comes here to see you every day?
Nora. Yes, I've told you.
Mrs. Linde. But how dare a man of his education be so forward?
Nora. What on earth are you talking about?
Mrs. Linde. Oh, stop pretending, Nora. Do you think I haven't guessed who it was who lent you that two hundred pounds?
Nora. Are you out of your mind? How could you imagine such a thing? A friend, someone who comes here every day! Why, that'd be an impossible situation!
Mrs. Linde. Then it really wasn't him?
Nora. No, of course not. I've never for a moment dreamed of—anyway, he hadn't any money to lend then. He didn't come into that till later.
Mrs. Linde. Well, I think that was a lucky thing for you, Nora dear.
Nora. No, I could never have dreamed of asking Dr. Rank—Though I'm sure that if ever I did ask him—
Mrs. Linde. But of course you won't.
Nora. Of course not. I can't imagine that it should ever become necessary. But I'm perfectly sure that if I did speak to Dr. Rank—
Mrs. Linde. Behind your husband's back?
Nora. I've got to get out of this other business—and *that's* been going on behind his back. I've *got* to get out of it.

Mrs. Linde. Yes, well, that's what I told you yesterday. But—
Nora (*walking up and down*). It's much easier for a man to arrange these things than a woman—
Mrs. Linde. One's own husband, yes.
Nora. Oh, bosh. (*stops walking*) When you've completely repaid a debt, you get your I.O.U. back, don't you?
Mrs. Linde. Yes, of course.
Nora. And you can tear it into a thousand pieces and burn the filthy, beastly thing!
Mrs. Linde (*looks hard at her, puts down her sewing and gets up slowly*). Nora, you're hiding something from me.
Nora. Can you see that?
Mrs. Linde. Something has happened since yesterday morning. Nora, what is it?
Nora (*goes towards her*). Christine! (*listens*) Ssh! There's Torvald. Would you mind going into the nursery for a few minutes? Torvald can't bear to see sewing around. Anne-Marie'll help you.
Mrs. Linde (*gathers some of her things together*). Very well. But I shan't leave this house until we've talked this matter out.

[*She goes into the nursery, left. As she does so,* HELMER *enters from the hall.*]

Nora (*runs to meet him*). Oh, Torvald dear, I've been so longing for you to come back!
Helmer. Was that the dressmaker?
Nora. No, it was Christine. She's helping me mend my costume. I'm going to look rather splendid in that.
Helmer. Yes, that was quite a bright idea of mine, wasn't it?
Nora. Wonderful! But wasn't it nice of me to give in to you?
Helmer (*takes her chin in his hand*). Nice—to give in to your husband? All right, little silly, I know you didn't mean it like that. But I won't disturb

you. I expect you'll be wanting to try it on.

Nora. Are you going to work now?

Helmer. Yes. (*shows her a bundle of papers*) Look at these. I've been down to the bank— (*turns to go into his study*)

Nora. Torvald.

Helmer (*stops*). Yes.

Nora. If little squirrel asked you really prettily to grant her a wish—

Helmer. Well?

Nora. Would you grant it to her?

Helmer. First I should naturally have to know what it was.

Nora. Squirrel would do lots of pretty tricks for you if you granted her wish.

Helmer. Out with it, then.

Nora. Your little skylark would sing in every room—

Helmer. My little skylark does that already.

Nora. I'd turn myself into a little fairy and dance for you in the moonlight, Torvald.

Helmer. Nora, it isn't that business you were talking about this morning?

Nora (*comes closer*). Yes, Torvald—oh, please! I beg of you!

Helmer. Have you really the nerve to bring that up again?

Nora. Yes, Torvald, yes, you must do as I ask! You must let Krogstad keep his place at the bank!

Helmer. My dear Nora, his is the job I'm giving to Mrs. Linde.

Nora. Yes, that's terribly sweet of you. But you can get rid of one of the other clerks instead of Krogstad.

Helmer. Really, you're being incredibly obstinate. Just because you thoughtlessly promised to put in a word for him, you expect me to—

Nora. No, it isn't that, Helmer. It's for your own sake. That man writes for the most beastly newspapers—you said so yourself. He could do you tremendous harm. I'm so dreadfully frightened of him—

Helmer. Oh, I understand, Memories of the past. That's what's frightening you.

Nora. What do you mean?

Helmer. You're thinking of your father, aren't you?

Nora. Yes, yes. Of course. Just think what those dreadful men wrote in the papers about Papa! The most frightful slanders. I really believe it would have lost him his job if the Ministry hadn't sent you down to investigate, and you hadn't been so kind and helpful to him.

Helmer. But, my dear little Nora, there's a considerable difference between your father and me. Your father was not a man of unassailable reputation. But I am. And I hope to remain so all my life.

Nora. But no one knows what spiteful people may not dig up. We could be so peaceful and happy now, Torvald—we could be free from every worry—you and I and the children. Oh, please, Torvald, please—!

Helmer. The very fact of your pleading his cause makes it impossible for me to keep him. Everyone at the bank already knows that I intend to dismiss Krogstad. If the rumor got about that the new vice-president had allowed his wife to persuade him to change his mind—

Nora. Well, what then?

Helmer. Oh, nothing, nothing. As long as my little Miss Obstinate gets her way—! Do you expect me to make a laughingstock of myself before my entire staff—give people the idea that I am open to outside influence? Believe me, I'd soon feel the consequences! Besides— there's something else that makes it impossible for Krogstad to remain in the bank while I am its manager.

Nora. What is that?

Helmer. I might conceivably have allowed myself to ignore his moral obloquies[1]—

---

1. **obloquies** (äb′lə·kwēz): verbal abuse; censure.

Nora. Yes, Torvald, surely?

Helmer. And I hear he's quite efficient at his job. But we—well, we were school friends. It was one of those friendships that one enters into over-hastily and so often comes to regret later in life. I might as well confess the truth. We—well, we're on Christian name terms. And the tactless idiot makes no attempt to conceal it when other people are present. On the contrary, he thinks it gives him the right to be familiar with me. He shows off the whole time, with "Torvald this" and "Torvald that." I can tell you, I find it damned annoying. If he stayed, he'd make my position intolerable.

Nora. Torvald, you can't mean this seriously.

Helmer. Oh? And why not?

Nora. But it's so petty.

Helmer. What did you say? Petty? You think *I* am petty?

Nora. No, Torvald dear, of course you're not. That's just why—

Helmer. Don't quibble! You call my motives petty. Then I must be petty too. Petty! I see. Well, I've had enough of this. (*goes to the door and calls into the hall*) Helen!

Nora. What are you going to do?

Helmer (*searching among his papers*). I'm going to settle this matter once and for all.

[*The* MAID *enters.*]

Helmer. Take this letter downstairs at once. Find a messenger and see that he delivers it. Immediately! The address is on the envelope. Here's the money.

Maid. Very good, sir. (*goes out with the letter*)

Helmer (*putting his papers in order*). There now, little Miss Obstinate.

Nora (*tensely*). Torvald—what was in that letter?

Helmer. Krogstad's dismissal.

Nora. Call her back, Torvald! There's still time. Oh, Torvald, call her back! Do it for my sake—

for your own sake—for the children! Do you hear me, Torvald? Please do it! You don't realize what this may do to us all!

Helmer. Too late.

Nora. Yes. Too late.

Helmer. My dear Nora, I forgive you this anxiety. Though it is a bit of an insult to me. Oh, but it is! Isn't it an insult to imply that I should be frightened by the vindictiveness of a depraved hack journalist? But I forgive you, because it so charmingly testifies to the love you bear me. (*takes her in his arms*) Which is as it should be, my own dearest Nora. Let what will happen, happen. When the real crisis comes, you will not find me lacking in strength or courage. I am man enough to bear the burden for us both.

Nora (*fearfully*). What do you mean?

Helmer. The whole burden, I say—

Nora (*calmly*). I shall never let you do that.

Helmer. Very well. We shall share it, Nora—as man and wife. And that's as it should be. (*caresses her*) Are you happy now? There, there, there; don't look at me with those frightened little eyes. You're simply imagining things. You go ahead now and do your tarantella, and get some practice on that tambourine. I'll sit in my study and close the door. Then I won't hear anything, and you can make all the noise you want. (*turns in the doorway*) When Dr. Rank comes, tell him where to find me. (*He nods to her, goes into his room with his papers and closes the door.*)

Nora (*desperate with anxiety, stands as though transfixed, and whispers*). He said he'd do it. He will do it. He will do it, and nothing'll stop him. No, never that. I'd rather anything. There must be some escape—Some way out—!

[*The bell rings in the hall.*]

Nora. Dr. Rank—! Anything but that! Anything, I don't care—!

[*She passes her hand across her face, composes herself, walks across and opens the door to the hall.* DR. RANK *is standing there, hanging up his fur coat. During the following scene it begins to grow dark.*]

Nora. Good evening, Dr. Rank. I recognized your ring. But you mustn't go in to Torvald yet. I think he's busy.

Rank. And—you?

Nora (*as he enters the room and she closes the door behind him*). Oh, you know very well I've always time to talk to you.

Rank. Thank you. I shall avail myself of that privilege as long as I can.

Nora. What do you mean by that? As long as you *can*?

Rank. Yes. Does that frighten you?

Nora. Well, it's rather a curious expression. Is something going to happen?

Rank. Something I've been expecting to happen for a long time. But I didn't think it would happen quite so soon.

Nora (*seizes his arm*). What is it? Dr. Rank, you must tell me!

Rank (*sits down by the stove*). I'm on the way out. And there's nothing to be done about it.

Nora (*sighs with relief*). Oh, it's you—?

Rank. Who else? No, it's no good lying to oneself. I am the most wretched of all my patients, Mrs. Helmer. These last few days I've been going through the books of this poor body of mine, and I find I am bankrupt. Within a month I may be rotting up there in the churchyard.

Nora. Ugh, what a nasty way to talk!

Rank. The facts aren't exactly nice. But the worst is that there's so much else that's nasty that's got to come first. I've only one more test to make. When that's done I'll have a pretty accurate idea of when the final disintegration is likely to begin. I want to ask you a favor. Helmer's a sensitive chap, and I know how he hates anything ugly.

I don't want him to visit me when I'm in hospital—

Nora. Oh but, Dr. Rank—

Rank. I don't want him there. On any pretext. I shan't have him allowed in. As soon as I know the worst, I'll send you my visiting card with a black cross on it, and then you'll know that the final filthy process has begun.

Nora. Really, you're being quite impossible this evening. And I did hope you'd be in a good mood.

Rank. With death on my hands? And all this to atone for someone else's sin? Is there justice in that? And in every single family, in one way or another, the same merciless law of retribution is at work—

Nora (*holds her hands to her ears*). Nonsense! Cheer up! Laugh!

Rank. Yes, you're right. Laughter's all the damned thing's fit for. My poor innocent spine must pay for the fun my father had as a gay young lieutenant.

Nora (*at the table, left*). You mean he was too fond of asparagus and *foie gras*?[2]

Rank. Yes; and truffles too.

Nora. Yes, of course, truffles, yes. And oysters too, I suppose?

Rank. Yes, oysters, oysters. Of course.

Nora. And all that port and champagne to wash them down. It's too sad that all those lovely things should affect one's spine.

Rank. Especially a poor spine that never got any pleasure out of them.

Nora. Oh yes, that's the saddest thing of all.

Rank (*looks searchingly at her*). Hm—

Nora (*after a moment*). Why did you smile?

Rank. No, it was you who laughed.

Nora. No, it was you who smiled, Dr. Rank!

---

2. *foie gras* (fwä grä): a pâté, or spread, made from goose liver.

Rank (*gets up*). You're a worse little rogue than I thought.

Nora. Oh, I'm full of stupid tricks today.

Rank. So it seems.

Nora (*puts both her hands on his shoulders*). Dear, dear Dr. Rank, you mustn't die and leave Torvald and me.

Rank. Oh, you'll soon get over it. Once one is gone, one is soon forgotten.

Nora (*looks at him anxiously*). Do you believe that?

Rank. One finds replacements, and then—

Nora. Who will find a replacement?

Rank. You and Helmer both will, when I am gone. You seem to have made a start already, haven't you? What was this Mrs. Linde doing here yesterday evening?

Nora. Aha! But surely you can't be jealous of poor Christine?

Rank. Indeed I am. She will be my successor in this house. When I have moved on, this lady will—

Nora. Ssh—don't speak so loud! She's in there!

Rank. Today again? You see!

Nora. She's only come to mend my dress. Good heavens, how unreasonable you are! (*sits on the sofa*) Be nice now, Dr. Rank. Tomorrow you'll see how beautifully I shall dance; and you must imagine that I'm doing it just for you. And for Torvald, of course; obviously. (*takes some things out of the box*) Dr. Rank, sit down here and I'll show you something.

Rank (*sits*). What's this?

Nora. Look here! Look!

Rank. Silk stockings!

Nora. Flesh-colored. Aren't they beautiful? It's very dark in here now, of course, but tomorrow—! No, no, no; only the soles. Oh well, I suppose you can look a bit higher if you want to.

Rank. Hm—

Nora. Why are you looking so critical? Don't you

think they'll fit me?

Rank. I can't really give you a qualified opinion on that.

Nora (*looks at him for a moment*). Shame on you! (*flicks him on the ear with the stockings*) Take that. (*puts them back in the box*)

Rank. What other wonders are to be revealed to me?

Nora. I shan't show you anything else. You're being naughty.

[*She hums a little and looks among the things in the box.*]

Rank (*after a short silence*). When I sit here like this being so intimate with you, I can't think—I cannot imagine what would have become of me if I had never entered this house.

Nora (*smiles*). Yes, I think you enjoy being with us, don't you?

Rank (*more quietly, looking into the middle distance*). And now to have to leave it all—

Nora. Nonsense. You're not leaving us.

Rank (*as before*). And not to be able to leave even the most wretched token of gratitude behind; hardly even a passing sense of loss; only an empty place, to be filled by the next comer.

Nora. Suppose I were to ask you to—? No—

Rank. To do what?

Nora. To give me proof of your friendship—

Rank. Yes, yes?

Nora. No, I mean—to do me a very great service—

Rank. Would you really for once grant me that happiness?

Nora. But you've no idea what it is.

Rank. Very well, tell me, then.

Nora. No, but, Dr. Rank, I can't. It's far too much—I want your help and advice, and I want you to do something for me.

Rank. The more the better. I've no idea what it can be. But tell me. You do trust me, don't you?

Nora. Oh, yes, more than anyone. You're my best and truest friend. Otherwise I couldn't tell you. Well then, Dr. Rank—there's something you must help me to prevent. You know how much Torvald loves me—he'd never hesitate for an instant to lay down his life for me—

Rank (*leans over towards her*). Nora—do you think he is the only one—?

Nora (*with a slight start*). What do you mean?

Rank. Who would gladly lay down his life for you?

Nora (*sadly*). Oh, I see.

Rank. I swore to myself I would let you know that before I go. I shall never have a better opportunity. . . . Well, Nora, now you know that. And now you also know that you can trust me as you can trust nobody else.

Nora (*rises; calmly and quietly*). Let me pass, please.

Rank (*makes room for her but remains seated*). Nora—

Nora (*in the doorway to the hall*). Helen, bring the lamp. (*goes over to the stove*) Oh, dear Dr. Rank, this was really horrid of you.

Rank (*gets up*). That I have loved you as deeply as anyone else has? Was that horrid of me?

Nora. No—but that you should go and tell me. That was quite unnecessary—

Rank. What do you mean? Did you know, then—?

[*The* MAID *enters with the lamp, puts it on the table and goes out.*]

Rank. Nora—Mrs. Helmer—I am asking you, did you know this?

Nora. Oh, what do I know, what did I know, what didn't I know—I really can't say. How could you be so stupid, Dr. Rank? Everything was so nice.

Rank. Well, at any rate now you know that I am ready to serve you, body and soul. So—please continue.

Nora (*looks at him*). After this?

Rank. Please tell me what it is.

Nora. I can't possibly tell you now.

Rank. Yes, yes! You mustn't punish me like this. Let me be allowed to do what I can for you.

Nora. You can't do anything for me now. Anyway, I don't need any help. It was only my imagination—you'll see. Yes, really. Honestly. (*sits in the rocking chair, looks at him and smiles*) Well, upon my word you *are* a fine gentleman, Dr. Rank, Aren't you ashamed of yourself, now that the lamp's been lit?

Rank. Frankly, no. But perhaps I ought to say—*adieu*?

Nora. Of course not. You will naturally continue to visit us as before. You know quite well how Torvald depends on your company.

Rank. Yes, but you?

Nora. Oh, I always think it's enormous fun having you here.

Rank. That was what misled me. You're a riddle to me, you know. I'd often felt you'd just as soon be with me as with Helmer.

Nora. Well, you see, there are some people whom one loves, and others whom it's almost more fun to be with.

Rank. Oh yes, there's some truth in that.

Nora. When I was at home, of course I loved Papa best. But I always used to think it was terribly amusing to go down and talk to the servants; because they never told me what I ought to do; and they were such fun to listen to.

Rank. I see. So I've taken their place?

Nora (*jumps up and runs over to him*). Oh, dear, sweet Dr. Rank, I didn't mean that at all. But I'm sure you understand—I feel the same about Torvald as I did about Papa.

Maid (*enters from the hall*). Excuse me, madam. (*whispers to her and hands her a visiting card*)

Nora (*glances at the card*). Oh! (*puts it quickly in her pocket*)

Rank. Anything wrong?

Nora. No, no, nothing at all. It's just something that—it's my new dress.

Rank. What? But your costume is lying over there.

Nora. Oh—that, yes—but there's another—I ordered it specially—Torvald mustn't know—

Rank. Ah, so that's your big secret?

Nora. Yes, yes. Go in and talk to him—he's in his study—keep him talking for a bit—

Rank. Don't worry. He won't get away from me. (*goes into* HELMER'*s study*)

Nora (*to the* MAID). Is he waiting in the kitchen?

Maid. Yes, madam, he came up the back way—

Nora. But didn't you tell him I had a visitor?

Maid. Yes, but he wouldn't go.

Nora. Wouldn't go?

Maid. No, madam, not until he'd spoken with you.

Nora. Very well, show him in; but quietly. Helen, you mustn't tell anyone about this. It's a surprise for my husband.

Maid. Very good, madam. I understand. (*goes*)

Nora. It's happening. It's happening after all. No, no, no, it can't happen, it mustn't happen.

[*She walks across and bolts the door of* HELMER'*s study. The* MAID *opens the door from the hall to admit* KROGSTAD, *and closes it behind him. He is wearing an overcoat, heavy boots and a fur cap.*]

Nora (*goes towards him*). Speak quietly. My husband's at home.

Krogstad. Let him hear.

Nora. What do you want from me?

Krogstad. Information.

Nora. Hurry up, then. What is it?

Krogstad. I suppose you know I've been given the sack.

Nora. I couldn't stop it, Mr. Krogstad. I did my best for you, but it didn't help.

Krogstad. Does your husband love you so little? He knows what I can do to you, and yet he dares to—

Nora. Surely you don't imagine I told him?

Krogstad. No, I didn't really think you had. It wouldn't have been like my old friend Torvald Helmer to show that much courage—

Nora. Mr. Krogstad, I'll trouble you to speak respectfully of my husband.

Krogstad. Don't worry, I'll show him all the respect he deserves. But since you're so anxious to keep this matter hushed up, I presume you're better informed than you were yesterday of the gravity of what you've done?

Nora. I've learned more than you could ever teach me.

Krogstad. Yes, a bad lawyer like me—

Nora. What do you want from me?

Krogstad. I just wanted to see how things were with you, Mrs. Helmer. I've been thinking about you all day. Even duns and hack journalists have hearts, you know.

Nora. Show some heart, then. Think of my little children.

Krogstad. Have you and your husband thought of mine? Well, let's forget that. I just wanted to tell you, you don't need to take this business too seriously. I'm not going to take any action, for the present.

Nora. Oh, no—you won't, will you? I knew it.

Krogstad. It can all be settled quite amicably. There's no need for it to become public. We'll keep it among the three of us.

Nora. My husband must never know about this.

Krogstad. How can you stop him? Can you pay the balance of what you owe me?

Nora. Not immediately.

Krogstad. Have you any means of raising the money during the next few days?

Nora. None that I would care to use.

Krogstad. Well, it wouldn't have helped anyway. However much money you offered me now I wouldn't give you back that paper.

Nora. What are you going to do with it?

Krogstad. Just keep it. No one else need ever

hear about it. So in case you were thinking of doing anything desperate—

Nora. I am.

Krogstad. Such as running away—

Nora. I am.

Krostad. Or anything more desperate—

Nora. How did you know?

Krogstad. —just give up the idea.

Nora. How did you know?

Krogstad. Most of us think of that at first. I did. But I hadn't the courage—

Nora (*dully*). Neither have I.

Krogstad (*relieved*). It's true, isn't it? You haven't the courage, either?

Nora. No. I haven't. I haven't.

Krogstad. It'd be a stupid thing to do anyway. Once the first little domestic explosion is over . . . I've got a letter in my pocket here addressed to your husband—

Nora. Telling him everything?

Krogstad. As delicately as possible.

Nora (*quickly*). He must never see that letter. Tear it up. I'll find the money somehow—

Krogstad. I'm sorry, Mrs. Helmer. I thought I'd explained—

Nora. Oh, I don't mean the money I owe you. Let me know how much you want from my husband, and I'll find it for you.

Krogstad. I'm not asking your husband for money.

Nora. What do you want, then?

Krogstad. I'll tell you. I want to get on my feet again, Mrs. Helmer. I want to get to the top. And your husband's going to help me. For eighteen months now my record's been clean. I've been in hard straits all that time: I was content to fight my way back inch by inch. Now I've been chucked back into the mud, and I'm not going to be satisfied with just getting back my job. I'm going to get to the top, I tell you. I'm going to get back into the bank, and it's going to be higher up. Your husband's going to create a new

job for me—

Nora. He'll never do that!

Krogstad. Oh yes, he will. I know him. He won't dare to risk a scandal. And once I'm in there with him, you'll see! Within a year I'll be his right-hand man. It'll be Nils Krogstad who'll be running that bank, not Torvald Helmer!

Nora. That will never happen.

Krogstad. Are you thinking of—?

Nora. Now I *have* the courage.

Krogstad. Oh, you can't frighten me. A pampered little pretty like you—

Nora. You'll see! You'll see!

Krogstad. Under the ice? Down in the cold, black water? And then, in the spring, to float up again, ugly, unrecognizable, hairless—?

Nora. You can't frighten me.

Krogstad. And you can't frighten me. People don't do such things, Mrs. Helmer. And anyway, what'd be the use? I've got him in my pocket.

Nora. But afterwards? When I'm no longer—?

Krogstad. Have you forgotten that then your reputation will be in my hands?

[*She looks at him speechlessly.*]

Krogstad. Well, I've warned you. Don't do anything silly. When Helmer's read my letter, he'll get in touch with me. And remember, it's your husband who has forced me to act like this. And for that I'll never forgive him. Goodbye, Mrs. Helmer. (*He goes out through the hall.*)

Nora (*runs to the hall door, opens it a few inches and listens*). He's going. He's not going to give him the letter. Oh, no, no, it couldn't possibly happen. (*opens the door, a little wider*) What's he doing? Standing outside the front door. He's not going downstairs. Is he changing his mind? Yes, he—!

[*A letter falls into the letter box.* KROGSTAD'*s footsteps die away down the stairs.*]

Nora. (*with a stifled cry, runs across the room towards the table by the sofa; a pause*). In the letter box. (*steals timidly over towards the hall door*) There it is! Oh, Torvald, Torvald! Now we're lost!

Mrs. Linde (*enters from the nursery with NORA's costume*). Well, I've done the best I can. Shall we see how it looks—?

Nora (*whispers hoarsely*). Christine, come here.

Mrs. Linde (*throws the dress on the sofa*). What's wrong with you? You look as though you'd seen a ghost!

Nora. Come here. Do you see that letter? There—look—through the glass of the letter box.

Mrs. Linde. Yes, yes, I see it.

Nora. That letter's from Krogstad—

Mrs. Linde. Nora! It was Krogstad who lent you the money!

Nora. Yes. And now Torvald's going to discover everything.

Mrs. Linde. Oh, believe me, Nora, it'll be best for you both.

Nora. You don't know what's happened. I've committed a forgery—

Mrs. Linde. But, for heaven's sake—!

Nora. Christine, all I want is for you to be my witness.

Mrs. Linde. What do you mean? Witness what?

Nora. If I should go out of my mind—and it might easily happen—

Mrs. Linde. Nora!

Nora. Or if anything else should happen to me—so that I wasn't here any longer—

Mrs. Linde. Nora, Nora, you don't know what you're saying!

Nora. If anyone should try to take the blame, and say it was all his fault—you understand—?

Mrs. Linde. Yes, yes—but how can you think—?

Nora. Then you must testify that it isn't true, Christine. I'm not mad—I know exactly what I'm saying—and I'm telling you, no one else knows anything about this. I did it entirely on my own. Remember that.

Mrs. Linde. All right. But I simply don't understand—

Nora. Oh, how could you understand? A—miracle—is about to happen.

Mrs. Linde. Miracle?

Nora. Yes. A miracle. But it's so frightening, Christine. It mustn't happen, not for anything in the world.

Mrs. Linde. I'll go over and talk to Krogstad.

Nora. Don't go near him. He'll only do something to hurt you.

Mrs. Linde. Once upon a time he'd have done anything for my sake.

Nora. He?

Mrs. Linde. Where does he live?

Nora. Oh, how should I know—? Oh yes, wait a moment—! (*feels in her pocket*) Here's his card. But the letter, the letter—!

Helmer (*from his study, knocks on the door*). Nora!

Nora (*cries in alarm*). What is it?

Helmer. Now, now, don't get alarmed. We're not coming in—you've closed the door. Are you trying on your costume?

Nora. Yes, yes—I'm trying on my costume. I'm going to look so pretty for you, Torvald.

Mrs. Linde (*who has been reading the card*). Why, he lives just round the corner.

Nora. Yes; but it's no use. There's nothing to be done now. The letter's lying there in the box.

Mrs. Linde. And your husband has the key?

Nora. Yes, he always keeps it.

Mrs. Linde. Krogstad must ask him to send the letter back unread. He must find some excuse—

Nora. But Torvald always opens the box at just about this time—

Mrs. Linde. You must stop him. Go in and keep him talking. I'll be back as quickly as I can.

[*She hurries out through the hall.*]

Nora (*goes over to* HELMER*'s door, opens it and peeps in*). Torvald!

Helmer (*offstage*). Well, may a man enter his own drawing room again? Come on, Rank, now we'll see what—(*in the doorway*) But what's this?

Nora. What, Torvald dear?

Helmer. Rank's been preparing me for some great transformation scene.

Rank (*in the doorway*). So I understood. But I seem to have been mistaken.

Nora. Yes, no one's to be allowed to see me before tomorrow night.

Helmer. But, my dear Nora, you look quite worn out. Have you been practicing too hard?

Nora. No, I haven't practiced at all yet.

Helmer. Well, you must.

Nora. Yes, Torvald, I must, I know. But I can't get anywhere without your help. I've completely forgotten everything.

Helmer. Oh, we'll soon put that to rights.

Nora. Yes, help me, Torvald. Promise me you will? Oh, I'm so nervous. All those people—! You must forget everything except me this evening. You mustn't think of business—I won't even let you touch a pen. Promise me, Torvald?

Helmer. I promise. This evening I shall think of nothing but you—my poor, helpless little darling. Oh, there's just one thing I must see to—(*goes towards the hall door*)

Nora. What do you want out there?

Helmer. I'm only going to see if any letters have come.

Nora. No, Torvald, no!

Helmer. Why what's the matter?

Nora. Torvald, I beg you. There's nothing there.

Helmer. Well, I'll just make sure.

[*He moves towards the door.* NORA *runs to the piano and plays the first bars of the* Tarantella.]

Helmer (*at the door, turns*). Aha!

Nora. I can't dance tomorrow if I don't practice with you now.

Helmer (*goes over to her*). Are you really so frightened, Nora dear?

Nora. Yes, terribly frightened. Let me start practicing now, at once—we've still time before dinner. Oh, do sit down and play for me, Torvald dear. Correct me, lead me, the way you always do.

Helmer. Very well, my dear, if you wish it.

[*He sits down at the piano.* NORA *seizes the tambourine and a long multicolored shawl from the cardboard box, wraps the shawl hastily around her, then takes a quick leap into the center of the room and cries:*]

Nora. Play for me! I want to dance!

[HELMER *plays and* NORA *dances.* DR. RANK *stands behind* HELMER *at the piano and watches her.*]

Helmer (*as he plays*). Slower, slower!

Nora. I can't!

Helmer. Not so violently, Nora.

Nora. I must!

Helmer (*stops playing*). No, no, this won't do at all.

Nora (*laughs and swings her tambourine*). Isn't that what I told you?

Rank. Let me play for her.

Helmer (*gets up*). Yes, would you? Then it'll be easier for me to show her.

[RANK *sits down at the piano and plays.* NORA *dances more and more wildly.* HELMER *has stationed himself by the stove and tries repeatedly to correct her, but she seems not to hear him. Her hair works loose and falls over her shoulders; she ignores it and continues to dance.* MRS. LINDE *enters.*]

Mrs. Linde (*stands in the doorway as though tongue-tied*). Ah—!

Nora (*as she dances*). Oh, Christine, we're having such fun!

Helmer. But, Nora darling, you're dancing as if your life depended on it.

Nora. It does.

Helmer. Rank, stop it! This is sheer lunacy. Stop it, I say!

[RANK *ceases playing.* NORA *suddenly stops dancing.*]

Helmer (*goes over to her*). I'd never have believed it. You've forgotten everything I taught you.

Nora (*throws away the tambourine*). You see!

Helmer. I'll have to show you every step.

Nora. You see how much I need you! You must show me every step of the way. Right to the end of the dance. Promise me you will, Torvald?

Helmer. Never fear. I will.

Nora. You mustn't think about anything but me—today or tomorrow. Don't open any letters—don't even open the letter box—

Helmer. Aha, you're still worried about that fellow—

Nora. Oh, yes, yes, him too.

Helmer. Nora, I can tell from the way you're behaving, there's a letter from him already lying there.

Nora. I don't know. I think so. But you mustn't read it now. I don't want anything ugly to come between us till it's all over.

Rank (*quietly to* HELMER). Better give her her way.

Helmer (*puts his arm round her*). My child shall have her way. But tomorrow night, when your dance is over—

Nora. Then you will be free.

Maid (*appears in the doorway, right*). Dinner is served, madam.

Nora. Put out some champagne, Helen.

Maid. Very good, madam. (*goes*)

Helmer. I say! What's this, a banquet?

Nora. We'll drink champagne until dawn! (*calls*) And, Helen! Put out some macaroons! Lots of macaroons—for once!

Helmer (*takes her hands in his*). Now, now, now. Don't get so excited. Where's my little songbird, the one I know?

Nora. All right. Go and sit down—and you, too, Dr. Rank. I'll be with you in a minute. Christine, you must help me put my hair up.

Rank (*quietly, as they go*). There's nothing wrong, is there? I mean, she isn't—er—expecting—?

Helmer. Good heavens no, my dear chap. She just gets scared like a child sometimes—I told you before—

[*They go out, right.*]

Nora. Well?

Mrs. Linde. He's left town.

Nora. I saw it from your face.

Mrs. Linde. He'll be back tomorrow evening. I left a note for him.

Nora. You needn't have bothered. You can't stop anything now. Anyway, it's wonderful really, in a way—sitting here and waiting for the miracle to happen.

Mrs. Linde. Waiting for what?

Nora. Oh, you wouldn't understand. Go in and join them. I'll be with you in a moment.

[MRS. LINDE *goes into the dining room.*]

Nora (*stands for a moment as though collecting herself. Then she looks at her watch*). Five o'clock. Seven hours till midnight. Then another twenty-four hours till midnight tomorrow. And then the tarantella will be finished. Twenty-four and seven? Thirty-one hours to live.

Helmer (*appears in the doorway, right*). What's happened to my little songbird?

Nora (*runs to him with her arms wide*). Your songbird is here!

ACT 3

The same room. The table which was formerly by the sofa has been moved into the center of the room; the chairs surround it as before. A lamp is burning on the table. The door to the hall stands open. Dance music can be heard from the floor above. MRS. LINDE *is seated at the table, absentmindedly glancing through a book. She is trying to read, but seems unable to keep her mind on it. More than once she turns and listens anxiously towards the front door.*

Mrs. Linde (*looks at her watch*). Not here yet. There's not much time left. Please God he hasn't—! (*listens again*) Ah, here he is.

[*Goes out into the hall and cautiously opens the front door. Footsteps can be heard softly ascending the stairs.*]

Mrs. Linde (*whispers*). Come in. There's no one here.

Krogstad (*in the doorway*). I found a note from you at my lodgings. What does this mean?

Mrs. Linde. I must speak with you.

Krogstad. Oh? And must our conversation take place in this house?

Mrs. Linde. We couldn't meet at my place; my room has no separate entrance. Come in. We're quite alone. The maid's asleep, and the Helmers are at the dance upstairs.

Krogstad (*comes into the room*). Well, well! So the Helmers are dancing this evening? Are they indeed?

Mrs. Linde. Yes, why not?

Krogstad. True enough. Why not?

Mrs. Linde. Well, Krogstad. You and I must have a talk together.

Krogstad. Have we two anything further to discuss?

Mrs. Linde. We have a great deal to discuss.

Krogstad. I wasn't aware of it.

Mrs. Linde. That's because you've never really understood me.

Krogstad. Was there anything to understand? It's the old story, isn't it—a woman chucking a man because something better turns up?

Mrs. Linde. Do you really think I'm so utterly heartless? You think it was easy for me to give you up?

Krogstad. Wasn't it?

Mrs. Linde. Oh, Nils, did you really believe that?

Krogstad. Then why did you write to me the way you did?

Mrs. Linde. I had to. Since I had to break with you, I thought it my duty to destroy all the feelings you had for me.

Krogstad (*clenches his fists*). So that was it. And you did this for money!

Mrs. Linde. You mustn't forget I had a helpless mother to take care of, and two little brothers. We couldn't wait for you, Nils. It would have been so long before you'd have had enough to support us.

Krogstad. Maybe. But you had no right to cast me off for someone else.

Mrs. Linde. Perhaps not. I've often asked myself that.

Krogstad (*more quietly*). When I lost you, it was just as though all solid ground had been swept from under my feet. Look at me. Now I'm a shipwrecked man, clinging to a spar.[1]

Mrs. Linde. Help may be near at hand.

Krogstad. It was near. But then you came, and stood between it and me.

Mrs. Linde. I didn't know, Nils. No one told me till today that this job I'd found was yours.

Krogstad. I believe you, since you say so. But now you know, won't you give it up?

Mrs. Linde. No—because it wouldn't help you

---

1. **spar:** a pole or mast that supports or extends the sail of a ship.

even if I did.

Krogstad. Wouldn't it? I'd do it all the same.

Mrs. Linde. I've learned to look at things practically. Life and poverty have taught me that.

Krogstad. And life has taught me to distrust fine words.

Mrs. Linde. Then it has taught you a useful lesson. But surely you still believe in actions?

Krogstad. What do you mean?

Mrs. Linde. You said you were like a shipwrecked man clinging to a spar.

Krogstad. I have good reason to say it.

Mrs. Linde. I'm in the same position as you. No one to care about, no one to care for.

Krogstad. You made your own choice.

Mrs. Linde. I had no choice—then.

Krogstad. Well?

Mrs. Linde. Nils, suppose we two shipwrecked souls could join hands?

Krogstad. What are you saying?

Mrs. Linde. Castaways have a better chance of survival together than on their own.

Krogstad. Christine!

Mrs. Linde. Why do you suppose I came to this town?

Krogstad. You mean—you came because of me?

Mrs. Linde. I must work if I'm to find life worth living. I've always worked, for as long as I can remember. It's been the greatest joy of my life—my only joy. But now I'm alone in the world, and I feel so dreadfully lost and empty. There's no joy in working just for oneself. Oh, Nils, give me something—someone—to work for.

Krogstad. I don't believe all that. You're just being hysterical and romantic. You want to find an excuse for self-sacrifice.

Mrs. Linde. Have you ever known me to be hysterical?

Krogstad. You mean you really—? Is it possible? Tell me—you know all about my past?

Mrs. Linde. Yes.

Krogstad. And you know what people think of me here?

Mrs. Linde. You said just now that with me you might have become a different person.

Krogstad. I know I could have.

Mrs. Linde. Couldn't it still happen?

Krogstad. Christine—do you really mean this? Yes—you do—I see it in your face. Have you really the courage—?

Mrs. Linde. I need someone to be a mother to; and your children need a mother. And you and I need each other. I believe in you, Nils. I am afraid of nothing—with you.

Krogstad (*clasps her hands*). Thank you, Christine—thank you! Now I shall make the world believe in me as you do! Oh—but I'd forgotten—

Mrs. Linde (*listens*). Ssh! The tarantella! Go quickly, go!

Krogstad. Why? What is it?

Mrs. Linde. You hear that dance? As soon as it's finished, they'll be coming down.

Krogstad. All right, I'll go. It's no good, Christine. I'd forgotten—you don't know what I've just done to the Helmers.

Mrs. Linde. Yes, Nils. I know.

Krogstad. And yet you'd still have the courage to—?

Mrs. Linde. I know what despair can drive a man like you to.

Krogstad. Oh, if only I could undo this!

Mrs. Linde. You can. Your letter is still lying in the box.

Krogstad. Are you sure?

Mrs. Linde. Quite sure. But—

Krogstad (*looks searchingly at her*). Is that why you're doing this? You want to save your friend at any price? Tell me the truth. Is that the reason?

Mrs. Linde. Nils, a woman who has sold herself once for the sake of others doesn't make the same mistake again.

Krogstad. I shall demand my letter back.

Mrs. Linde. No, no.

Krogstad. Of course I shall. I shall stay here till Helmer comes down. I'll tell him he must give me back my letter—I'll say it was only to do with my dismissal, and that I don't want him to read it—

Mrs. Linde. No, Nils, you mustn't ask for that letter back.

Krogstad. But—tell me—wasn't that the real reason you asked me to come here?

Mrs. Linde. Yes—at first, when I was frightened. But a day has passed since then, and in that time I've seen incredible things happen in this house. Helmer must know the truth. This unhappy secret of Nora's must be revealed. They must come to a full understanding. There must be an end of all these shiftings and evasions.

Krogstad. Very well. If you're prepared to risk it. But one thing I can do—and at once—

Mrs. Linde (*listens*). Hurry! Go, go! The dance is over. We aren't safe here another moment.

Krogstad. I'll wait for you downstairs.

Mrs. Linde. Yes, do. You can see me home.

Krogstad. I've never been so happy in my life before!

[*He goes out through the front door. The door leading from the room into the hall remains open.*]

Mrs. Linde (*tidies the room a little and gets her hat and coat*). What a change! Oh, what a change! Someone to work for—to live for! A home to bring joy into! I won't let this chance of happiness slip through my fingers. Oh, why don't they come? (*listens*) Ah, here they are. I must get my coat on.

[*She takes her hat and coat.* HELMER's *and* NORA's *voices become audible outside. A key is turned in the lock and* HELMER *leads* NORA *almost forcibly into the hall. She is dressed in an Italian costume with a large black shawl. He is in evening dress, with a black coat.*]

Nora (*still in the doorway, resisting him*). No, no, no—not in here! I want to go back upstairs. I don't want to leave so early.

Helmer. But my dearest Nora—

Nora. Oh, please, Torvald, please! Just another hour!

Helmer. Not another minute, Nora, my sweet. You know what we agreed. Come along, now. Into the drawing room. You'll catch cold if you stay out here.

[*He leads her, despite her efforts to resist him, gently into the room.*]

Mrs. Linde. Good evening.

Nora. Christine!

Helmer. Oh, hullo, Mrs. Linde. You still here?

Mrs. Linde. Please forgive me. I did so want to see Nora in her costume.

Nora. Have you been sitting here waiting for me?

Mrs. Linde. Yes. I got here too late. I'm afraid. You'd already gone up. And I felt I really couldn't go home without seeing you.

Helmer (*takes off* NORA's *shawl*). Well, take a good look at her. She's worth looking at, don't you think? Isn't she beautiful, Mrs. Linde?

Mrs. Linde. Oh, yes, indeed—

Helmer. Isn't she unbelievably beautiful? Everyone at the party said so. But dreadfully stubborn she is, bless her pretty little heart. What's to be done about that? Would you believe it, I practically had to use force to get her away!

Nora. Oh, Torvald, you're going to regret not letting me stay—just half an hour longer.

Helmer. Hear that, Mrs. Linde? She dances her tarantella—makes a roaring success—and very well deserved—though possibly a trifle too realistic—more so than was aesthetically necessary, strictly speaking. But never mind that. Main thing is—she had a success—roaring success. Was I going to let her stay on after that and spoil the impression? No, thank you! I took my beautiful little Capri signorina—my capricious little Capricienne,[2] what?—under my arm—a swift round of the ballroom, a curtsy to the company, and, as they say in novels, the beautiful apparition disappeared! An exit should always be dramatic, Mrs. Linde. But unfortunately that's just what I can't get Nora to realize. I say, it's hot in here. (*throws his cloak on a chair and opens the door to his study*) What's this? It's dark in here. Ah, yes, of course—excuse me. (*goes in and lights a couple of candles*)

Nora (*whispers softly, breathlessly*). Well?

Mrs. Linde (*quietly*). I've spoken to him.

Nora. Yes?

Mrs. Linde. Nora—you must tell your husband everything.

Nora (*dully*). I knew it.

Mrs. Linde. You have nothing to fear from Krogstad. But you must tell him.

Nora. I shan't tell him anything.

Mrs. Linde. Then the letter will.

Nora. Thank you, Christine. Now I know what I must do. Ssh!

Helmer (*returns*). Well, Mrs. Linde, finished admiring her?

Mrs. Linde. Yes. Now I must say good night.

Helmer. Oh, already? Does this knitting belong to you?

Mrs. Linde (*takes it*). Thank you, yes. I nearly forgot it.

Helmer. You knit, then?

Mrs. Linde. Why, yes.

Helmer. Know what? You ought to take up embroidery.

Mrs. Linde. Oh? Why?

Helmer. It's much prettier. Watch me, now. You hold the embroidery in your left hand, like this, and then you take the needle in your right hand and go in and out in a slow, easy movement— like this. I am right, aren't I?

Mrs. Linde. Yes, I'm sure—

Helmer. But knitting, now—that's an ugly business—can't help it. Look—arms all huddled up—great clumsy needles going up and down— I say that really was a magnificent champagne they served us.

Mrs. Linde. Well, good night, Nora. And stop being stubborn! Remember!

Helmer. Quite right, Mrs. Linde!

Mrs. Linde. Good night, Mr. Helmer.

Helmer (*accompanies her to the door*). Good night, good night! I hope you'll manage to get home all right? I'd gladly—but you haven't far to go, have you? Good night, good night.

[*She goes. He closes the door behind her and returns.*]

Helmer. Well, we've got rid of her at last. Dreadful bore that woman is!

Nora. Aren't you very tired, Torvald?

Helmer. No, not in the least.

Nora. Aren't you sleepy?

Helmer. Not a bit. On the contrary, I feel extraordinarily exhilarated. But what about you? Yes, you look very sleepy and tired.

Nora. Yes, I am very tired. Soon I shall sleep.

Helmer. You see, you see! How right I was not to let you stay longer!

Nora. Oh, you're always right, whatever you do.

Helmer (*kisses her on the forehead*). Now my little songbird's talking just like a real big human being. I say, did you notice how cheerful Rank was this evening?

Nora. Oh? Was he? I didn't have a chance to speak with him.

Helmer. I hardly did. But I haven't seen him in

---

2. **Capri...Capricienne:** "Capri signorina" and "Capricienne" both refer to a lady from Capri, a small island off the coast of Italy. Helmer is playing on the similarities in the words *capricious* and *Capricienne*.

such a jolly mood for ages. (*looks at her for a moment, then comes closer*) I say, it's nice to get back to one's home again, and be all alone with you. Upon my word, you're a distractingly beautiful young woman.

Nora. Don't look at me like that, Torvald!

Helmer. What, not look at my most treasured possession? At all this wonderful beauty that's mine, mine alone, all mine.

Nora (*goes round to the other side of the table*). You mustn't talk to me like that tonight.

Helmer (*follows her*). You've still the tarantella in your blood, I see. And that makes you even more desirable. Listen! Now the other guests are beginning to go. (*more quietly*) Nora—soon the whole house will be absolutely quiet.

Nora. Yes, I hope so.

Helmer. Yes, my beloved Nora, of course you do! You know—when I'm out with you among other people like we were tonight, do you know why I say so little to you, why I keep so aloof from you, and just throw you an occasional glance? Do you know why I do that? It's because I pretend to myself that you're my secret mistress, my clandestine little sweetheart, and that nobody knows there's anything at all between us.

Nora. Oh, yes, yes, yes—I know you never think of anything but me.

Helmer. And then when we're about to go, and I wrap the shawl round your lovely young shoulders, over this wonderful curve of your neck—then I pretend to myself that you are my young bride, that we've just come from the wedding, that I'm taking you to my house for the first time—that, for the first time, I am alone with you—quite alone with you, as you stand there young and trembling and beautiful. All evening I've had no eyes for anyone but you. When I saw you dance the tarantella, like a huntress, a temptress, my blood grew hot, I couldn't stand it any longer! That was why I

seized you and dragged you down here with me—

Nora. Leave me, Torvald! Get away from me! I don't want all this.

Helmer. What? Now, Nora, you're joking with me. Don't want, don't want—? Aren't I your husband?

[*There is a knock on the front door.*]

Nora (*starts*). What was that?

Helmer (*goes towards the hall*). Who is it?

Dr. Rank (*outside*). It's me. May I come in for a moment?

Helmer (*quietly, annoyed*). Oh, what does he want now? (*calls*) Wait a moment. (*walks over and opens the door*) Well! Nice of you not to go by without looking in.

Rank. I thought I heard your voice, so I felt I had to say goodbye. (*His eyes travel swiftly around the room.*) Ah, yes—these dear rooms, how well I know them. What a happy, peaceful home you two have.

Helmer. You seemed to be having a pretty happy time yourself upstairs.

Rank. Indeed I did. Why not? Why shouldn't one make the most of this world? As much as one can, and for as long as one can. The wine was excellent—

Helmer. Especially the champagne.

Rank. You noticed that, too? It's almost incredible how much I managed to get down.

Nora. Torvald drank a lot of champagne, too, this evening.

Rank. Oh?

Nora. Yes. It always makes him merry afterwards.

Rank. Well, why shouldn't a man have a merry evening after a well-spent day?

Helmer. Well-spent? Oh, I don't know that I can claim that.

Rank (*slaps him across the back*). I can, though, my dear fellow!

Nora. Yes, of course, Dr. Rank—you've been carrying out a scientific experiment today, haven't you?

Rank. Exactly.

Helmer. Scientific experiment! Those are big words for my little Nora to use!

Nora. And may I congratulate you on the finding?

Rank. You may indeed.

Nora. It was good then?

Rank. The best possible finding—both for the doctor and the patient. Certainty.

Nora (*quickly*). Certainty?

Rank. Absolute certainty. So aren't I entitled to have a merry evening after that?

Nora. Yes, Dr. Rank. You were quite right to.

Helmer. I agree. Provided you don't have to regret it tomorrow.

Rank. Well, you never get anything in this life without paying for it.

Nora. Dr. Rank—you like masquerades, don't you?

Rank. Yes, if the disguises are sufficiently amusing.

Nora. Tell me. What shall we two wear at the next masquerade?

Helmer. You little gadabout! Are you thinking about the next one already?

Rank. We two? Yes, I'll tell you. You must go as the Spirit of Happiness—

Helmer. You try to think of a costume that'll convey that.

Rank. Your wife need only appear as her normal, everyday self—

Helmer. Quite right! Well said! But what are you going to be? Have you decided that?

Rank. Yes, my dear friend. I have decided that.

Helmer. Well?

Rank. At the next masquerade, I shall be invisible.

Helmer. Well, that's a funny idea.

Rank. There's a big, black hat—haven't you heard of the invisible hat? Once it's over your head, no one can see you any more.

Helmer (*represses a smile*). Ah yes, of course.

Rank. But I'm forgetting what I came for. Helmer, give me a cigar. One of your black Havanas.

Helmer. With the greatest pleasure. (*offers him the box*)

Rank (*takes one and cuts off the tip*). Thank you.

Nora (*strikes a match*). Let me give you a light.

Rank. Thank you. (*She holds out the match for him. He lights his cigar.*) And now—goodbye.

Helmer. Goodbye, my dear chap, goodbye.

Nora. Sleep well, Dr. Rank.

Rank. Thank you for that kind wish.

Nora. Wish me the same.

Rank. You? Very well—since you ask. Sleep well. And thank you for the light. (*He nods to them both and goes.*)

Helmer (*quietly*). He's been drinking too much.

Nora (*abstractedly*). Perhaps.

[HELMER *takes his bunch of keys from his pocket and goes out into the hall.*]

Nora. Torvald, what do you want out there?

Helmer. I must empty the letter box. It's absolutely full. There'll be no room for the newspapers in the morning.

Nora. Are you going to work tonight?

Helmer. You know very well I'm not. Hullo, what's this? Someone's been at the lock.

Nora. At the lock—

Helmer. Yes, I'm sure of it. Who on earth—? Surely not one of the maids? Here's a broken hairpin. Nora, it's yours—

Nora (*quickly*). Then it must have been the children.

Helmer. Well, you'll have to break them of that habit. Hm, hm. Ah, that's done it. (*takes out the contents of the box and calls into the kitchen*) Helen! Helen! Put out the light on the staircase. (*comes back into the drawing room and closes the door to the hall*)

Helmer (*with the letters in his hand*). Look at this! You see how they've piled up? (*glances through them*) What on earth's this?

Nora (*at the window*). The letter! Oh no, Torvald, no!

Helmer. Two visiting cards—from Rank.

Nora. From Dr. Rank?

Helmer (*looks at them*). Peter Rank, M.D. They were on top. He must have dropped them in as he left.

Nora. Has he written anything on them?

Helmer. There's a black cross above his name. Rather gruesome, isn't it? It looks just as though he was announcing his death.

Nora. He is.

Helmer. What? Do you know something? Has he told you anything?

Nora. Yes. When these cards come, it means he's said goodbye to us. He wants to shut himself up in his house and die.

Helmer. Ah, poor fellow. I knew I wouldn't be seeing him for much longer. But so soon—! And now he's going to slink away and hide like a wounded beast.

Nora. When the time comes, it's best to go silently. Don't you think so, Torvald?

Helmer (*walks up and down*). He was so much a part of our life. I can't realize that he's gone. His suffering and loneliness seemed to provide a kind of dark background to the happy sunlight of our marriage. Well, perhaps it's best this way. For him, anyway. (*stops walking*) And perhaps for us too, Nora. Now we have only each other. (*embraces her*) Oh, my beloved wife—I feel as though I could never hold you close enough. Do you know, Nora, often I wish some terrible danger might threaten you, so that I could offer my life and my blood, everything, for your sake.

Nora (*tears herself loose and says in a clear, firm voice*). Read your letters now, Torvald.

Helmer. No, no. Not tonight. Tonight I want to be with you, my darling wife—

Nora. When your friend is about to die—?

Helmer. You're right. This news has upset us both. An ugliness has come between us; thoughts of death and dissolution. We must try to forget them. Until then—you go to your room; I shall go to mine.

Nora (*throws her arms round his neck*). Good night, Torvald! Good night!

Helmer (*kisses her on the forehead*). Good night, my darling little songbird. Sleep well, Nora. I'll go and read my letters.

[*He goes into the study with the letters in his hand, and closes the door.*]

Nora (*wild-eyed, fumbles around, seizes* HELMER'*s cloak, throws it round herself and whispers quickly, hoarsely*). Never see him again. Never. Never. Never. (*throws the shawl over her head*) Never see the children again. Them, too. Never. Never. Oh—the icy black water! Oh—that bottom-less—that—! Oh, if only it were all over! Now he's got it—he's reading it. Oh no, no! Not yet! Goodbye, Torvald! Goodbye, my darlings!

[*She turns to run into the hall. As she does so,* HELMER *throws open his door and stands there with an open letter in his hand.*]

Helmer. Nora!

Nora (*shrieks*). Ah—!

Helmer. What is this? Do you know what is in this letter?

Nora. Yes, I know. Let me go! Let me go!

Helmer (*holding her back*). Go? Where?

Nora (*tries to tear herself loose*). You mustn't try to save me, Torvald!

Helmer (*staggers back*). Is it true? Is it true, what he writes? Oh, my God! No, no—it's impossible, it can't be true!

Nora. It *is* true. I've loved you more than anything else in the world.

Helmer. Oh, don't try to make silly excuses.

Nora (*takes a step towards him*). Torvald—

Helmer. Wretched woman! What have you done?

Nora. Let me go! You're not going to suffer for my sake. I won't let you!

Helmer. Stop being theatrical. (*locks the front door*) You're going to stay here and explain yourself. Do you understand what you've done? Answer me! Do you understand?

Nora (*looks unflinchingly at him and, her expression growing colder, says*). Yes. Now I am beginning to understand.

Helmer (*walking round the room*). Oh, what a dreadful awakening! For eight whole years—she who was my joy and pride—a hypocrite, a liar—worse, worse—a criminal! Oh, the hideousness of it! Shame on you, shame!

[NORA *is silent and stares unblinkingly at him.*]

Helmer (*stops in front of her*). I ought to have guessed that something of this sort would happen. I should have foreseen it. All your father's recklessness and instability—be quiet!—I repeat, all your father's recklessness and instability he has handed on to you! No religion, no morals, no sense of duty! Oh, how I have been punished for closing my eyes to his faults! I did it for your sake. And now you reward me like this.

Nora. Yes. Like this.

Helmer. Now you have destroyed all my happiness. You have ruined my whole future. Oh, it's too dreadful to contemplate! I am in the power of a man who is completely without scruples. He can do what he likes with me, demand what he pleases, order me to do anything—I dare not disobey him. I am condemned to humiliation and ruin simply for the weakness of a woman.

Nora. When I am gone from this world, you will be free.

Helmer. Oh, don't be melodramatic. Your father was always ready with that kind of remark. How would it help me if you were "gone from this world," as you put it? It wouldn't assist me in the slightest. He can still make all the facts public; and if he does, I may quite easily be suspected of having been an accomplice in your crime. People may think that I was behind it—that it was I who encouraged you! And for all this I have to thank you, you whom I have carried on my hands through all the years of our marriage! Now do you realize what you've done to me?

Nora (*coldly calm*). Yes.

Helmer. It's so unbelievable I can hardly credit it. But we must try to find some way out. Take off that shawl. Take it off, I say! I must try to buy him off somehow. This thing must be hushed up at any price. As regards our relationship—we must appear to be living together just as before. Only *appear*, of course. You will therefore continue to reside here. That is understood. But the children shall be taken out of your hands. I dare no longer entrust them to you. Oh, to have to say this to the woman I once loved so dearly—and whom I still—! Well, all that must be finished. Henceforth there can be no question of happiness, we must merely strive to save what shreds and tatters—

[*The front door bell rings.* HELMER *starts.*]

Helmer. What can that be? At this hour? Surely not—? He wouldn't—? Hide yourself, Nora. Say you're ill.

[NORA *does not move.* HELMER *goes to the door of the room and opens it. The* MAID *is standing half-dressed in the hall.*]

Maid. A letter for madam.

Helmer. Give it to me. (*seizes the letter and shuts*

the door) Yes, it's from him. You're not having it. I'll read this myself.

Nora. Read it.

Helmer (*by the lamp*). I hardly dare to. This may mean the end for us both. No. I must know. (*tears open the letter hastily; reads a few lines; looks at a piece of paper which is enclosed with it; utters a cry of joy*) Nora! (*She looks at him questioningly.*) Nora! No—I must read it once more. Yes, yes, it's true! I am saved! Nora, I am saved!

Nora. What about me?

Helmer. You too, of course. We're both saved, you and I. Look! He's returning your I.O.U. He writes that he is sorry for what has happened—a happy accident has changed his life—oh, what does it matter what he writes? We are saved, Nora! No one can harm you now. Oh, Nora, Nora—no, first let me destroy this filthy thing. Let me see—! (*glances at the I.O.U.*) No, I don't want to look at it. I shall merely regard the whole business as a dream. (*He tears the I.O.U. and both letters into pieces, throws them into the stove and watches them burn.*) There. Now they're destroyed. He wrote that ever since Christmas Eve you've been—oh, these must have been three dreadful days for you, Nora.

Nora. Yes. It's been a hard fight.

Helmer. It must have been terrible—seeing no way out except—no, we'll forget the whole sordid business. We'll just be happy and go on telling ourselves over and over again: "It's over! It's over!" Listen to me, Nora. You don't seem to realize. It's over! Why are you looking so pale? Ah, my poor little Nora, I understand. You can't believe that I have forgiven you. But I have, Nora. I swear it to you. I have forgiven you everything. I know that what you did you did for your love of me.

Nora. That is true.

Helmer. You have loved me as a wife should love her husband. It was simply that in your inexperience you chose the wrong means. But do you think I love you any the less because you don't know how to act on your own initiative? No, no. Just lean on me. I shall counsel you. I shall guide you. I would not be a true man if your feminine helplessness did not make you doubly attractive in my eyes. You mustn't mind the hard words I said to you in those first dreadful moments when my whole world seemed to be tumbling about my ears. I have forgiven you, Nora. I swear it to you; I have forgiven you.

Nora. Thank you for your forgiveness. (*She goes out through the door, right.*)

Helmer. No, don't go—(*looks in*) What are you doing there?

Nora (*offstage*). Taking off my fancy dress.

Helmer (*by the open door*). Yes, do that. Try to calm yourself and get your balance again, my frightened little songbird. Don't be afraid. I have broad wings to shield you. (*begins to walk around near the door*) How lovely and peaceful this little home of ours is, Nora. You are safe here; I shall watch over you like a hunted dove which I have snatched unharmed from the claws of the falcon. Your wildly beating little heart shall find peace with me. It will happen, Nora; it will take time; but it will happen, believe me. Tomorrow all this will seem quite different. Soon everything will be as it was before. I shall no longer need to remind you that I have forgiven you; your own heart will tell you that it is true. Do you really think I could ever bring myself to disown you, or even to reproach you? Ah, Nora, you don't understand what goes on in a husband's heart. There is something indescribably wonderful and satisfying for a husband in knowing that he has forgiven his wife—forgiven her unreservedly, from the bottom of his heart. It means that she has become his property in a double sense; he has, as it were, brought her into the world anew; she is now not only his wife but also his child.

From now on that is what you shall be to me, my poor, helpless, bewildered little creature. Never be frightened of anything again, Nora. Just open your heart to me. I shall be both your will and your conscience. What's this? Not in bed? Have you changed?

Nora (*in her everyday dress*). Yes, Torvald. I've changed.

Helmer. But why now—so late—?

Nora. I shall not sleep tonight.

Helmer. But, my dear Nora—

Nora (*looks at her watch*). It isn't that late. Sit down there, Torvald. You and I have a lot to talk about.

[*She sits down on one side of the table.*]

Helmer. Nora, what does this mean? You look quite drawn—

Nora. Sit down. It's going to take a long time. I've a lot to say to you.

Helmer (*sits down on the other side of the table*). You alarm me, Nora. I don't understand you.

Nora. No, that's just it. You don't understand me. And I've never understood you—until this evening. No, don't interrupt me. Just listen to what I have to say. You and I have got to face facts, Torvald.

Helmer. What do you mean by that?

Nora (*after a short silence*). Doesn't anything strike you about the way we're sitting here?

Helmer. What?

Nora. We've been married for eight years. Does it occur to you that this is the first time we two, you and I, man and wife, have ever had a serious talk together?

Helmer. Serious? What do you mean, serious?

Nora. In eight whole years—no, longer—ever since we first met—we have never exchanged a serious word on a serious subject.

Helmer. Did you expect me to drag you into all my worries—worries you couldn't possibly have helped me with?

Nora. I'm not talking about worries. I'm simply saying that we have never sat down seriously to try to get to the bottom of anything.

Helmer. But, my dear Nora, what on earth has that got to do with you?

Nora. That's just the point. You have never understood me. A great wrong has been done to me, Torvald. First by Papa, and then by you.

Helmer. What? But we two have loved you more than anyone in the world!

Nora (*shakes her head*). You have never loved me. You just thought it was fun to be in love with me.

Helmer. Nora, what kind of a way is this to talk?

Nora. It's the truth, Torvald. When I lived with Papa, he used to tell me what he thought about everything, so that I never had any opinions but his. And if I did have any of my own, I kept them quiet, because he wouldn't have liked them. He called me his little doll, and he played with me just the way I played with my dolls. Then I came here to live in your house—

Helmer. What kind of a way is that to describe our marriage?

Nora (*undisturbed*). I mean, then I passed from Papa's hands into yours. You arranged everything the way you wanted it, so that I simply took over your taste in everything—or pretended I did—I don't really know—I think it was a little of both—first one and then the other. Now I look back on it, it's as if I've been living here like a pauper, from hand to mouth. I performed tricks for you, and you gave me food and drink. But that was how you wanted it. You and Papa have done me a great wrong. It's your fault that I have done nothing with my life.

Helmer. Nora, how can you be so unreasonable and ungrateful? Haven't you been happy here?

Nora. No; never. I used to think I was. But I haven't ever been happy.

Helmer. Not—not happy?

Nora. No. I've just had fun. You've always been very kind to me. But our home has never been anything but a playroom. I've been your doll-wife, just as I used to be Papa's doll-child. And the children have been my dolls. I used to think it was fun when you came in and played with me, just as they think it's fun when I go in and play games with them. That's all our marriage has been, Torvald.

Helmer. There may be a little truth in what you say, though you exaggerate and romanticize. But from now on it'll be different. Playtime is over. Now the time has come for education.

Nora. Whose education? Mine or the children's?

Helmer. Both yours and the children's, my dearest Nora.

Nora. Oh, Torvald, you're not the man to educate me into being the right wife for you.

Helmer. How can you say that?

Nora. And what about me? Am I fit to educate the children?

Helmer. Nora!

Nora. Didn't you say yourself a few minutes ago that you dare not leave them in my charge?

Helmer. In a moment of excitement. Surely you don't think I meant it seriously?

Nora. Yes. You were perfectly right. I'm not fitted to educate them. There's something else I must do first. I must educate myself. And you can't help me with that. It's something I must do by myself. That's why I'm leaving you.

Helmer (*jumps up*). What did you say?

Nora. I must stand on my own feet if I am to find out the truth about myself and about life. So I can't go on living here with you any longer.

Helmer. Nora, Nora!

Nora. I'm leaving you now, at once. Christine will put me up for tonight—

Helmer. You're out of your mind! You can't do this! I forbid you!

Nora. It's no use your trying to forbid me any more. I shall take with me nothing but what is mine. I don't want anything from you, now or ever.

Helmer. What kind of madness is this?

Nora. Tomorrow I shall go home—I mean, to where I was born. It'll be easiest for me to find some kind of a job there.

Helmer. But you're blind! You've no experience of the world—

Nora. I must try to get some, Torvald.

Helmer. But to leave your home, your husband, your children! Have you thought what people will say?

Nora. I can't help that. I only know that I must do this.

Helmer. But this is monstrous! Can you neglect your most sacred duties?

Nora. What do you call my most sacred duties?

Helmer. Do I have to tell you? Your duties towards your husband, and your children.

Nora. I have another duty which is equally sacred.

Helmer. You have not. What on earth could that be?

Nora. My duty towards myself.

Helmer. First and foremost you are a wife and mother.

Nora. I don't believe that any longer. I believe that I am first and foremost a human being, like you—or anyway, that I must try to become one. I know most people think as you do, Torvald, and I know there's something of the sort to be found in books. But I'm no longer prepared to accept what people say and what's written in books. I must think things out for myself, and try to find my own answer.

Helmer. Do you need to ask where your duty lies in your own home? Haven't you an infallible guide in such matters—your religion?

Nora. Oh, Torvald, I don't really know what religion means.

Helmer. What are you saying?

Nora. I only know what Pastor Hansen told me when I went to confirmation. He explained that religion meant this and that. When I get away from all this and can think things out on my own, that's one of the questions I want to look into. I want to find out whether what Pastor Hansen said was right—or anyway, whether it is right for me.

Helmer. But it's unheard of for so young a woman to behave like this! If religion cannot guide you, let me at least appeal to your conscience. I presume you have some moral feelings left? Or—perhaps you haven't? Well, answer me.

Nora. Oh, Torvald, that isn't an easy question to answer. I simply don't know. I don't know where I am in these matters. I only know that these things mean something quite different to me from what they do to you. I've learned now that certain laws are different from what I'd imagined them to be; but I can't accept that such laws can be right. Has a woman really not the right to spare her dying father pain, or save her husband's life? I can't believe that.

Helmer. You're talking like a child. You don't understand how society works.

Nora. No, I don't. But now I intend to learn. I must try to satisfy myself which is right, society or I.

Helmer. Nora, you're ill. You're feverish. I almost believe you're out of your mind.

Nora. I've never felt so sane and sure in my life.

Helmer. You feel sure that it is right to leave your husband and your children?

Nora. Yes. I do.

Helmer. Then there is only one possible explanation.

Nora. What?

Helmer. That you don't love me any longer.

Nora. No, that's exactly it.

Helmer. Nora! How can you say this to me?

Nora. Oh, Torvald, it hurts me terribly to have to say it, because you've always been so kind to me. But I can't help it. I don't love you any longer.

Helmer (*controlling his emotions with difficulty*). And you feel quite sure about this, too?

Nora. Yes, absolutely sure. That's why I can't go on living here any longer.

Helmer. Can you also explain why I have lost your love?

Nora. Yes, I can. It happened this evening, when the miracle failed to happen. It was then that I realized you weren't the man I'd thought you to be.

Helmer. Explain more clearly. I don't understand you.

Nora. I've waited so patiently, for eight whole years—well, good heavens, I'm not such a fool as to suppose that miracles occur every day. Then this dreadful thing happened to me, and then I *knew*: "Now the miracle will take place!" When Krogstad's letter was lying out there, it never occurred to me for a moment that you would let that man trample over you. I *knew* that you would say to him: "Publish the facts to the world!" And when he had done this—

Helmer. Yes, what then? When I'd exposed my

wife's name to shame and scandal—

Nora. Then I was certain that you would step forward and take all the blame on yourself, and say: "I am the one who is guilty!"

Helmer. Nora!

Nora. You're thinking I wouldn't have accepted such a sacrifice from you? No, of course I wouldn't! But what would my word have counted for against yours? That was the miracle I was hoping for, and dreading. And it was to prevent it happening that I wanted to end my life.

Helmer. Nora, I would gladly work for you night and day, and endure sorrow and hardship for your sake. But no man can be expected to sacrifice his honor, even for the person he loves.

Nora. Millions of women have done it.

Helmer. Oh, you think and talk like a stupid child.

Nora. That may be. But you neither think nor talk like the man I could share my life with. Once you'd got over your fright—and you weren't frightened of what might threaten me, but only of what threatened you—once the danger was past, then as far as you were concerned it was exactly as though nothing had happened. I was your little songbird just as before—your doll whom henceforth you would take particular care to protect from the world because she was so weak and fragile. (*gets up*) Torvald, in that moment I realized that for eight years I had been living here with a complete stranger, and had borne him three children—! Oh, I can't bear to think of it! I could tear myself to pieces!

Helmer (*sadly*). I see it, I see it. A gulf has indeed opened between us. Oh, but Nora—couldn't it be bridged?

Nora. As I am now, I am no wife for you.

Helmer. I have the strength to change.

Nora. Perhaps—if your doll is taken from you.

Helmer. But to be parted—to be parted from you! No, no, Nora. I can't conceive of it happening!

Nora (*goes into the room, right*). All the more necessary that it should happen.

[*She comes back with her outdoor things and a small traveling bag, which she puts down on a chair by the table.*]

Helmer. Nora, Nora, not now! Wait till tomorrow!

Nora (*puts on her coat*). I can't spend the night in a strange man's house.

Helmer. But can't we live here as brother and sister, then—?

Nora (*fastens her hat*). You know quite well it wouldn't last. (*puts on her shawl*) Goodbye, Torvald. I don't want to see the children. I know they're in better hands than mine. As I am now, I can be nothing to them.

Helmer. But some time, Nora—some time—?

Nora. How can I tell? I've no idea what will happen to me.

Helmer. But you are my wife, both as you are and as you will be.

Nora. Listen, Torvald. When a wife leaves her husband's house, as I'm doing now, I'm told that according to the law he is freed of any obligations towards her. In any case, I release you from any such obligations. You mustn't feel bound to me in any way however small, just as I shall not feel bound to you. We must both be quite free. Here is your ring back. Give me mine.

Helmer. That too?

Nora. That too.

Helmer. Here it is.

Nora. Good. Well, now it's over. I'll leave the

keys here. The servants know about everything to do with the house—much better than I do. Tomorrow, when I have left town, Christine will come to pack the things I brought here from home. I'll have them sent on after me.

Helmer. This is the end, then! Nora, will you never think of me any more?

Nora. Yes, of course. I shall often think of you and the children and this house.

Helmer. May I write to you, Nora?

Nora. No. Never. You mustn't do that.

Helmer. But at least you must let me send you—

Nora. Nothing, Nothing.

Helmer. But if you should need help—?

Nora. I tell you, no. I don't accept things from strangers.

Helmer. Nora—can I never be anything but a stranger to you?

Nora (*picks up her bag*). Oh, Torvald! Then the miracle of miracles would have to happen.

Helmer. The miracle of miracles!

Nora. You and I would both have to change so much that—oh, Torvald, I don't believe in miracles any longer.

Helmer. But I want to believe in them. Tell me. We should have to change so much that—!

Nora. That life together between us two could become a marriage. Goodbye.

[*She goes out through the hall.*]

Helmer (*sinks down on a chair by the door and buries his face in his hands*). Nora! Nora! (*looks round and gets up*) Empty! She's gone! (*a hope strikes him*) The miracle of miracles—?

[*The street door is slammed shut downstairs.*]

The Proposal

Meet the Playwright

Anton Chekhov (1860–1904)

It's difficult to judge whether the writer Anton Chekhov made a bigger impact in the world of drama or fiction. The craft revealed in his short stories, which fill volumes, influenced writers throughout the twentieth century. And although he wrote relatively few plays, these works are often credited with revolutionizing modern drama.

His beginnings gave no hint of his potential, though. Born in the small Russian city of Taganrog, Chekhov was the son of a grocer and the grandson of a serf, or peasant slave. Although his younger siblings would later disagree with his assessment of their upbringing, Chekhov remembered a childhood made difficult by his father's strict discipline and long hours working in his store. Chekhov found two escapes— listening to his mother tell stories and going to the theater.

As a young man, Chekhov studied medicine and the sciences and became a doctor. By 1875, however, he had to find other sources of income to support his family after his father's business failed. To raise money, Chekhov turned to writing comic scenes and anecdotes for the many popular humor magazines published in Russia at that time.

Early Writings and Enduring Themes

In the 1870s and 1880s, Chekhov wrote hundreds of short stories and comic scenes and published them not under his own name but under such pseudonyms as A Man Without a Spleen, My Brother's Brother, and The Doctor Without Patients. In these brief, humorous works, Chekhov sharpened his style and explored themes that would interest him for the rest of his life—the lives of the poor, the pettiness of government officials, and the continual ups and downs of daily life. By 1885, Chekhov was surprised to learn that the intellectuals who had read his stories considered him talented and expected greater things from him. At that point, Chekhov turned to the theater. *Ivanov*, a four-act play, opened in 1887 to great success in Moscow.

Chekhov's response to sudden fame was simple—he ran away. First, he returned to his home city of Taganrog. Then, in 1890, he embarked on an 8,000-mile journey to Sakhalin, a penal colony off the coast of Siberia. He went as a scientist and doctor, to research and report on the suffering and hardship he found there. Of course, the adventure shaped him as an artist as well, directly and indirectly influencing subsequent works.

After a circuitous trip home by sea and a subsequent trip to Italy and France, Chekhov returned to Russia, bought a large estate and, over the next decade, wrote the three plays that changed Russian theater forever: *The Seagull, The Three Sisters,* and *The Cherry Orchard.* Though the characters in these plays sometimes seem tragically isolated or misguided, Chekhov considered the plays comedies. He objected to the gloomy characterizations served up by the actors of his day.

Dissatisfied with Success

Chekhov did not enjoy his theatrical success or his life in general during this time. He struggled to control the tuberculosis he had been diagnosed with as a young man, and which had killed one of his brothers. He secretly married the leading actress of the day, Olga Knipper, but they rarely spent time together. He grew distant from the directors and producers who had first championed his plays. Chekhov's life ended in the way that one of his plays might have, with an understated mixture of sadness and irony. After suffering a heart attack at a spa in Germany in July 1904, Chekhov sipped champagne and announced quietly that he was dying. A moment later, he was dead. His body was shipped home to Russia in an ice-filled box that was marked "Oysters."

Background to *The Proposal*

In the centuries before the Russian Revolution in 1917, Russia was a feudal society ruled by a czar (zär). After the nobility, the highest social class was made up of landowners who owned serfs, or peasant workers, much as plantation owners in the American South owned enslaved workers. In 1861, Czar Alexander II emancipated the serfs, but the social structure built on slavery continued long afterward. As a result, Chekhov's plays often reflect the lingering distinctions—and resentments—among the social classes.

Until the end of the nineteenth century, the power of the czars was absolute. The government censored newspapers and journals to suppress critics. Exceptions to this rule, however, were the comic magazines that Chekhov wrote for. Under the guise of comedy, the writers often slipped political satire beneath the watchful eyes of government censors. Chekhov, however, considered himself apolitical. If he wrote about banal and corrupt bureaucrats, he said, it was because he knew such people, not because he had any political point to make.

A Russian Brand of Naturalism

Like Russian society, the theater experienced a revolution of sorts at the end of the nineteenth century, thanks in great part to Chekhov. His plays *The Seagull, The Three Sisters*, and *The Cherry Orchard* brought worldwide recognition to the Moscow Art Theater and its director Konstantin Stanislavsky. In these plays, Chekhov ignored accepted dramatic conventions. For example, there is no one central character; the plays are ensemble (än·säm'bəl) pieces in which each part is a significant piece of the whole. The characters themselves are ordinary people from all levels of Russian society—fading aristocrats, corrupt bureaucrats, ignorant peasants, lonely spinsters, doctors, and struggling artists. The action of the plays does not push toward a significant climax; instead, the plays simply drift to their conclusions, much as life does. In championing this anticlimatic, hyperrealistic style, Chekhov ushered in a movement called naturalism. Naturalism aims to capture "a slice of life"; Chekhov himself aimed to reveal the drama that pulsed beneath the mundane aspects of daily life. In doing so, he gave the theater a uniquely Russian voice.

Unlike Chekhov's greatest plays, *The Proposal*—also known as *A Marriage Proposal*—is a farce. An early play, it shows the influence of both the French farces he saw on the stage as a youth and the comic scenes he had written for comic magazines in the 1870s. But even as *The Proposal* borrows from the tradition of farce, this short play has a few hallmarks of Chekhov's later works. The comedy features three ordinary people and their tendency to communicate at cross-purposes.

The Proposal

A FARCE IN ONE ACT

Anton Chekhov

Translated by **Carol Rocamora**

CHARACTERS

Stepan Stepanovich[1] Chubukov (ste·pän′ ste·pä′nō·vıdı cho͞o·bo͞o·kôf′), landowner

Natalya Stepanovna (nä·täl′yə ste·pä′nōv·nə), his daughter, twenty-five years of age

Ivan Vasilyevich Lomov (i·vän′ vä·sil′ē·yich lō′mōf), a neighbor of CHUBUKOV, a healthy, rather portly landowner, but somewhat of a hypochondriac

1. **Stepanovich:** *Stepanovich* is a patronymic—a name based on a father's or male ancestor's name. All Russians have patronymic names.

The action takes place on CHUBUKOV's estate, in the drawing room of CHUBUKOV's house.

Enter LOMOV, *in tails and white gloves.* CHUBUKOV *goes to greet him.*

Chubukov. Why look who's here, my dear dear fellow! Ivan Vasilyevich! I'm so delighted! (*Shakes his hand.*) Such a surprise, my dear dear man, yes, indeed . . . And how are you?

Lomov. Very well, thank you. And permit me to inquire, how are you?

Chubukov. Not bad, not bad at all, my angel, thank you for asking, etcetera etcetera. Sit down, sit down, I beg of you. . . . Mustn't forget one's neighbors, my dear fellow, no indeed. But my dear man, why so formal? Tails and gloves, etcetera etcetera. Planning on going somewhere?

Lomov. No, only to visit you, my esteemed Stepan Stepanich.

Chubukov. But why the tails, my dear boy? You look like it's New Year's eve!

Lomov. Well, you see, here's the thing. (*Takes his arm.*) I have come to see you, my esteemed Stepan Stepanich, to trouble you with a certain request. On more than one occasion I have had the honor of turning to you for your help, and you have always been, well, what can I say . . . forgive me, I'm a bit agitated. I'll just have a drink of water, my esteemed Stepan Stepanich. (*Drinks water.*)

Chubukov (*aside*). He's come to ask for money! Well, I'm not giving him any! (*To* LOMOV) What's up, my dear friend?

Lomov. Well, you see, my esteemed Stepanich . . . sorry, my Stepan Esteem'dich . . . what I mean is, I'm terribly agitated, as you can plainly see. . . . In a word, you and you alone can help me, although, of course, I don't deserve it. . . . I have no right, no right at all to rely upon your assistance. . . .

Chubukov. Oh, will you please stop beating around the bush, my dear man? I mean, really! Tell me this instant! What is it?

Lomov. Yes, this instant . . . right away. The fact of the matter is, that I have come here today to ask for the hand of your daughter, Natalya Stepanovna.

Chubukov (*ecstatically*). My dearest fellow! Ivan Vasilyevich! Would you kindly repeat that—I didn't quite hear you!

Lomov. I have the honor of asking . . .

Chubukov (*interrupting him*). My dear dear fellow . . . I'm so very happy, etcetera etcetera. . . . Yes, indeed, and so on and so on. (*Embraces and kisses him.*) I've waited for this moment for so long. It has been my fondest dream. (*Sheds tears.*) I have always loved you, dear boy, like my own son. May God bless you, and may you live happily ever after, etcetera etcetera. . . . I have longed for this day. . . . What am I doing, standing around like a blockhead for? I'm dumbfounded, simply dumbfounded with joy! With all my heart, I wish you . . . all sorts of things. . . . I'll go call Natasha, and so on and so on.

Lomov (*deeply moved*). My esteemed Stepan Stepanich, do you think I can count on her acceptance?

Chubukov. A handsome young man like you— what's not to accept? She'll curl up like a kitten, etcetera etcetera. . . . Be right back! (*Exits.*)

Lomov (*alone*). It's cold. . . . I'm trembling, like a schoolboy before an exam. Act now . . . that's the main thing. He who hesitates is lost: Wait around for true love, for ideal love, and you'll never get married. . . . Brrrrr! . . . It's cold. . . . Natalya Stepanovna is an excellent housekeeper, she's not bad looking, she's educated . . . what more could I want? Only now I'm so agitated I've got ringing in my ears. (*Takes a drink of water.*) Anyway, I can't *not* get married. . . . I mean, first of all, I'm already thirty-five years old—I'm at the critical age, so to speak. Second of all, I've got to settle down, lead an orderly life. . . . I've got heart trouble, constant palpitations, I get agitated easily, I'm always worked up about something or other. . . . Look, right now, how my lips are trembling and my right eyelid is twitching. . . . But the worst thing is, trying to get some sleep. No sooner do I get into bed and start to fall asleep, when all of a sudden I get this pain in my left side, and—whoosh!—it goes right to my shoulder and then to my head. . . . I leap up, like some sort of madman, I walk around for a bit, and then I lie down again, but no sooner do I start to fall asleep, when suddenly—whoosh!—there it is again! I mean, if it happens once, it happens twenty times. . . .

[*Enter* NATALYA STEPANOVNA.]

Natalya Stepanovna. Well, look who's here! You! Papa said: "Go inside—there's a merchant come to collect his goods." Hello, Ivan Vasilyevich!
Lomov. Hello, esteemed Natalya Stepanovna!
Natalya Stepanovna. Excuse my apron, I look like a mess. . . . We're shelling peas for drying. Why haven't you come to visit in so long? Sit down. . . .

[*They sit.*]

Natalya Stepanovna. Would you like something to eat?
Lomov. No, thank you, I've already eaten.
Natalya Stepanovna. Do smoke, if you want to. . . . Here . . . matches. . . . The weather's wonderful, but it rained so hard yesterday that the workers haven't been able to do a thing all day. How much haying have you gotten done? Imagine, I got so carried away, I mowed our entire meadow, but now I'm sorry I did it, I'm afraid it's all going to rot. I should have waited. Oh, well. So look at you, all dressed up in tails!

Aren't you something! Where are you going, to a ball? Not bad, not bad at all. . . . No really, what are you all dressed up for?
Lomov (*agitated*). Well, you see, my esteemed Natalya Stepanovna . . . it's like this. . . . The fact of the matter is, I've decided to ask you to . . . actually, to listen to what I'm going to say to you. . . . Now, of course, it may come as a surprise to you, and indeed it might offend you, but I . . . (*Aside*) It's freezing in here!
Natalya Stepanovna. What's up? (*Pause*) Well?
Lomov. I'll try to make it brief. As you know, my esteemed Natalya Stepanovna, I have long had the honor of knowing your family, ever since my childhood, in fact. My late aunt and her husband, from whom, as you may well know, I have inherited my land, have always held your father and your dear departed mother in the highest esteem. The Lomovs and the Chubukovs have always been on the most friendly, why you might even say, affectionate terms. Moreover, as you may well know, my land actually borders on yours. And furthermore, as you may also recall, my Oxen Meadows actually adjoin your birch groves.
Natalya Stepanovna. Sorry, but I'm going to interrupt you. You just said "*my* Oxen Meadows" . . . But surely they're not yours?
Lomov. Well of course they're mine.
Natalya Stepanovna. What do you mean? Oxen Meadows are ours, not yours!
Lomov. I beg your pardon, my esteemed Natalya Stepanovna, they're mine.
Natalya Stepanovna. Well, that's news to me. And how did it come to pass, that they happen to be yours?
Lomov. What do you mean, "how did it come to pass?" I'm talking about Oxen Meadows, you know, the land that's wedged in between your birch groves and Burnt Swamp.
Natalya Stepanovna. Right, right. . . . They're ours.

Lomov. No, I believe you are mistaken, my esteemed Natalya Stepanovna—they're mine.

Natalya Stepanovna. Oh, come on, Ivan Vasilyevich! Since when have they been yours?

Lomov. Since when? Since as long as I can remember, they've always been ours.

Natalya Stepanovna. Excuse me, but now you've really gone too far!

Lomov. It's all in the records, my esteemed Natalya Stepanovna. The ownership of Oxen Meadows was once under dispute, it's true; but now everyone knows that they're mine. There's no disputing that any more. And as I am sure you are aware, my late aunt's grandmother granted those Meadows to your father's grandfather indefinitely, for use by the peasants free of charge, in return for baking her bricks. Your father's grandfather's peasants made good use of those meadows free of charge for forty years, and had come to consider them as theirs. But then, when the new land registry was published . . .

Natalya Stepanovna. What are you talking about, it isn't like that at all! My grandfather and great-grandfather considered that their land extended all the way to Burnt Swamp—meaning, that Oxen Meadows belonged to us. What's there to quarrel about?—I don't understand it. I mean, really, it's very annoying!

Lomov. I'll show you the papers, Natalya Stepanovna!

Natalya Stepanovna. No, really, you're just kidding me, you're only joking, right. . . . It's all some kind of a game! We've owned that land for thirty years and now suddenly we're being told that it's no longer ours! Ivan Vasilyevich, forgive me, please, but I cannot believe my own ears. . . . I mean, it's hardly worth arguing about these Meadows. They're not more than a dozen acres or so, and they're worth only three hundred rubles,[2] but it's the injustice of it all that upsets

me. Say whatever you like, but injustice I cannot bear.

Lomov. Listen to me, I beg of you! Your father's grandfather's peasants, as I have already had the honor of telling you, baked bricks for my late aunt's grandmother. My late aunt's grandmother, wishing to return the favor . . .

Natalya Stepanovna. Grandfather, grandmother, dead aunt . . . I don't know what you're talking about! The Meadows are ours, and that's all there is to it.

Lomov. They're mine!

Natalya Stepanovna. They're ours! You can stand here arguing for two days, you can put on fifteen pairs of tails, they'll still be ours, ours, ours! . . . I have no desire to take what's yours, and by the same token, I do not intend to lose what's mine. . . . So say whatever you like.

Lomov. I do not need these Oxen Meadows, Natalya Stepanovna, but it's the principle of the thing. If you want them, then by all means, I shall give them to you.

Natalya Stepanovna. Well if you want to put it that way, then *I* can very well give them to *you*, because they're *mine*! All this is really very very strange, to say the least, Ivan Vasilyevich! Up until now we've thought of you as a good neighbor, as a friend, we even lent you our threshing machine last year, which meant, it just so happens, that we had to finish threshing in November, and now you treat us as if we were gypsies! Trying to give me my own land! Sorry, but that is not a very neighborly thing to do! In my opinion, it's downright impertinent, if you really want to know. . . .

Lomov. So now you're telling me that, in your opinion, I'm stealing your land, is that what you're telling me? My dear dear madam, never in my entire life have I ever stolen anyone else's land, and I shall never allow anyone to accuse me of such a thing. . . . (*Hurries over to the carafe, and drinks some water.*) Oxen Meadows are mine!

---

2. **rubles** (ro͞o′bəlz): Russian currency.

Natalya Stepanovna. That's a lie! They're ours!

Lomov. They're mine!

Natalya Stepanovna. A lie! I can prove it! Today I shall send my mowers out to work these meadows!

Lomov. What did you say?

Natalya Stepanovna. I shall have my mowers on that land today!

Lomov. And I'll throw them out by their necks!

Natalya Stepanovna. You wouldn't dare!

Lomov (*clutches at his heart*). Oxen Meadows are mine! Understand? Mine!

Natalya Stepanovna. Stop shouting, please! You can shout yourself blue in the face in your own house, if you want to, but here I must ask you to control yourself!

Lomov. My dear lady, if I weren't having absolutely agonizing palpitations right now, if my veins weren't popping right out of my head, then I would be talking very differently to you! (*Shouts.*) Oxen Meadows are mine!

Natalya Stepanovna. Ours!

Lomov. Mine!

Natalya Stepanovna. Ours!

Lomov. Ours!

[*Enter* CHUBUKOV.]

Chubukov. What's going on here? What's all this shouting about?

Natalya Stepanovna. Papa, tell this gentleman, will you, please: to whom do Oxen Meadows belong—to us or to him?

Chubukov (*to* LOMOV). My dear sweet fellow, they're ours!

Lomov. For goodness's sake, Stepan Stepanich, how do they come to be yours? At least *you* be reasonable, please! My late aunt's grandmother gave the Meadows to your grandfather's peasants for temporary use, free of charge, for a certain period of time only. The peasants made use of that land for forty years, they regarded it as their own, but then when the new land registry was published . . .

Chubukov. Permit me to say, my precious man . . . You're forgetting the fact that these peasants didn't pay your grandmother and so on and so on for the very reason that the Meadows were under disputed ownership, etcetera etcetera. . . . And anyway, every dog in the district knows that those Meadows are ours, yes, indeed. It's obvious you haven't looked at the land registry!

Lomov. And I can prove it to you that they're mine!

Chubukov. You can prove nothing of the kind, my darling fellow!

Lomov. Oh yes I can!

Chubukov. My dear sweet fellow, why are you shouting? Shouting proves absolutely nothing, no, indeed. I'm not after anything that is yours and by the same token I don't intend to give up what is mine. Why should I? If it comes to that, my dear dear fellow, if you really intend to dispute the ownership of the Meadows etcetera etcetera, why then I'd sooner give it to the peasants than to you. So there!

Lomov. I don't understand! What right have you to give away someone else's property?

Chubukov. That's my business, whether I have the right to or not. And by the way, young man, I am not accustomed to being spoken to in that tone of voice, no, indeed, I'm not. I'm twice as old as you are, young man, and I must ask you to speak to me with civility, and so on and so on.

Lomov. Oh no you don't, you're making a fool of me, you're laughing at me! You say that my land belongs to you—and then you have the nerve to ask me to calm down and speak civilly to you! Good neighbors don't behave that way, Stepan Stepanich! And anyway, you're not a neighbor, you're a landsnatcher!

Chubukov. What? What did you say?

Natalya Stepanovna. Papa, send the men out right away to mow Oxen Meadows!

Chubukov (*to* LOMOV). What did you say, sir?
Natalya Stepanovna. Oxen Meadows are ours, and I will not give them up, I won't, I won't!
Lomov. We'll see about that! I'll prove it in court that they're mine.
Chubukov. In court? So you just might go to court, sir, and so on and so on! Is that what you just might do! Really! I know your kind, indeed, I do, you've been waiting for this, the chance to go to court, etcetera etcetera. . . . You trouble-maker, you! You come from a whole line of rabblerousers![3] The whole lot of you!
Lomov. I must ask you not to insult my family. Everyone in the Lomov family is an honest man, we've never had anyone who's been tried for embezzling, no, not like your uncle!
Chubukov. But you've had plenty in the Lomov family who've been certified lunatics!
Natalya Stepanovna. All of you! All of you! All of you!
Chubukov. Your uncle was a drunk, and as for your other aunt, Nastasya Mikhailovna, yes indeed, the younger one, she ran off with an architect, etcetera etcetera. . . .
Lomov. And your mother was a hunchback. (*Clutches at his heart.*) There's a pain in my side. . . . My head is pounding. . . . Good heavens! . . . Water! . . .
Chubukov. And your father was a gambler and a glutton.
Natalya Stepanovna. And your aunt is the greatest gossip in the district!
Lomov. My left leg is paralyzed. . . . You conniver, you. . . . Ach, my heart! . . . And it's no secret around here that you help fix the elections. . . . I'm seeing stars. . . . Where is my hat?
Natalya Stepanovna. Lowlife! Cheat! Villain!

Chubukov. And you're a spiteful, two-faced schemer, yes indeed! That's what you are!
Lomov. My hat, here it is. . . . My heart . . . Where am I going? Where's the door? Ach! . . . I think I'm dying. . . . My foot isn't working. . . . (*Walks toward the door.*)
Chubukov (*following after him*). And may you never set foot in this house again! Ever!
Natalya Stepanovna. Go on, take us to court! Then we'll see!

[*Exit* LOMOV, *staggering.*]

Chubukov. To hell with him! (*Walks about the stage in agitation.*)
Natalya Stepanovna. Did you ever meet such a scoundrel! And that's what they call "a good neighbor!"
Chubukov. The miserable swindler! The scare-crow!
Natalya Stepanovna. The monster! He takes your land, and then he has the nerve to curse at you.
Chubukov. And this nightmare, this—this aberration, has the audacity to make a proposal to you, etcetera etcetera! Can you imagine? A proposal!
Natalya Stepanovna. What proposal?
Chubukov. What do you mean, "what proposal?" He came to make a proposal to you.
Natalya Stepanovna. A proposal? To me? Why didn't you say so before?
Chubukov. And all stuffed up in a pair of tails! The sausage! The mushroom!
Natalya Stepanovna. A proposal? To me? Ach! (*Collapses into the armchair and moans.*) Bring him back! Bring him back! Ach! Bring him back!
Chubukov. Who? Bring who back?
Natalya Stepanovna. Hurry, hurry! I'm fainting! Bring him back! (*Hysterics.*)
Chubukov. What's going on here? What's the matter with you? (*Grasps his head in his hands.*)

---

3. **rabblerousers** (rabʹəl·rouzʹərz): People who try to stir up a crowd by appealing to prejudices and strong emotions.

Oh, what a wretched creature am I! I shall shoot myself! Hang myself! I'm exhausted!

Natalya Stepanovna. I'm dying! Bring him back!

Chubukov. All right, all right! Stop howling! (*Runs offstage.*)

Natalya Stepanovna (*alone, moaning*). What have we done? Bring him back! Bring him back!

Chubukov (*runs in*). He's coming, he's coming, damn him! Ugh! You talk to him, I have no desire to, no indeed, I don't. . . .

Natalya Stepanovna (*moans*). Bring him back!

Chubukov (*shouting*). He's coming, I tell you. "O, what a trial it is, dear Lord, to be the father of a full-grown daughter!" I shall kill myself! I shall absolutely positively kill myself! We've cursed the man, we've disgraced him, we've thrown him out, all this is your doing . . . yours!

Natalya Stepanovna. No, yours!

Chubukov. I am to blame, of course!

[LOMOV *appears at the door.*]

Go speak to him yourself! (*Exits.*)

Lomov (*enters, exhausted*). Terrible palpitations . . . My foot's gone numb. . . . there's a pain in my side. . . .

Natalya Stepanovna. Forgive me, Ivan Vasilyevich, I think we overreacted. . . . Now I remember: Oxen Meadows are yours, actually.

Lomov. My heart is pounding, terribly. . . . *My* Meadows . . . I'm seeing stars . . . in both eyes. . . .

Natalya Stepanovna. They're your Meadows, yours. . . . Sit down. . . .

[*They sit.*]

We made a mistake.

Lomov. It's the principle of the thing. . . . It's not the land that matters, it's the principle. . . .

Natalya Stepanovna. Yes, yes, of course, the principle . . . Let's talk about something else.

Lomov. Moreover, I have proof. My aunt's grandmother gave your father's grandfather's peasants . . .

Natalya Stepanovna. Enough, enough with all this. . . . (*Aside*) I don't know, how should I bring it up? . . . (*To* LOMOV) Are you planning to go hunting soon?

Lomov. For grouse,[4] yes, most esteemed Natalya Stepanovna, after the harvest, I hope. Oh, have you heard? Imagine, what a misfortune has befallen me! My dog, Spotter, whom of course you may remember, has gone lame.

Natalya Stepanovna. What a pity! How come?

Lomov. Don't know. . . . He probably twisted his leg, or else another dog bit him. . . . (*Sighs.*) The best dog I ever had, never mind how much I paid for him! I bought him from Mironov—actually paid one hundred and twenty-five rubles.

Natalya Stepanovna. Too much, Ivan Vasilyevich, too much!

Lomov. Actually, I thought it was quite cheap. He's a marvelous dog.

Natalya Stepanovna. Papa paid seventy-five rubles for his Sprinter, and Sprinter's better than your Spotter any old day.

Lomov. Sprinter better than Spotter? What are you saying! (*Laughs.*) Sprinter better than Spotter!

Natalya Stepanovna. Well, of course, he's better! Sprinter is young, it's true, he's not yet fully grown, but on points and on pedigree there isn't a better dog in the district, why Volchanetsky can't even match him.

Lomov. Forgive me, Natalya Stepanovna, but truly you've forgotten, he's got an overbite, and dogs with an overbite never make good hunters.

Natalya Stepanovna. Overbite? That's the first I've heard of it!

Lomov. I assure you, his lower jaw is shorter than his upper one.

---

4. **grouse** (grous): a game bird.

Natalya Stepanovna. Have you measured it?

Lomov. Yes, I have, I have measured it. He's good enough for pointing, of course, but when it comes to retrieving . . .

Natalya Stepanovna. First of all, our Sprinter is a pedigree, a borzoi,[5] he's the son of Harness and Chisel, whereas you'll never find a pedigree for that spotted mongrel of yours. . . . And anyway, he's old and ugly as death. . . .

Lomov. All right, he's old, but I wouldn't swap him for five of your Sprinters. . . . Am I really hearing this? Spotter's a dog, but Sprinter . . . I mean, it's ridiculous even to argue about it. . . . Dogs like your Sprinter are as common as . . . as dogs. Every hunter has one. If you'd paid a quarter of that price, the former owner was lucky.

Natalya Stepanovna. You seemed to be possessed by the demon of contradiction today, Ivan Vasilyevich. First you got it into your head that the Meadows were yours, now you're saying that Spotter is better than Sprinter. I don't like it when a man doesn't say what he really thinks. You know very well that Sprinter is a hundred times better than . . . than your stupid Spotter. Why do you say the opposite?

Lomov. I see, Natalya Stepanovna, that either you think I'm blind or else I'm a fool. Face it, your Sprinter has an overbite.

Natalya Stepanovna. That's a lie!

Lomov. Overbite!

Natalya Stepanovna (*shouts*). Lie!

Lomov. Why are you shouting, madam?

Natalya Stepanovna. Why are you talking nonsense? Really, it's shocking! Your Spotter should be put to sleep already, and you're comparing him with Sprinter!

Lomov. Forgive me, I cannot continue this discussion. I'm having palpitations.

---

5. **borzoi** (bôr′zoi′): breed of large dog, also called a Russian wolfhound.

Natalya Stepanovna. Well, you know what they say about hunters: It's the ones who argue the most, that know the least.

Lomov. I beg of you, madam, be quiet. . . . I'm having a heart attack. . . . (*Shouts.*) Be quiet!

Natalya Stepanovna. I shall not be quiet, not until you admit that Sprinter is one hundred times better than your Spotter!

Lomov. One hundred times worse! I hope he dies, your Sprinter! My head . . . my eyes . . . my shoulder . . .

Natalya Stepanovna. Well, there's no need for your stupid Spotter to die, because he's dead already!

Lomov (*weeps*). Be quiet! I'm having heart failure!!

Natalya Stepanovna. I shall *not* be quiet!

[*Enter* CHUBUKOV.]

Chubukov. *Now* what's going on?

Natalya Stepanovna. Papa, tell the truth, honestly: Which dog is better—our Sprinter or his Spotter?

Lomov. Stepan Stepanovich, I beseech you, tell me only one thing: Does your dog Sprinter have an overbite or doesn't he? Yes or no?

Chubukov. And what if he does? So what! There isn't a better dog in the district, etcetera etcetera.

Lomov. But truly, isn't my Spotter better? Honestly!

Chubukov. Don't get excited, my precious man. . . . Permit me to explain. . . . Your Sprinter has his good features, indeed he does. . . . He's a pedigree, sure-footed, strong-flanked, and so on and so on. But this dog, if you really must know, my lovely fellow, has two fundamental flaws: He's old, and he's got a short muzzle.

Lomov. Excuse me, I'm having palpitations. . . . Let's look at the facts. . . . I beg to remind you, that in Marusky's Meadows, my Spotter was running neck and neck with the Count's

Springer, while your Sprinter was running a good two-thirds of a mile behind.

Chubukov. He was behind, because the Count's huntsman was whipping him, that's why he was behind.

Lomov. Yes, and why! Because all the other dogs were chasing the foxes, while your Sprinter was running after sheep!

Chubukov. That's a lie! . . . My dear dear man, I've got a very bad temper, indeed I have, and I beg of you, let's cut this conversation short. The Count's huntsman whipped him, simply because everyone's jealous of everyone else's dog. . . . Yes! Everyone hates everyone else! And you, my dear sir, are not above it all, either! Yes, indeed, the moment you notice that somebody else's dog is better than your Spotter, right away you start in with this, that, the other thing, and so on and so on. . . . You see, I remember everything!

Lomov. And I remember everything, too!

Chubukov (*mimics him*). I remember everything, too. . . . What? What do you remember?

Lomov. Palpitations. . . My foot's paralyzed. . . . I can't bear it any more.

Natalya Stepanovna (*mimics him*). Palpitations . . . What kind of a hunter are you, anyway? You should be home, lying on top of the stove[6] squashing cockroaches, not out hunting foxes! Palpitations . . .

Chubukov. That's right. What kind of a hunter are you, anyway? You should be sitting home with your palpitations, not chasing around in a saddle. It's fine to go out hunting and all that, but all you want to do is go out and argue with your neighbors and bother their dogs, etcetera etcetera. I've got a very bad temper, so let us quit this conversation, shall we? Hunter "my foot"; I'll say you're no hunter!

Lomov. And you call yourself a hunter? You only go out hunting so you can fawn all over the Count, and plot and scheme. . . . My heart! . . . Schemer!

Chubukov. What did you say? I, a schemer? (*Shouts*) Be quiet!

Lomov. Schemer!

Chubukov. Crybaby! Puppy dog!

Lomov. You old rat! You Jesuit![7]

Chubukov. Be quiet; or else I'll shoot you down like a partridge! Blabbermouth!

Lomov. Everyone in the world knows that—ach! my heart!—that your wife, may her soul rest in peace, used to beat you. . . . My foot . . . my head . . . I see stars. . . . I'm fainting, I'm fainting! . . .

Chubukov. And your housekeeper has you tied to her apron strings!

Lomov. You see, you see, you see . . . my heart's exploding! My shoulder's falling off. . . . Where's my shoulder? I'm dying! (*Collapses into the armchair.*) Get a doctor! (*Faints.*)

Chubukov. Crybaby! Infant! Blabbermouth! I feel faint! (*Drinks water.*) Faint!

Natalya Stepanovna. What kind of a hunter are you, anyway? You can't even sit on a horse! (*To* CHUBUKOV) Papa! What's the matter with him? Papa! Look, Papa! (*Screams.*) Ivan Vasilyevich! He's dead!

Chubukov. I feel faint! . . . . I can't breathe! . . . Air, give me air!

Natalya Stepanovna. He's dead! (*Tugs at* LOMOV's *sleeve.*) Ivan Vasilyich! Ivan Vasilyich! What have we done! He's dead! (*Collapses into the armchair.*) A doctor, get a doctor! (*Hysterics.*)

---

6. **lying on top of the stove:** The stoves in serf dwellings were like fireplaces. At night, the warmest place to sleep was on the flat top of the stove.

---

7. **Jesuit** (jezh′oo·it): member of the Society of Jesus, a Roman Catholic order. Russians were Russian Orthodox; some used the term *Jesuit* disparagingly to mean "schemer."

Chubukov. Ach!. . .What's going on? What's the matter with you?

Natalya Stepanovna (*moans*). He's dead! . . . dead!

Chubukov. Who's dead? (*Looks at* LOMOV.) He really *is* dead. Good heavens! Water! A doctor! (*Puts a glass to* LOMOV's *lips.*) Drink! . . . No, he's not drinking. . . . That means he's dead, and so on and so on. . . . Oh misfortune! Why haven't I put a bullet through my brain! Why haven't I put an end to it all? What am I waiting for? Give me a knife! Give me a pistol!

[LOMOV *stirs.*]

I think he's coming 'round! . . . Here, drink this water! . . . That's it. . . .

Lomov. Stars . . . mist . . . Where am I?

Chubukov. Please, just marry her as soon as possible—and get it over with! She accepts! (*Joins* LOMOV's *hand with* NATALYA STEPANOVNA's.) She accepts, and so on and so on. My blessings, etcetera etcetera. Only now, leave me in peace!

Lomov. Eh? What? (*Gets up.*) Who?

Chubukov. She accepts! So? Kiss each other. . . . and to hell with you both!

Natalya Stepanovna (*moans*). He's alive. . . . Yes, yes, I accept. . . .

Chubukov. Kiss!

Lomov. Eh? Who? (*Kisses* NATALYA STEPANOVNA.) Delighted, I'm sure. . . . Excuse me, what's going on? Ach, yes, now I understand. . . . My heart . . . I see stars. . . . I'm so happy, Natalya Stepanovna. . . . (*Kisses her hand.*) My foot was paralyzed. . . .

Natalya Stepanovna. I'm . . . I'm happy too. . . .

Chubukov. That's a load off my shoulders. . . . Ugh!

Natalya Stepanovna. Anyway . . . let's get it straight: Spotter is a worse dog than Sprinter.

Lomov. No, he's not!

Natalya Stepanovna. Yes, he is!

Chubukov. And so, the beginnings of marital bliss! Champagne!

Lomov. Is not!

Natalya Stepanovna. Is too! Is too! Is too!

Chubukov (*attempting to shout them down*). Champagne! Champagne!

CURTAIN.

BEFORE YOU READ

The Spy

Meet the Playwright

Bertolt Brecht (1898–1956)

Bertolt Brecht was a German playwright, poet, drama theorist, and political activist whose ideas and techniques have had a profound impact on twentieth-century theater. Brecht's activism landed him in trouble early on; he was nearly expelled from high school for objecting to the Roman poet Horace's sentiment "Dulce et decorum est pro patria mori" ("It is sweet and proper to die for one's country"). Soon afterward, in a grand irony, he was drafted into the German army and served during the last grueling months of World War I. Like many other members of his generation, Brecht was appalled by the devastation caused by the war. After the war, Brecht took up the life of a bohemian artist and discovered communism, the political movement that views history in terms of class conflict.

From Berlin to Hollywood

Brecht's political beliefs impelled his writing. His earliest plays commented on Germany's dark postwar period. His first play produced, *Drums in the Night*, brought direct language, ordinary characters, and blatant symbolism to the German stage. By the mid-1920s, Brecht had moved to Berlin, the capital of Germany, where he honed his political and dramatic theories. Out of this period came *The Threepenny Opera*, a play he created in 1928 with composer Kurt Weill (vīl). The play, a mixture of songs and dialogue, is a tale of petty criminals in London. Like most of Brecht's plays, *The Threepenny Opera* has a social agenda—to expose corruption in capitalist society—but its agenda is eclipsed by the play's humor and music, including songs like "Mack the Knife." The play was an enormous success.

Because of Brecht's anti-war views and his political leanings, he was a target of the emerging Nazi Party. His works appeared on the Nazis' blacklist and were among the materials destroyed in a massive book burning by the Nazis in 1933. In that same year, communists were blamed for the burning of the Reichstag (parliament). (Historians believe that the Nazis set the fire themselves to provide an excuse for arresting communists and other government opponents.) The day after the Reichstag burned, Brecht and his family fled Germany for their lives. They lived for several years in the relatively safe haven of Scandinavia. In 1941, with World War II raging in Europe, Brecht moved himself and his family to Santa Monica, California, where he wrote for the stage and screen.

Brecht's years in exile were productive. During this time he wrote *Mother Courage and Her Children*, *The Good Woman of Setzuan*, and *The Caucasian Chalk Circle*—the plays most identified with his major contribution to dramatic theory, epic theater (see next page). These plays are highly critical of the economic and political forces that shape the lives of ordinary people.

Suspicion and Recognition

In 1947, Brecht was called before the House Un-American Activities Committee, a Congressional committee that investigated internal threats against the government, especially by communists. The day after he gave his testimony—by most accounts a masterfully comic performance— Brecht was ready to leave the United States. He returned to East Germany, where he reestablished himself in the theater scene, setting up his own production company. During the last years of Brecht's life, critics from both Western Europe and communist-dominated Eastern Europe praised his work. In 1954, for example, the Berliner Ensemble's production of *Mother Courage* caused a sensation in Paris, assuring Brecht's position as one of Europe's foremost directors. A year later, he won the Soviet Union's Stalin Peace Prize. He died in East Berlin in 1956.

Background to *The Spy*

Brecht's plays were deeply influenced by an artistic movement called expressionism. **Expressionism** was a direct response to the realism that had dominated the stage since the late nineteenth century, when Henrik Ibsen had transformed Western drama. Instead of showing a realistic slice of external life, German expressionist drama conveys an individual's inner vision—often a nightmarish one. Characters in German expressionist drama often represent abstract ideas—especially social ills—and directors use lighting effects, dreamlike sets, dance-like gestures, and singing to represent subjective states of mind on the stage. Expressionism was a deliberate protest against the established social order. Playwrights, disillusioned by World War I, used expressionism to show how middle-class values contributed to the horrors of war and its bleak aftermath.

Revolutionary Ideas and Techniques

Brecht's plays took expressionism to a new level. His melding of art and politics led to the development of a new kind of theater—epic theater. In spite of its name, **epic theater** is not a heroic, romantic, larger-than-life form of drama. Instead, it is drama stripped of the elements that make audiences respond emotionally to a play. According to Brecht's theory of drama, an audience that was emotionally involved could not see or respond rationally to the problem at the center of the play. The epic play's plot does not rise to an emotional climax, because Brecht did not want his audience to get carried away by a feeling of suspense; rather, it consists of a series of scenes that could each stand alone (as the scenes in an epic poem can stand alone—hence the name "epic theater"). The epic play also tends to end without a resolution. Neatly tied-up plot strings, Brecht believed, made for complacent audiences.

The A-Effect

Brecht also used what he called the **alienation effect** (or **A-effect**) to keep audiences aware that they were watching a play. He achieved the A-effect by using theatrical devices such as bright lights, signs, quick scene changes, and minimal stage settings. He borrowed dramatic techniques from theater in other cultures, particularly from Japan and China. Because audiences were not familiar with the techniques, he believed they would be forced to stop and think about them while watching the play. He also intended for his characters (The Man, The Son, The Wife) to be viewed as inhabitants of their social roles and not as individuals with unique personalities. He encouraged his actors to play their parts with detachment. On occasion, Brecht did allow a character to inspire an emotional response in the audience, but he was sure to undercut the emotion's impact with a joke, a speech, or a lighting effect.

Fear and Misery of the Third Reich

Unlike Brecht's epic plays, which he set in the past to highlight parallels with the present, *The Spy* was a timely drama. He wrote the short play some time between 1935 and 1941, during the height of the Nazi regime that he had recently fled. In the play, a husband and wife become increasingly paranoid about their son, who has joined an organization called the Hitler Youth. Hitler established this organization to instill Nazi values in young boys (a parallel organization existed for girls). By 1939, membership was compulsory. Parents saw their influence over their children erode as loyalty to the Nazi regime was stressed above all else.

The Spy is part of a larger work called *Fear and Misery of the Third Reich*, a series of sketches. Though each sketch is powerful enough to stand alone, none of the sketches ends with resolution. In Brecht's view, it would be the audience's job to draw their own conclusions, finding the connections among the episodes and considering the total effect of the work.

As much as Brecht desired through his plays to teach his audiences a lesson—and ultimately to transform society—his skill as an artist may have worked against him. To this day, audiences tend to take his politics with a grain of salt and, despite his keenest wishes, open their hearts to the pathos and poetry of his plays.

The Spy

Bertolt Brecht

Translated by **John Willett**

CHARACTERS
The Man
The Wife
The Boy
The Maidservant

Scene. Cologne[1] 1935. A wet Sunday afternoon. THE MAN, THE WIFE, and THE BOY have finished lunch. THE MAIDSERVANT enters.

The Maidservant. Mr. and Mrs. Klimbtsch[2] are asking if you are at home.
The Man (*snarls*). No.

[THE MAIDSERVANT *goes out.*]

The Wife. You should have gone to the phone yourself. They must know we couldn't possibly have gone out yet.
The Man. Why couldn't we?
The Wife. Because it's raining.
The Man. That's no reason.
The Wife. Where could we have gone to? That's the first thing they'll ask.
The Man. Oh, masses of places.
The Wife. Let's go then.
The Man. Where to?
The Wife. If only it wasn't raining.
The Man. And where'd we go if it wasn't raining?
The Wife. At least in the old days you could go and meet someone. (*Pause.*) It was a mistake you not going to the phone. Now they'll realize we don't want to have them.
The Man. Suppose they do?
The Wife. Then it wouldn't look very nice, our dropping them just when everyone else does.
The Man. We're not dropping them.
The Wife. Why shouldn't they come here in that case?
The Man. Because Klimbtsch bores me to tears.
The Wife. He never bored you in the old days.
The Man. In the old days . . . All this talk of the old days gets me down.
The Wife. Well anyhow you'd never have cut

him just because the school inspectors are after him.
The Man. Are you telling me I'm a coward? (*Pause.*) All right, ring up and tell them we've just come back on account of the rain.

[THE WIFE *remains seated.*]

The Wife. What about asking the Lemkes[3] to come over?
The Man. And have them go on telling us we're slack about civil defense?[4]
The Wife (*to* THE BOY). Klaus-Heinrich,[5] stop fiddling with the wireless.

[THE BOY *turns his attention to the newspapers.*]

The Man. It's a disaster, its raining like this. It's quite intolerable, living in a country where it's a disaster when it rains.
The Wife. Do you really think it's sensible to go round making remarks like that?
The Man. I can make what remarks I like between my own four walls. This is my home, and I shall damn well say . . .

[*He is interrupted.* THE MAIDSERVANT *enters with coffee things. So long as she is present they remain silent.*]

Have we got to have a maid whose father is the block warden?[6]
The Wife. We've been over that again and again. The last thing you said was that it had its advantages.

---

1. **Cologne** (kə·lōn′).
2. **Klimbtsch** (klimpch).
3. **Lemkes** (lem′kəz).
4. **civil defense:** a system for warning and protecting civilians in case of war.
5. **Klaus-Heinrich** (klous hīn′rik).
6. **block warden:** similar to a neighborhood watch leader, appointed by the police department.

The Man. What aren't I supposed to have said? If you mentioned anything of the sort to your mother we could land in a proper mess.

The Wife. The things I talk about to my mother . . .

[*Enter* THE MAIDSERVANT *with the coffee.*]

The Wife. That's all right, Erna. You can go now, I'll see to it.

The Maidservant. Thank you very much, ma'am.

The Boy (*looking up from his paper*). Is that how vicars[7] always behave, dad?

The Man. How do you mean?

The Boy. Like it says here.

The Man. What's that you're reading? (*snatches the paper from his hands*)

The Boy. Hey, our group leader[8] said it was all right for us to know about anything in that paper.

The Man. I don't have to go by what your group leader says. It's for me to decide what you can or can't read.

The Wife. There's ten pfennigs,[9] Klaus-Heinrich, run over and get yourself something.

The Boy. But it's raining. (*He hangs round the window, trying to make up his mind.*)

The Man. If they go on reporting these cases against priests I shall cancel the paper altogether.

The Wife. Which are you going to take, then? They're all reporting them.

The Man. If all the papers are full of this kind of filth I'd sooner not read a paper at all. And I wouldn't be any worse informed about what's going on in the world.

The Wife. There's something to be said for a bit of a clean-up.

The Man. Clean-up indeed. The whole thing's politics.

The Wife. Well, it's none of our business anyway. After all, we're protestants.[10]

The Man. It matters to our people all right if it can't hear the word vestry[11] without being reminded of dirt like this.

The Wife. But what do you want them to do when this kind of thing happens?

The Man. What do I want them to do? Suppose they looked into their own back yard. I'm told it isn't all so snowy white in that Brown House[12] of theirs.

The Wife. But that only goes to show how far our people's recovery has gone, Karl.

The Man. Recovery! A nice kind of recovery. If that's what recovery looks like, I'd sooner have the disease any day.

The Wife. You're so on edge today. Did something happen at the school?

The Man. What on earth could have happened at school? And for God's sake don't keep saying I'm on edge, it makes me feel on edge.

The Wife. We oughtn't to keep on quarreling so, Karl. In the old days . . .

The Man. Just what I was waiting for. In the old days. Neither in the old days nor now did I wish to have my son's imagination perverted for him.

The Wife. Where has he got to, anyway?

The Man. How am I to know?

The Wife. Did you see him go?

The Man. No.

The Wife. I can't think where he can have gone. (*She calls.*) Klaus-Heinrich! (*She hurries out of the room, and is heard calling. She returns.*) He really has left.

---

7. **vicars:** leaders of a parish, like priests.
8. **group leader:** a local leader of the Hitler Youth.
9. **pfennigs** (fen′igz): a small unit of German money.

10. **protestants:** members of any of numerous Protestant churches.
11. **vestry:** a room in a church where church garments are kept or where prayer meetings are held.
12. **Brown House:** Hitler's headquarters.

The Man. Why shouldn't he?

The Wife. But it's raining buckets.

The Man. Why are you so on edge at the boy's having left?

The Wife. You remember what we were talking about?

The Man. What's that got to do with it?

The Wife. You've been so careless lately.

The Man. I have certainly not been careless, but even if I had what's that got to do with the boy's having left?

The Wife. You know how they listen to everything.

The Man. Well?

The Wife. Well. Suppose he goes round telling people? You know how they're always dinning[13] it into them in the Hitler Youth. They deliberately encourage the kids to repeat everything. It's so odd his going off so quietly.

The Man. Rubbish.

The Wife. Didn't you see when he went?

The Man. He was hanging round the window for quite a time.

The Wife. I'd like to know how much he heard.

The Man. But he must know what happens to people who get reported.

The Wife. What about that boy the Schmulkes[14] were telling us about? They say his father's still in a concentration camp.[15] I wish we knew how long he was in the room.

The Man. The whole thing's a load of rubbish. (*He hastens to the other rooms and calls* THE BOY.)

The Wife. I just can't see him going off somewhere without saying a word. It wouldn't be like him.

The Man. Mightn't he be with a school friend?

The Wife. Then he'd have to be at the Mummer-manns'. I'll give them a ring. (*She telephones.*)

The Man. It's all a false alarm, if you ask me.

The Wife (*telephoning*). Is that Mrs. Mummer-mann? It's Mrs. Furcke[16] here. Good afternoon. Is Klaus-Heinrich with you? He isn't?— Then where on earth can the boy be?—Mrs. Mummermann do you happen to know if the Hitler Youth place is open on Sunday afternoons?—It is?—Thanks a lot, I'll ask them. (*She hangs up. They sit in silence.*)

The Man. What do you think he overheard?

The Wife. You were talking about the paper. You shouldn't have said what you did about the Brown House. He's so patriotic about that kind of thing.

The Man. What am I supposed to have said about the Brown House?

The Wife. You remember perfectly well. That things weren't all snowy white in there.

The Man. Well, nobody can take that as an attack, can they? Saying things aren't all white, or snowy white rather, as I qualified it—which makes a difference, quite a substantial one at that—well, it's more a kind of jocular remark like the man in the street makes in the vernacular, sort of, and all it really means is that probably not absolutely everything even there is always exactly as the Führer[17] would like it to be. I quite deliberately emphasized that this was only "probably" so by using the phrase, as I very well remember, "I'm told" things aren't all—and that's another obvious qualification—so snowy white there. "I'm told"; that doesn't mean it's necessarily so. How could I say things aren't snowy white? I haven't any proof. Wherever

---

13. **dinning:** teaching by repeating information constantly.

14. **Schmulkes** (shmo͞ol′kəz).

15. **concentration camp:** prison camp. The Nazis imprisoned Jews, Romanies, political opponents, and others designated as enemies. In these concentration camps millions died from poison gas or starvation and disease.

16. **Furcke** (für′kə).

17. **the Führer** (fyo͞or′ər): "leader," in German; Hitler.

there are human beings there are imperfections. That's all I was suggesting, and in very qualified form. And in any case there was a certain occasion when the Führer himself expressed the same kind of criticisms a great deal more strongly.

The Wife. I don't understand you. You don't need to talk to me in that way.

The Man. I'd like to think I don't. I wish I knew to what extent you gossip about all that's liable to be said between these four walls in the heat of the moment. Of course I wouldn't dream of accusing you of casting ill-considered aspersions on your husband, any more than I'd think my boy capable for one moment of doing anything to harm his own father. But doing harm and doing it wittingly are unfortunately two very different matters.

The Wife. You can stop that right now! What about the kind of things you say yourself? Here am I worrying myself silly whether you made that remark about life in Nazi Germany being intolerable before or after the one about the Brown House.

The Man. I never said anything of the sort.

The Wife. You're acting absolutely as if I were the police. All I'm doing is racking my brains about what the boy may have overheard.

The Man. The term Nazi Germany just isn't in my vocabulary.

The Wife. And that stuff about the warden of our block and how the papers print nothing but lies, and what you were saying about civil defense the other day—when does the boy hear a single constructive remark? That just doesn't do any good to a child's attitude of mind, it's simply demoralizing, and at a time when the Führer keeps stressing that Germany's future lies in Germany's youth. He really isn't the kind of boy to rush off and denounce one just like that. It makes me feel quite ill.

The Man. He's vindictive, though.

The Wife. What on earth has he got to be vindictive about?

The Man. God knows, but there's bound to be something. The time I confiscated his tree-frog perhaps.

The Wife. But that was a week ago.

The Man. It's that kind of thing that sticks in his mind, though.

The Wife. What did you confiscate it for, anyway?

The Man. Because he wouldn't catch any flies for it. He was letting the creature starve.

The Wife. He really is run off his feet, you know.

The Man. There's not much the frog can do about that.

The Wife. But he never came back to the subject, and I gave him ten pfennigs only a moment ago. He only has to want something and he gets it.

The Man. Exactly. I call that bribery.

The Wife. What do you mean by that?

The Man. They'll simply say we were trying to bribe him to keep his mouth shut.

The Wife. What do you imagine they could do to you?

The Man. Absolutely anything. There's no limit. My God! And to think I'm supposed to be a teacher. An educator of our youth. Our youth scares me stiff.

The Wife. But they've nothing against you.

The Man. They've something against everyone. Everyone's suspect. Once the suspicion's there, one's suspect.

The Wife. But a child's not a reliable witness. A child hasn't the faintest idea what it's talking about.

The Man. So you say. But when did they start having to have witnesses for things?

The Wife. Couldn't we work out what you could have meant by your remarks? Then he could just have misunderstood you.

The Man. Well, what did I say? I can't even remember. It's all the fault of that damned rain. It puts one in a bad mood. Actually I'm the last person to say anything against the moral resurgence the German people is going through these days. I foresaw the whole thing as early as the winter of 1932.

The Wife. Karl, there just isn't time to discuss that now. We must straighten everything out right away. There's not a minute to spare.

The Man. I don't believe Klaus-Heinrich's capable of it.

The Wife. Let's start with the Brown House and all the filth.

The Man. I never said a word about filth.

The Wife. You said the paper's full of filth and you want to cancel it.

The Man. Right, the paper. But not the Brown House.

The Wife. Couldn't you have been saying that you won't stand for such filth in the churches? And that you think the people now being tried could quite well be the same as used to spread malicious rumors about the Brown House suggesting things weren't all that snowy white there? And that they ought to have started looking into their own place instead? And what you were telling the boy was that he should stop fiddling with the wireless and read the paper because you're firmly of the opinion that the youth of the Third Reich should have a clear view of what's happening round about them.

The Man. It wouldn't be any use.

The Wife. Karl, you're not to give up now. You should be strong, like the Führer keeps on . . .

The Man. I'm not going to be brought before the law and have my own flesh and blood standing in the witness box and giving evidence against me.

The Wife. There's no need to take it like that.

The Man. It was a great mistake our seeing so much of the Klimbtsches.

The Wife. But nothing whatever has happened to him.

The Man. Yes, but there's talk of an inquiry.

The Wife. What would it be like if everybody got in such a panic as soon as there was talk of an inquiry?

The Man. Do you think our block warden has anything against us?

The Wife. You mean, supposing they asked him? He got a box of cigars for his birthday the other day and his Christmas box was ample.

The Man. The Gauffs gave him fifteen marks.[18]

The Wife. Yes, but they were still taking a socialist paper[19] in 1932, and as late as May 1933 they were hanging out the old nationalist flag.[20]

[*The phone rings.*]

The Man. That's the phone.

The Wife. Shall I answer it?

The Man. I don't know.

The Wife. Who could be ringing us?

The Man. Wait a moment. If it rings again, answer it.

[*They wait. It doesn't ring again.*]

We can't go on living like this!

The Wife. Karl!

The Man. A Judas,[21] that's what you've borne me. Sitting at the table listening, gulping down the soup we've given him and noting down whatever his father says, the little spy.

The Wife. That's a dreadful thing to say. (*Pause.*)

---

18. **marks:** German currency.

19. **socialist paper:** a newspaper that reflects the political leanings of the Socialist Party, the "party of the worker."

20. **nationalist flag:** the flag of the nation of Germany, not the Nazi flag. After 1935, the Nazi flag, with its swastika, became the official German flag. To fly the nationalist flag in 1933 would have been a sign of protest or resistance.

21. **Judas:** a traitor or betrayer, like Judas Iscariot in the New Testament.

Do you think we ought to make any kind of preparations?

The Man. Do you think he'll bring them straight back with him?

The Wife. Could he really?

The Man. Perhaps I'd better put on my Iron Cross.[22]

The Wife. Of course you must, Karl.

[*He gets it and puts it on with shaking hands.*]

But they've nothing against you at school, have they?

The Man. How's one to tell? I'm prepared to teach whatever they want taught; but what's that? If only I could tell . . . How am I to know what they want Bismarck[23] to have been like? When they're taking so long to publish the new text books. Couldn't you give the maid another ten marks? She's another who's always listening.

The Wife (*nodding*). And what about the picture of Hitler; shouldn't we hang it above your desk? It'd look better.

The Man. Yes, do that.

[THE WIFE *starts taking down the picture.*]

The Wife. Suppose the boy goes and says we deliberately rehung it, though, it might look as if we had a bad conscience.

[THE WIFE *puts the picture back on its old hook.*]

The Man. Wasn't that the door?

The Wife. I didn't hear anything.

The Man. It was.

The Wife. Karl! (*She embraces him.*)

The Man. Keep a grip on yourself. Pack some things for me.

[*The door of the flat opens.* MAN *and* WIFE *stand rigidly side by side in the corner of the room. The door opens and enter* THE BOY, *a paper bag in his hand. Pause.*]

The Boy. What's the matter with you people?

The Wife. Where have you been?

[THE BOY *shows her the bag, which contains chocolate.*]

Did you simply go out to buy chocolate?

The Boy. Wherever else? Obvious, isn't it?

[*He crosses the room munching, and goes out. His parents look inquiringly after him.*]

The Man. Do you suppose he's telling the truth?

[THE WIFE *shrugs her shoulders.*]

22. **Iron Cross:** a traditional German medal awarded to soldiers who displayed bravery in combat; the fact that The Man has one suggests that he fought for Germany in World War I.

23. **Bismarck:** the German leader who united Germany in the late nineteenth century. The remark refers to Nazi efforts to rewrite German history books.

The Jewels of the Shrine

Meet the Playwright

James Ene Henshaw (1924–)

James Ene Henshaw was born in Calabar, Nigeria. His works for the theater include *This Is Our Chance: Plays from West Africa* (1957), *Children of the Goddess and Other Plays* (1964), and *Medicine for Love* (1964). *The Jewels of the Shrine*, one of Henshaw's earliest plays, won first prize at the All Nigerian Festival of the Arts in 1952.

Theater for Young Africans

In his plays, Henshaw strives to achieve a basic, honest communication with young Africans, his primary audience. Henshaw believes that plays should have an air of reality and truthfulness, making the audience feel as if the events in the play could have happened to them that day. Henshaw, who has great faith in traditional values, has said, "These good traditions, such as the respect for the older person . . . and the obligatory sharing of the other person's burdens, should not merely make the young African distinct, but should continue to be the earth he walks on, and the air he breathes."

Drama as Diversion

For Henshaw, who is also a medical doctor, writing plays offers a welcome diversion from practicing medicine. From his medical practice he draws inspiration; the profession offers him "a lot of opportunity to observe and to interpret all kinds of human behavior and attitudes." In addition to plays, he has written "Matron's Darling," a short story that appeared in a medical magazine, the *Eastern Nigerian Medical Journal*. He has also contributed articles to medical journals in Africa and England and has served as the editor of a major Nigerian medical publication. In 1978, Henshaw was appointed to the Order of the Niger in honor of his contributions as a doctor and a writer.

Background to *The Jewels of the Shrine*

Long before the Europeans began to colonize the African continent in the 1800s, African cultures had developed theatrical traditions of their own. Storytelling, religious rituals and ceremonies, enactments of daily events intended to instruct young people—these theatrical practices were and are key elements of traditional African cultures. Though *The Jewels of the Shrine* belongs more to the tradition of European realist theater that overtook African drama for a time in the twentieth century, it does feature a staple of the African tradition: the trickster character.

The Trickster

Trickster characters are mischievous figures who tend to leave chaos and confusion in their wake. They are neither wholly good nor wholly bad, but are clever, creative, and rebellious. They appear in literature the world over and feature prominently in the traditional oral narratives performed by African storytellers as well as in the highly theatrical rituals known as spirit cult performances. These ritual performances involve a medium, a person who, while in a trance, contacts the spirit world. The medium, dressed in a colorful costume and speaking in a "spirit tongue," can assume the identities of various spirits—including trickster spirits. It's little wonder that the wily trickster, one of the most enduring characters of world drama, survived the turbulent era of colonization from which a new theater would emerge.

European Forms, African Themes

By the end of the nineteenth century, European dramatic forms had been introduced to Africa. In Nigeria, for example, theater groups sprang up that produced musicals and comedies by English and other European writers. Though there was a call to see African themes presented in the European-style forums, it was not until the 1950s that Nigerian playwrights began to claim the stage as their own. Plays of this period used the realistic style of conventional European drama to showcase their ideas. Playwrights like James Ene Henshaw created dramas that were a hybrid of European and Nigerian theater, using European forms to explore such themes as how Nigerian life and society had changed as a result of colonization. Henshaw's plays show families struggling to come to terms with the place of tradition in the modern world. The schoolchildren of the 1960s and 1970s saw Henshaw's plays, and members of that generation went on to create a new and vital Nigerian theater.

A New Day for Nigerian Drama

Since the 1960s, postcolonial Nigerian drama has finally broken free from the constraints of European drama. Playwrights like Nobel laureate Wole Soyinka and others have mined traditional African dramatic forms for inspiration and updated them in innovative ways. Nigerian plays since the 1960s have been steeped in political issues and have unapologetically explored the effects of colonization. The new Nigerian playwrights boldly employ symbolism, poetry, folklore, music, dance, and other traditional African forms to explore religion, inequality, corruption, and other social issues. Their goal, like Henshaw's, has been to make theater relevant to Nigerian audiences.

The Jewels of the Shrine

A Play in One Act

James Ene Henshaw

CHARACTERS

Okorie (ō·ko·rē·e), an old man
Arob (a·rob)
Ojima (ō·jē·mə) } Okorie's grandsons
Bassi (bä·sē), a woman
A Stranger

Setting: An imaginary village close to a town in Nigeria. All the scenes of this play take place in OKORIE's mud-walled house. The time is the present.

SCENE 1

The hall in OKORIE's *house. There are three doors. One leads directly into* OKORIE's *room. The two others are on either side of the hall. Of these, one leads to his grandsons' apartment, while the other acts as a general exit.*

The chief items of furniture consist of a wide bamboo bed—on which is spread a mat—a wooden chair, a low table, and a few odds and ends, including three hoes.

OKORIE, *an old man of about eighty years of age, with scanty grey hair and dressed in the way his village folk do, is sitting at the edge of the bed. He holds a stout, rough walking-stick and a horn filled with palm wine.*

On the wooden chair near the bed sits a STRANGER, *a man of about forty-five years of age. He too occasionally sips wine from a calabash[1] cup. It is evening. The room is rather dark, and a cloth-in-oil lantern hangs from a hook on the wall.*

Okorie. Believe me, Stranger, in my days things were different. It was a happy thing to become an old man, because young people were taught to respect elderly men.

Stranger (*sipping his wine*). Here in the village you should be happier. In the town where I come from, a boy of ten riding a hired bicycle will knock down a man of fifty years without any feeling of pity.

---

1. **calabash** (kal′ə·bash′): a fruit whose hard shell is often used as a dish or a cup.

Okorie. Bicycle. That is why I have not been to town for ten years. Town people seem to enjoy rushing about doing nothing. It kills them.

Stranger. You are lucky that you have your grandchildren to help you. Many people in town have no one to help them.

Okorie. Look at me, Stranger, and tell me if these shabby clothes and this dirty beard show that I have good grandchildren. Believe me, Stranger, in my younger days things were different. Old men were happy. When they died they were buried with honor. But in my case, Stranger, my old age has been unhappy. And my only fear now is that when I die my grandsons will not accord me the honor due to my age. It will be a disgrace to me.

Stranger. I will now go on my way, Okorie. May God help you.

Okorie. I need help, Stranger, for although I have two grandsons I am lonely and unhappy because they do not love or care for me. They tell me that I am from an older world. Farewell, Stranger. If you call again and I am alive, I will welcome you back. (*Exit* STRANGER.)

[BASSI, *a beautiful woman, of about thirty years, enters.*]

Bassi. Who was that man, Grandfather?

Okorie. He was a stranger.

Bassi. I do not trust strangers. They may appear honest when the lights are on. But as soon as there is darkness, they creep back as thieves.

[OKORIE *smiles and drinks his wine.*]

Bassi (*pointing to him*). What has happened, Grandfather? When I left you this afternoon, you were old, your mind was worried, and your eyes were swollen. Where now are the care, the sorrow, the tears in your eyes? You never smiled before, but now——

Okorie. The stranger has brought happiness

back into my life. He has given me hope again.

Bassi. But don't they preach in town that it is only God who gives hope? Every other thing gives despair.

Okorie. Perhaps that stranger was God. Don't the preachers say that God moves like a stranger?

Bassi. God moves in strange ways.

Okorie. Yes, I believe it, because since that stranger came, I have felt younger again. You know, woman, when I worshipped at our forefathers' shrine I was happy. I knew what it was all about. It was my life. Then the preachers came, and I abandoned the beliefs of our fathers. The old ways did not leave me; the new ways did not wholly accept me. I was therefore unhappy. But soon I felt the wings of God carrying me high. And with my loving and helpful son, I thought that my old age would be as happy as that of my father before me. But death played me a trick. My son died and I was left to the mercy of his two sons. Once more unhappiness gripped my life. With all their education my grandsons lacked one thing—respect for age. But today the stranger who came here has once more brought happiness to me. Let me tell you this—

Bassi. It is enough, Grandfather. Long talks make you tired. Come, your food is now ready.

Okorie (*happily*). Woman, I cannot eat. When happiness fills your heart, you cannot eat.

[*Two voices are heard outside, laughing and swearing.*]

Bassi. Your grandchildren are coming back.

Okorie. Don't call them my grandchildren. I am alone in this world.

[*Door flings open. Two young men, about eighteen and twenty, enter the room. They are in shirt and trousers.*]

Arob. By our forefathers, Grandfather, you are still awake!

Bassi. Why should he not keep awake if he likes?

Arob. But Grandfather usually goes to bed before the earliest chicken thinks of it.

Ojima. Our good grandfather might be thinking of his youthful days when all young men were fond of farming and all young women loved the kitchen.

Bassi. Shame on both of you for talking to an old man like that. When you grow old, your own children will laugh and jeer at you. Come, Grandfather, and take your food.

[OKORIE *stands up with difficulty and limps with the aid of his stick through the exit followed by* BASSI, *who casts a reproachful look on the two men before she leaves.*]

Arob. I wonder what Grandfather and the woman were talking about.

Ojima. It must be the usual thing. We are bad boys. We have no regard for the memory of our father, and so on.

Arob. Our father left his responsibility to us. Nature had arranged that he should bury Grandfather before thinking of himself.

Ojima. But would Grandfather listen to Nature when it comes to the matter of death? Everybody in his generation, including all his wives, have died. But Grandfather has made a bet with death. And it seems that he will win.

Okorie (*calling from offstage*). Bassi! Bassi! Where is that woman?

Ojima. The old man is coming. Let us hide ourselves. (*Both rush under the bed.*)

Okorie (*comes in, limping on his stick as usual*). Bassi, where are you? Haven't I told that girl never . . .

Bassi (*entering*). Don't shout so. It's not good for you.

Okorie. Where are the two people?

Bassi. You mean your grandsons?

Okorie. My, my, well, call them what you like.

Bassi. They are not here. They must have gone into their room.

Okorie. Bassi, I have a secret for you. (*He narrows his eyes.*) A big secret. (*His hands tremble.*) Can you keep a secret?

Bassi. Of course I can.

Okorie (*rubbing his forehead*). You can, what can you? What did I say?

Bassi (*holding him and leading him to sit on the bed*). You are excited. You know that whenever you are excited you begin to forget things.

Okoric. That is not my fault. It is old age. Well, but what was I saying?

Bassi. You asked me if I could keep a secret.

Okorie. Yes, yes, a great secret. You know, Bassi, I have been an unhappy man.

Bassi. I have heard it all before.

Okorie. Listen, woman. My dear son died and left me to the mercy of his two sons. They are the worst grandsons in the land. They have sold all that their father left. They do not care for me. Now when I die what will they do to me? Don't you think that they will abandon me in disgrace? An old man has a right to be properly cared for. And when he dies he has a right to a good burial. But my grandchildren do not think of these things.

Bassi. See how you tremble, Grandfather! I have told you not to think of such things.

Okorie. Why should I not? But sh! . . . I hear a voice.

Bassi. It's only your ears deceiving you, Grandfather.

Okorie. It is not my ears, woman. I know when old age hums in my ears and tired nerves ring bells in my head, but I know also when I hear a human voice.

Bassi. Go on, Grandfather, there is no one.

Okorie. Now, listen. You saw the stranger that came here. He gave me hope. But wait, look around, Bassi. Make sure that no one is listening to us.

Bassi. No one, Grandfather.

Okorie. Open the door and look.

Bassi (*opens the exit door*). No one.

Okorie. Look into that corner.

Bassi (*looks*). There is no one.

Okorie. Look under the bed.

Bassi (*irritably*). I won't, Grandfather. There is no need. I have told you that there is nobody in the house.

Okorie (*pitiably*). I have forgotten what I was talking about.

Bassi (*calmly*). You have a secret from the stranger.

Okorie. Yes, the stranger told me something. Have you ever heard of the "Jewels of the Shrine"?

Bassi. Real jewels?

Okorie. Yes. Among the beads which my father got from the early white men were real jewels. When war broke out, and a great fever invaded all our lands, my father made a sacrifice in the village Shrine. He promised that if this village were spared he would offer his costly jewels to the Shrine. Death roamed through all the other villages, but not one person in this village died of the fever. My father kept his promise. In a big ceremony, the jewels were placed on our Shrine. But it was not for long. Some said they were stolen. But the stranger who came here knew where they were. He said that they were buried somewhere near the big oak-tree in our farm. I must go out and dig for them. They can be sold for fifty pounds[2] these days.

Bassi. But, Grandfather; it will kill you to go out in this cold and darkness. You must get someone to do it for you. You cannot lift a hoe.

Okorie (*infuriated*). So, you believe I am too old

---

2. **pounds:** Until 1960, Nigeria was a colony and protectorate of Britain, and its monetary unit was the pound. The basic monetary unit in Nigeria today is the naira (nīʹrə).

to lift a hoe. You, you, oh, I . . .

Bassi (*coaxing him*). There now, young man, no temper. If you wish, I myself will dig up the whole farm for you.

Okorie. Every bit of it?

Bassi. Yes.

Okorie. And hand over to me all that you will find?

Bassi. Yes.

Okorie. And you will not tell my grandsons?

Bassi. No, Grandfather, I will not.

Okorie. Swear, woman, swear by our Fathers' Shrine.

Bassi. I swear.

Okorie (*relaxing*). Now life is becoming worthwhile. Tell no one about it, woman. Begin digging tomorrow morning. Dig inch by inch until you bring out the jewels of our Forefathers' Shrine.

Bassi. I am tired, Grandfather, I must sleep now. Good night.

Okorie (*with feeling*). Good night. God and our Fathers' Spirits keep you. When dangerous bats alight on the roofs of wicked men, let them not trouble you in your sleep. When far-seeing owls hoot the menace of future days, let their evil prophecies keep off your path. (BASSI *leaves.*)

Okorie (*standing up and trembling, moves to a corner and brings out a small hoe; and struggling with his senile joints he tries to imitate a young man digging*). Oh, who said I was old? After all, I am only eighty years. And I feel younger than most young men. Let me see how I can dig. (*He tries to dig again.*) Ah! I feel aches all over my hip. Maybe the soil here is too hard. (*He listens.*) How I keep on thinking that I hear people whispering in this room! I must rest now. (*Carrying the hoe with him, he goes into his room.* AROB *and* OJIMA *crawl out from under the bed.*)

Arob (*stretching his hip*). My hip, oh my hip!

Ojima. My legs!

Arob. So there is a treasure in our farm; we must waste no time. We must begin digging soon.

Ojima. Soon? We must begin tonight; now. The old man has taken one hoe. (*Pointing to the corner.*) There are two over there. (*They fetch two hoes from among the heap of things in a corner of the room.*) If we can only get the jewels we can go and live in town and let the old man manage as he can. Let's move now.

[*As they are about to go out, each holding a hoe,* OKORIE *comes out with his own hoe. For a moment the three stare at each other in silence and surprise.*]

Arob. Now, Grandfather, where are you going with a hoe at this time of night?

Ojima (*impudently*). Yes, Grandfather, what is the idea?

Okorie. I should ask you; this is my house. Why are you creeping about like thieves?

Arob. All right, Grandfather, we are going back to bed.

Okorie. What are you doing with hoes? You were never fond of farming.

Ojima. We intend to go to the farm early in the morning.

Okorie. But the harvest is over. When everybody in the village was digging out the crops, you were going around the town with your hands in your pockets. Now you say you are going to the farm.

Ojima. Digging is good for the health, Grandfather.

Okorie (*re-entering his room*). Good night.

Arob and Ojima. Good night, Grandfather.

[*They return to their room. After a short time* AROB *and* OJIMA *come out, each holding a hoe, and tip-toe out through the exit. Then, gently,* OKORIE *too comes out on his toes, and placing his hoe on the shoulder, warily leaves the hall.*]

[*Curtain.*]

SCENE 2

The same, the following morning.

Bassi (*knocking at* OKORIE's *door. She is holding a hoe*). Grandfather, wake up. I am going to the farm.

Okorie (*opening the door*). Good morning. Where are you going so early in the morning?

Bassi. I am going to dig up the farm. You remember the treasure, don't you?

Okorie. Do you expect to find a treasure while you sleep at night? You should have dug at night, woman. Treasures are never found in the day.

Bassi. But you told me to dig in the morning, Father.

Okorie. My grandsons were in this room somewhere. They heard what I told you about the Jewels of the Shrine.

Bassi. They could not have heard us. I looked everywhere. The stranger must have told them.

Okorie (*rubbing his forehead*). What stranger?

Bassi. The stranger who told you about the treasure in the farm.

Okorie. So it was a stranger who told me! Oh yes, a stranger! (*He begins to dream.*) Ah, I remember him now. He was a great man. His face shone like the sun. It was like the face of God.

Bassi. You are dreaming, Grandfather. Wake up! I must go to the farm quickly.

Okorie. Yes, woman, I remember the jewels in the farm. But you are too late.

Bassi (*excitedly*). Late? Have your grandsons discovered the treasure?

Okorie. They have not, but I have discovered it myself.

Bassi (*amazed*). You?

[OKORIE *nods his head with a smile on his face.*]

Bassi. Do you mean to say that you are now a rich man?

Okorie. By our Fathers' Shrine, I am.

Bassi. So you went and worked at night. You should not have done it, even to forestall your grandchildren.

Okorie. My grandsons would never have found it.

Bassi. But you said that they heard us talking of the treasure.

Okorie. You see, I suspected that my grandsons were in this room. So I told you that the treasure was in the farm but in actual fact it was in the little garden behind this house, where the village Shrine used to be. My grandsons traveled half a mile last night to the farm for nothing.

Bassi. Then I am glad I did not waste my time.

Okorie (*with delight*). How my grandsons must have toiled in the night! (*He is overcome with laughter.*) My grandsons, they thought I would die in disgrace, a pauper, unheard of. No, not now. (*Then boldly*) But those wicked children must change, or when I die I shall not leave a penny for them.

Bassi. Oh, Grandfather, to think you are a rich man!

Okorie. I shall send you to buy me new clothes. My grandsons will not know me again. Ha— ha—ha—ha! (OKORIE *and* BASSI *leave.*)

[AROB *and* OJIMA *crawl out from under the bed, where for a second time they have hidden. They look rough, their feet dirty with sand and leaves. Each comes out with his hoe.*]

Arob. So the old man fooled us.

Ojima. Well, he is now a rich man, and we must treat him with care.

Arob. We have no choice. He says that unless we change, he will not leave a penny to us.

[*A knock at the door.*]

Arob and Ojima. Come in.

Okorie (*comes in, and seeing them so rough and dirty, bursts out laughing. The others look surprised*). Look how dirty you are, with hoes and all. "Gentlemen" like you should not touch hoes. You should wear white gloves and live in towns. But see, you look like two pigs. Ha—ha—ha— ha—ha! oh what grandsons! How stupid they look! Ha—ha—ha! (AROB *and* OJIMA *are dumbfounded.*[3]) I saw both of you a short while ago under the bed. I hope you now know that I have got the Jewels of the Shrine.

Arob. We, too, have something to tell you, Grandfather.

Okorie. Yes, yes, "gentlemen." Come, tell me. (*He begins to move away.*) You must hurry up. I am going to town to buy myself some new clothes and a pair of shoes.

Arob. New clothes?

Ojima. And shoes?

Okorie. Yes, Grandsons, it is never too late to wear new clothes.

Arob. Let us go and buy them for you. It is too hard for you to—

Okorie. If God does not think that I am yet old enough to be in the grave, I do not think l am too old to go to the market in town. I need some clothes and a comb to comb my beard. I am happy, Grandchildren, very happy.

[AROB *and* OJIMA *are dumbfounded.*]

Okorie. Now, "gentlemen," why don't you get drunk and shout at me as before? (*Growing bolder*) Why not laugh at me as if I were nobody? You young puppies, I am now somebody, somebody. What is somebody? (*Rubbing his forehead as usual.*)

Arob (*to* OJIMA). He has forgotten again.

Okorie. Who has forgotten what?

Ojima. You have forgotten nothing. You are a good man, Grandfather, and we like you.

Okorie (*shouting excitedly*). Bassi! Bassi! Bassi! Where is that silly woman? Bassi, come and hear this. My grandchildren like me, I am now a good man. Ha—ha—ha—ha! (*He limps into his room.*)

[AROB *and* OJIMA *look at each other. It is obvious to them that the old man has all the cards now.*]

Arob. What has come over the old man?

Ojima. Have you not heard that when people have money, it scratches them on the brain? That is what has happened to our grandfather now.

Arob. He does not believe that we like him. How can we convince him?

Ojima. You know what he likes most; someone to scratch his back. When he comes out, you will scratch his back, and I will use his big fan to fan at him.

Arob. Great idea. (OKORIE *coughs from the room.*) He is coming now.

Okorie (*comes in*). I am so tired.

Arob. You said you were going to the market, Grandfather.

Okorie. You do well to remind me. I have sent Bassi to buy the things I want.

Ojima. Grandfather, you look really tired. Lie down here. (OKORIE *lies down and uncovers his back.*) Grandfather, from now on, I shall give you all your breakfast and your midday meals.

Arob (*jealously*). By our Forefathers' Shrine, Grandfather, I shall take care of your dinner and supply you with wine and clothing.

Okorie. God bless you, little sons. That is how it should have been all the time. An old man has a right to live comfortably in his last days.

Ojima. Grandfather, it is a very long time since we scratched your back.

---

3. **dumbfounded:** amazed, astonished.

Arob. Yes, it is a long time. We have not done it since we were infants. We want to do it now. It will remind us of our younger days when it was a pleasure to scratch your back.

Okorie. Scratch my back? Ha—ha—ha—ha. Oh go on, go on; by our Fathers' Shrine you are now good men. I wonder what has happened to you.

Ojima. It's you, Grandfather. You are such a nice man. As a younger man you must have looked very well. But in your old age you look simply wonderful.

Arob. That is right, Grandfather, and let us tell you again. Do not waste a penny of yours any more. We will keep you happy and satisfied to the last hour of your life.

[OKORIE *appears pleased.* AROB *now begins to pick at, and scratch,* OKORIE's *back.* OJIMA *kneels near the bed and begins to fan the old man. After a while, a slow snore is heard. Then, as* AROB *warms up to his task,* OKORIE *jumps up.*]

Okorie. Oh, that one hurts. Gently, children, gently. (*He relaxes and soon begins to snore again.* OJIMA *and* AROB *gradually stand up.*)

Arob. The old fogy[4] is asleep.

Ojima. That was clever of us. I am sure he believes us now.

[*They leave.* OKORIE *opens an eye and peeps at them. Then he smiles and closes it again.* BASSI *enters, bringing some new clothes, a pair of shoes, a comb and brush, a tin of face powder, etc. She pushes* OKORIE.]

Bassi. Wake up, Grandfather.

Okorie (*opening his eyes*). Who told you that I was asleep? Oh! you have brought the things. It is so long since I had a change of clothes. Go on,

___
4. **fogy** (fō´gē): someone whose habits and ideas are considered old-fashioned.

woman, and call those grandsons of mine. They must help me to put on my new clothes and shoes.

[BASSI *leaves.* OKORIE *begins to comb his hair and beard, which have not been touched for a long time.* BASSI *re-enters with* AROB *and* OJIMA. *Helped by his grandsons and* BASSI, OKORIE *puts on his new clothes and shoes. He then sits on the bed and poses majestically like a Chief.*]

[*Curtain.*]

SCENE 3

The same, a few months later. OKORIE *is lying on the bed. He is well dressed and looks happy, but it is easily seen that he is nearing his end. There is a knock at the door.* OKORIE *turns and looks at the door, but cannot speak loudly. Another knock; the door opens and the* STRANGER *enters.*

Okorie. Welcome back, Stranger. You have come in time. Sit down. I will tell you of my Will.

[*Door opens slowly.* BASSI *walks in.*]

Bassi (*to* STRANGER). How is he?

Stranger. Just holding on.

Bassi. Did he say anything?

Stranger. He says that he wants to tell me about his Will. Call his grandsons. (BASSI *leaves.*)

Okorie. Stranger.

Stranger. Yes, Grandfather.

Okorie. Do you remember what I told you about my fears in life?

Stranger. You were afraid your last days would be miserable, and that you would not have a decent burial.

Okorie. Now, Stranger, all that is past. Don't you see how happy I am? I have been very well cared for since I saw you last. My grandchildren have done everything for me, and I am sure they will bury me with great ceremony and rejoicing. I want you to be here when I am making my Will. Bend to my ears, I will whisper something to you. (STRANGER *bends for a moment.* OKORIE *whispers. Then he says aloud*) Is that clear, Stranger?

Stranger. It is clear.

Okorie. Will you remember?

Stranger. I will.

Okorie. Do you promise?

Stranger. I promise.

Okorie (*relaxing on his pillow*). There now. My end will be more cheerful than I ever expected.

[*A knock.*]

Stranger. Come in.

[AROB, OJIMA, *and* BASSI *enter. The two men appear as sad as possible. They are surprised to meet the* STRANGER, *and stare at him for a moment.*]

Okorie (*with effort*). This man may be a stranger to you, but not to me. He is my friend. Arob, look how sad you are! Ojima, how tight your lips are with sorrow! Barely a short while ago, you would not have cared whether I lived or died.

Arob. Don't speak like that, Grandfather.

Okorie. Why should I not? Remember, these are my last words on earth.

Ojima. You torture us, Grandfather.

Okorie. Since my son, your father, died, you have tortured me. But now you have changed, and it is good to forgive you both.

Stranger. You wanted to make a Will.

Okorie. Will? Yes, Will. Where is Bassi? Has that woman run away already?

Bassi (*standing above the bed*). No, Grandfather, I am here.

Okorie. Now there is my family complete.

Stranger. The Will, Grandfather, the Will.

Okorie. Oh, the Will; the Will is made.

Arob. Made? Where is it?

Okorie. It is written out on paper.

Arob and Ojima (*together*). Written? What?

Okorie (*coolly*). Yes, someone wrote it for me soon after I had discovered the treasure.

Arob. Where is it, Grandfather?

Ojima. Are you going to show us, Grandfather?

Okorie. Yes, I will. Why not? But not now, not until I am dead.

Arob and Ojima. What?

Okorie. Listen here. The Will is in a small box buried somewhere. The box also contains all my wealth. These are my wishes. Make my burial the best you can. Spend as much as is required, for you will be compensated. Do not forget that I am the oldest man in this village. An old man has a right to be decently buried. Remember, it was only after I had discovered the Jewels of the Shrine that you began to take good care of me. You should, by carrying out all my last wishes, atone for all those years when you left me poor, destitute, and miserable.

(*To the* STRANGER, *in broken phrases*) Two weeks after my death, Stranger, you will come and unearth the box of my treasure. Open it in the presence of my grandsons. Read out the division of the property and share it among them. Bassi, you have nothing. You have a good husband and a family. No reward or treasure is greater than a good marriage and a happy home. Stranger, I have told you where the box containing the Will is buried. That is all. May God——

Arob and Ojima (*rushing to him*). Grandfather, Grandfather——

[BASSI, *giving out a scream, rushes from the room.*]

Stranger. I must go now. Don't forget his Will. Unless you bury him with great honor, you may not touch his property. (*He leaves.*)

[*Curtain.*]

SCENE 4

All in this scene are dressed in black. AROB, OJIMA, *and* BASSI *are sitting around the table. There is one extra chair. The bed is still there, but the mat is taken off, leaving it bare. The hoe with which* GRANDFATHER *dug out the treasure is lying on the bed as a sort of memorial.*

Arob. Thank God, today is here at last. When I get my own share, I will go and live in town.

Ojima. If only that foolish stranger would turn up! Why a stranger should come into this house and—

Bassi. Remember, he was your grandfather's friend.

Ojima. At last, poor Grandfather is gone. I wonder if he knew that we only played up just to get something from his Will.

Arob. Well, it didn't matter to him. He believed us, and that is why he has left his property to us. A few months ago, he would rather have thrown it all into the sea.

Ojima. Who could have thought, considering the way we treated him, that the old man had such a kindly heart!

[*There is a knock. All stand.* STRANGER *enters from* GRANDFATHER'S *room. He is grim, dressed in black, and carries a small wooden box under his arm.*]

Arob. Stranger, how did you come out from Grandfather's room?

Stranger. Let us not waste time on questions. This box was buried in the floor of your grandfather's room. (*He places the box on the table;* AROB *and* OJIMA *crowd together. Sternly*) Give me room, please. Your grandfather always wanted you to crowd around him. But no one would, until he was about to die. Step back, please. (*Both* AROB *and* OJIMA *step back.* OJIMA *accidentally steps on* AROB.)

Arob (*to* OJIMA). Don't you step on me!

Ojima (*querulously*[5]). Don't you shout at me!

[STRANGER *looks at both.*]

Arob. When I sat day and night watching Grandfather in his illness, you were away in town, dancing and getting drunk. Now you want to be the first to grab at everything.

Ojima. You liar! It was I who took care of him.

Arob. You only took care of him when you knew that he had come to some wealth.

Bassi. Why can't both of you—

Arob (*very sharply*). Keep out of this, woman. That pretender (*pointing to* OJIMA) wants to bring trouble today.

Ojima. I, a pretender? What of you, who began to scratch the old man's back simply to get his money?

Arob. How dare you insult me like that! (*He throws out a blow.* OJIMA *parries.*[6] *They fight and roll on the floor: The* STRANGER *looks on.*)

Bassi. Stranger, stop them.

Stranger (*calmly looking at them*). Don't interfere, woman. The mills of God,[7] the preachers tell us, grind slowly.

Bassi. I don't know anything about the mills of God. Stop them, or they will kill themselves.

Stranger (*clapping his hands*). Are you ready to proceed with your grandfather's Will, or should I wait till you are ready? (*They stop fighting and stand up, panting.*) Before I open this box, I want to know if all your grandfather's wishes have been kept. Was he buried with honor?

Arob. Yes, the greatest burial any old man has had in this village.

---

5. **querulously** (kwer′yo͞o·ləs·lē): in a complaining voice.
6. **parries** (par′ēz): fends off a blow.
7. **mills of God:** This metaphor refers to divine vengeance, which would be delivered slowly, as mills grind grain.

Ojima. You may well answer, but I spent more money than you did.

Arob. No, you did not. I called the drummers and the dancers.

Ojima. I arranged for the shooting of guns.

Arob. I paid for the wine for the visitors and the mourners.

Ojima. I——

Stranger. Please, brothers, wait. I ask you again, was the old man respectably buried?

Bassi. I can swear to that. His grandsons have sold practically all they have in order to give him a grand burial.

Stranger. That is good. I shall now open the box. (*There is silence. He opens the box and brings out a piece of paper.*)

Arob (*in alarm*). Where are the jewels, the money, the treasure?

Stranger. Sh!—Listen. This is the Will. Perhaps it will tell us where to find everything. Listen to this.

Arob. But you cannot read. Give it to me.

Ojima. Give it to me.

Stranger. I can read. I am a school-teacher.

Arob. Did you write this Will for Grandfather?

Stranger. Questions are useless at this time. I did not.

Arob. Stop talking, man. Read it.

Stranger (*reading*). Now, my grandsons; now that I have been respectably and honorably buried, as all grandsons should do to their grandfathers, I can tell you a few things.

First of all, I have discovered no treasure at all. There was never anything like the "Jewels of the Shrine."

[AROB *makes a sound as if something had caught him in the throat.* OJIMA *sneezes violently.*]

There was no treasure hidden in the farm or anywhere else. I have had nothing in life, so I can only leave you nothing. The house which you now live in was my own. But I sold it some months ago and got a little money for what I needed. That money was my "Jewels of the Shrine." The house belongs now to the stranger who is reading this Will to you. He shall take possession of this house two days after the Will has been read. Hurry up, therefore, and pack out of this house. You young puppies, do you think I never knew that you had no love for me, and that you were only playing up in order to get the money which you believed I had acquired?

When I was a child, one of my first duties was to respect people who were older than myself. But you have thrown away our traditional love and respect for the elderly person. I shall make you pay for it. Shame on you, young men, who believe that because you can read and write, you need not respect old age as your forefathers did! Shame on healthy young men like you, who leave the land to go to waste because they will not dirty their hands with work!

Ojima (*furiously*). Stop it, Stranger, stop it, or I will kill you! I am undone. I have not got a penny left. I have used all I had to feed him and to bury him. But now I have not even got a roof to stay under. You confounded[8] Stranger, how dare you buy this house?

Stranger. Do you insult me in my own house?

Arob (*miserably*). The old cheat! He cheated us to the last. To think that I scratched his back only to be treated like this! We are now poorer than he had ever been.

Ojima. It is a pity. It is a pity.

Stranger. What is a pity?

Ojima. It is a pity we cannot dig him up again.

[*Suddenly a hoarse, unearthly laugh is heard from somewhere. Everybody looks in a different direction. They listen. And then again——*]

---

8. **confounded:** cursed.

Voice. Ha—ha—ha—ha!

[*They all look up.*]

Voice. Ha—ha—ha—ha!

[*The voice is unmistakably Grandfather* OKORIE's *voice. Seized with terror, everybody except* BASSI *runs in confusion out of the room, stumbling over the table, box, and everything. As they run away, the voice continues.*]

Ha—ha—ha—ha!

[BASSI, *though frightened, boldly stands her ground. She is very curious to know whether someone has been playing them a trick.*]

Voice (*louder*). Ha—ha—ha—ha!

[BASSI *too is terrorized and runs in alarm off the stage.*]

Voice (*continues*). Ha—ha—ha—ha!!!

[*Curtain.*]

The Man Who Turned into a Dog

Meet the Playwright

Osvaldo Dragún (1929–1999)

One of the most important playwrights to emerge in Argentina in the 1950s and 1960s, Osvaldo Dragún wrote plays that raised questions about society and the human condition. Born in Entre Ríos, a northern province of Argentina, Dragún first aspired to become a lawyer; after moving to the city of Buenos Aires in 1945, however, he decided to become a playwright. He eventually wrote thirty plays in a wide range of styles, including social realism, historical drama, and theater of the absurd.

Veiled Messages

Dragún's earliest works were earnest historical plays that also commented on the political situation of his day. The first, *The Plague Comes from Melos*, though set during the ancient Peloponnesian Wars, is said to be a veiled criticism of U.S. interventions in Latin America. His next play, *Túpac Amaru*, tells the story of the eighteenth-century Incan leader who becomes a martyr in his people's struggle for independence from Spain. Both plays focus on individuals fighting an oppressive power.

For his next project, Dragún moved away from historical drama and wrote a series of absurdist one-act plays called *Stories to Be Told*, in which *The Man Who Turned into a Dog* appears. Dragún's absurdist plays are his best-known plays, and they have been performed and acclaimed around the world.

Open Criticism

Dragún's later works became increasingly more realistic. They depict characters dealing with tough social, economic, and political issues in contemporary Latin America. In these plays, Dragún openly criticizes the institutional corruption and violence that was prevalent in Latin America in the 1950s and 1960s. Dragún's best-known play from this time is *Epic of Buenos Aires*, the story of a mother who works ceaselessly to provide for her ungrateful children. The play is inspired by Bertolt Brecht's epic-theater drama *Mother Courage and Her Children*.

After the 1960s, Dragún's creative output slowed. In addition to a handful of plays, he wrote television screenplays and remained influential in the theatrical world until his death in 1999.

Background to *The Man Who Turned into a Dog*

For centuries, Spanish imperial culture influenced the literature and drama of Latin America. Although Argentina declared its independence from Spain in 1816 and began to develop a unique and thriving national theater, European art still influenced playwrights like Dragún. Dragún turned to the theater of the absurd in the 1950s because its techniques helped him comment on his country's social, economic, and political problems. These problems were the result of the instability caused by a series of political and military coups overthrowing the Argentine government. Between 1930 and 1966, Argentina's government changed hands more than a dozen times, often by force.

Theater of the Absurd

The theater of the absurd originated in Europe, particularly France, and reflected disillusionment immediately after World War II. Writers of the time, such as Eugène Ionesco, Samuel Beckett, Edward Albee, and Dragún, felt they lived in a world in which human life had lost all value. In their eyes, reason and logic did not apply to a world devastated by war. They wrote darkly humorous plays that portray existence as meaningless and all efforts to make sense of a chaotic universe as pointless.

Theater of the absurd is marked by an absence of plot, unresolved conflicts, and characters that are symbols or abstractions. Absurdist plays are frequently performed on empty stages with black backdrops that symbolize the void of nothingness. The dialogue is often disjointed or nonsensical, and the plays contain images that suggest the senseless, irrational nature of the world. A human character, for example, can literally and inexplicably turn into a rhinoceros (as actually happens in Eugène Ionesco's play *Rhinoceros*).

Dual Goals

The goals of the theater of the absurd are twofold. The first goal is to criticize a society in which human existence is a petty, mechanical, undignified affair and in which institutions such as government, business, and the church are corrupt and useless. The other goal is to reveal that underneath the meaningless trappings of daily life, existence remains a mystery. Like the ancient classical dramatists Sophocles and Euripides, absurdist dramatists ask their audiences to ponder the uncertain nature of human life. Unlike classical drama, however, theater of the absurd doesn't offer explanations. It demands that we strip away accepted notions about the meaning of existence and ask afresh what our place in the universe is.

Dragún was particularly concerned with the snares and pitfalls of a dehumanizing industrial society. He believed humans were born to create but spend too much of their lives in mindless and useless activity. In *The Man Who Turned into a Dog*, the protagonist, based on Dragún's own father, agrees to act as a watchdog and, in the end, loses his own humanity. The premise is at once completely absurd and totally logical. The image of a man becoming a dog is striking. It sticks with audiences and makes them realize that their own humanity is at risk, and that one bad choice can lead to events that strip their lives of meaning.

The Man Who
Turned into a Dog

Osvaldo Dragún

Translated by **Francesca Colecchia and Julio Matas**

CHARACTERS
First Actor
Second Actor
Third Actor
Actress

Second Actor. Friends, let's tell the story this way . . .

Third Actor. The way they told it to us this afternoon.

Actress. It's the tale of "The Man Who Turned Into a Dog."

Third Actor. It began two years ago on a bench in a square. There, sir . . . , where today you were trying to fathom the secret of a leaf.

Actress. There, where stretching out our arms, we held the world by its head and its feet, and said to it, "Play, accordion, play!"

Second Actor. We met him there. (FIRST ACTOR *enters.*) He was . . . (*He points to the* FIRST ACTOR.) . . . the way you see him, nothing more. And he was very sad.

Actress. He became our friend. He was looking for work, and we were actors.

Third Actor. He had to support his wife, and we were actors.

Second Actor. He would dream of life, and he would awaken during the night, screaming. And we were actors.

Actress. He became our friend, of course. Just like that. . . . (*She points to him.*) Nothing more.

All. And he was very sad!

Third Actor. Time went by. Fall . . .

Second Actor. Summer . . .

Actress. Winter . . .

Third Actor. Spring . . .

First Actor. Lie! I never knew spring.

Second Actor. Fall . . .

Actress. Winter . . .

Third Actor. Summer. And we returned. And we went to visit him because he was our friend.

Second Actor. And we asked, "Is he all right?" And his wife told us . . .

Actress. I don't know . . .

Third Actor. Is he sick?

Actress. I don't know.

Second and Third Actors. Where is he?

Actress. In the dog pound.

[FIRST ACTOR *enters on all fours.*]

Second and Third Actors. Uhh!

Third Actor (*observing him*).
I am the director of the pound.
And that's okay with me.
He arrived barking like a dog
(the main requirement).
Even if he wears a suit,
he is a dog, beyond a doubt.

Second Actor (*stuttering*).
I am the veterinarian,
and th-this is cl-clear to me.
Al-although he s-seems a man,
wh-what is here is a d-dog.

First Actor (*to the audience*). And I, what can I tell you? I don't know whether I'm a man or a dog. And I believe that in the end not even you will be able to tell me. Because it all began in the most ordinary fashion. I went to a factory to look for a job. I hadn't found anything in three months, and I went there to look for work.

Third Actor. Didn't you read the sign? There Are No Openings.

First Actor. Yes, I read it. Don't you have anything for me?

Third Actor. If it says There Are No Openings, there are none.

First Actor. Of course. Don't you have anything for me?

Third Actor. Not for you, not for the president!

First Actor. Okay. Don't you have anything for me?

Third Actor. No!

First Actor. Lathe operator . . .

Third Actor. No!

First Actor. Mechanic . . .

Third Actor. No!

First Actor. S[ecretary] . . .

Third Actor. No!

First Actor. Er[rand boy] . . .

Third Actor. N[o]!

First Actor. F[oreman] . . .

Third Actor. N[o]!

First Actor. Night watchman! Night watchman! Even if it's just a night watchman!

Actress (*as if she were playing a horn*). Toot, toot, toooot. The boss! (*The* SECOND *and* THIRD ACTORS *make signs to each other.*)

Third Actor (*to the audience*). Ladies and gentlemen, the night watchman's dog had died the night before, after twenty-five years of dedication.

Second Actor. He was a very old dog.

Actress. Amen.

Second Actor (*to the* FIRST ACTOR). Do you know how to bark?

First Actor. Lathe operator.

Second Actor. Do you know how to bark?

First Actor. Mechanic . . .

Second Actor. Do you know how to bark?

First Actor. Bricklayer . . .

Second and Third Actors. There are no openings!

First Actor (*pausing*). Bowwow . . . Bowwow! . . .

Second Actor. Very good, I congratulate you . . .

Third Actor. We'll give you ten pesos[1] a day, the doghouse, and your food.

Second Actor. As you see, he earned ten pesos a day more than the real dog.

Actress. When he returned home, he told me of the job he had gotten. He was drunk.

First Actor (*to his wife*). But they promised me that as soon as the first worker would retire, die, or be fired, they would give me his job. Amuse yourself, Maria, amuse yourself! Bowwow . . . bow-wow! . . . Amuse yourself, Maria, amuse yourself.

Second and Third Actors. Bowwow . . . bowwow . . . Amuse yourself, Maria, amuse yourself!

Actress. He was drunk, poor dear . . .

First Actor. And the following night I began to work. . . . (*He gets down on all fours.*)

Second Actor. Is the doghouse too small for you?

First Actor. I can't stoop so much.

Third Actor. Does it crowd you here?

First Actor. Yes.

Third Actor. All right, but look, don't tell me yes. You must begin to get used to the new you. Tell me, bowwow . . . bowwow! . . .

Second Actor. Does it crowd you here? (*The* FIRST ACTOR *does not answer.*) Does it crowd you here?

First Actor. Bowwow . . . bowwow! . . .

Second Actor. Fine . . . (*He leaves.*)

First Actor. But that night it rained, and I had to get into the doghouse.

Second Actor (*to the* THIRD ACTOR). It no longer crowds him . . .

Third Actor. And he is in the doghouse.

Second Actor (*to the* FIRST ACTOR). Did you see how one can get used to anything?

Actress. One gets used to anything . . .

Second and Third Actors. Amen . . .

Actress. And he did begin to get used to it.

Third Actor. Then, when you see someone come in, bark at me: bowwow . . . bowwow! Let's see . . .

First Actor (*as the* SECOND ACTOR *runs past*). Bowwow . . . bow-wow! (*The* SECOND ACTOR *passes by silently.*) Bowwow . . . wow . . . wow! (FIRST ACTOR *leaves.*)

Third Actor (*to the* SECOND ACTOR). It's ten pesos a day extra in our budget . . .

Second Actor. Hmmm!

Third Actor. . . . but the poor guy's so conscientious, he deserves them . . .

Second Actor. Hmmm!

Third Actor. Besides he doesn't eat any more than the dead one . . .

Second Actor. Hmmm!

Third Actor. We ought to help his family!

Second Actor. Hmmm! Hmmm! Hmmm!

---

1. **pesos** (pā′sōz): plural of peso, the currency of Argentina.

[*They leave.*]

Actress. Nevertheless, I found him very sad, and I tried to comfort him when he returned home. (*The* FIRST ACTOR *enters.*) We had visitors today! . . .

First Actor. Really?

Actress. The dances at the club, do you remember?

First Actor. Yes.

Actress. What was our tango?

First Actor. I don't know.

Actress. What do you mean, you don't know! "Love, you abandoned me. . . ." (*The* FIRST ACTOR *is on all fours.*) And one day you brought me a carnation. . . . (*She looks at him and is horrified.*) What are you doing?

First Actor. What?

Actress. You're on all fours . . . (*She leaves.*)

First Actor. I can't bear this any more! I'm going to talk with the boss!

[*The* SECOND *and* THIRD ACTORS *enter.*]

Third Actor. The fact is that there's nothing available. . . .

First Actor. They told me that an old man died.

Third Actor. Yes, but we're on an austerity budget. Wait a little more time, huh?

Actress. And he waited. He returned in three months.

First Actor (*to the* SECOND ACTOR). They told me that one guy retired . . .

Second Actor. Yes, but we intend to close that section. Wait a little more, huh?

Actress. And he waited. He returned in two months.

First Actor (*to the* THIRD ACTOR). Give me the job of one of the guys you fired because of the strike . . .

Third Actor. Impossible. Their positions will remain unfilled . . .

Second and Third Actors. As punishment! (*They leave.*)

First Actor. Then I couldn't take any more . . . and I quit!

Actress. It was our happiest night in a long time. (*She takes him by the arm.*) What's the name of this flower?

First Actor. Flower . . .

Actress. And what's the name of that star?

First Actor. Maria.

Actress (*laughing*). Maria's my name!

First Actor. The star's too, the star's too! (*He takes her hand and kisses it.*)

Actress (*pulls back her hand*). Don't bite me!

First Actor. I wasn't going to bite you. . . . I was going to kiss you, Maria . . .

Actress. Ah! I thought that you were going to bite me. . . .

[*She leaves. The* SECOND *and* THIRD ACTORS *enter.*]

Second Actor. Of course . . .

Third Actor. . . . and the next morning . . .

Second and Third Actors. He had to look for a job again.

First Actor. I went around to several places, until in one of them . . .

Third Actor. Look, . . . we don't have anything. Except . . .

First Actor. Except what?

Third Actor. Last night the night watchman's dog died.

Second Actor. He was thirty-five, the poor wretch . . .

Second and Third Actors. The poor wretch.

First Actor. And I had to accept again.

Second Actor. We did pay him, fifteen pesos a day. (*The* SECOND *and* THIRD ACTORS *walk back and forth.*) Hmmm! . . . Hmmm! . . . Hmmm! . . .

Second and Third Actors. All right, let it be fifteen! (*They leave.*)

Actress (*enters*). Of course the four hundred and fifty pesos won't be enough for us to pay the rent . . .

First Actor. Look, since I have the doghouse, move to a room with four or five other girls, all right?

Actress. There's no other solution. And since your salary isn't even enough for us to eat on . . .

First Actor. Look, since I've gotten used to bones, I'm going to bring the meat to you, all right?

Second and Third Actors (*entering*). The board of directors agreed!

First Actor and Actress. The board of directors agreed . . . hurrah for the board of directors!

[SECOND *and* THIRD ACTORS *leave.*]

First Actor. I'd already gotten used to it. The doghouse seemed larger to me. Walking on all fours wasn't very different from walking upright. Maria and I would meet each other in the square. . . . (*He goes toward her.*) You can't come into my doghouse, and since I can't come into your room. . . . Until one night. . . .

Actress. We were walking. And suddenly I felt sick . . .

First Actor. What's the matter with you?

Actress. I feel sick.

First Actor. How come?

Actress (*weeping*). I think . . . that I'm going to have a baby . . .

First Actor. And that's why you're crying?

Actress. I'm afraid . . . , I'm afraid!

First Actor. But, why?

Actress. I'm afraid . . . , I'm afraid! I don't want to have a baby!

First Actor. Why, Maria? Why?

Actress. I'm afraid . . . that it will be . . . (*She whispers.*) "a dog." (*The* FIRST ACTOR *looks at her terrified and leaves running and barking. She falls to the floor. She gets up.*) He left . . . , he

left running! Sometimes he'd stand up, and sometimes he'd run on all fours . . .

First Actor. It isn't true, I didn't stand up. I couldn't stand up! My back hurt me if I stood up! Bowwow! . . . Cars almost ran over me . . . People stared at me . . . (*The* SECOND *and* THIRD ACTORS *enter.*) Go away! Didn't you ever see a dog?

Second Actor. He's mad! Call a doctor! (*He leaves.*)

Third Actor. He's drunk! Call a policeman! (*He leaves.*)

Actress. Later they told me that a man had pity on him and approached him kindly.

Second Actor (*entering*). Do you feel sick, friend? You can't remain on all fours. Do you know how many beautiful things there are to see, standing up, with your eyes turned upward? Let's see, stand up. . . . I'll help you. . . . Come on, stand up . . .

First Actor (*beginning to stand up, when suddenly*). Bowwow . . . bowwow! (*He bites the* SECOND ACTOR.) Bowwow . . . bowwow! . . . (*He leaves.*)

Third Actor (*entering*). Finally, when after two years without seeing him, we asked his wife, "How is he?" she answered . . .

Actress. I don't know.

Second Actor. Is he all right?

Actress. I don't know.

Third Actor. Is he sick?

Actress. I don't know.

Second and Third Actors. Where is he?

Actress. In the dog pound.

Third Actor. And as we were coming here, a boxer passed by . . .

Second Actor. And they told us that he didn't know how to read, but that it didn't matter because he was a boxer.

Third Actor. And a draftee passed by . . .

Actress. And a policeman passed by . . .

Second Actor. And they all passed by . . . , and they passed by . . . , and you passed by. And we thought that perhaps the story of our friend would matter to you.

Actress. Because perhaps among you there may now be a woman who thinks: "Won't I have . . . , won't I have . . . ?" (*She whispers.*) "A dog."

Third Actor. Or someone who's been offered the job of the night watchman's dog . . .

Actress. If it isn't so, we're happy.

Second Actor. But if it's so, if there is someone among you whom others want to change into a dog, like our friend, then . . . but well, then that . . . that's another story!

Curtain.

A Solid Home

Meet the Playwright

Elena Garro (1920–1998)

The playwright, novelist, and journalist Elena Garro was drawn to the dramatic arts at a young age. She studied acting, choreography, and playwriting at the National Autonomous University in Mexico City in the 1930s. While in school, she became actively involved in politics, showing particular interest in the issues of indigenous, or native, peoples' rights.

In 1937, the teenaged Garro married Octavio Paz, the Nobel Prize–winning poet. For many years, the two enjoyed a globe-trotting lifestyle as diplomats and writers. In the mid-1940s, the pair lived in the United States; in the late 1940s, Garro was part of a Mexican diplomatic corps in France; in the early 1950s, she accompanied Paz in his posting as Mexico's ambassador to Japan.

Garro and Paz shared a passionate devotion to many of the same political causes—including opposition to the right-wing government of Mexico—but at times the marriage between the two artists was fraught with bitter rivalry. In 1959, while Garro was in New York, Paz informed her by mail that he wanted to separate. They eventually divorced, never to see each other again.

Pioneer of Magic Realism

While she was abroad, Garro wrote articles, plays, screenplays, and novels. She had often returned to Mexico during the 1940s, '50s, and '60s, and her writing both influenced and was influenced by Mexican and Latin American culture. According to some critics, her 1963 prize-winning novel, *Recollections of Things to Come*, is the first masterwork of magic realism. Magic realism is a literary technique that weaves supernatural ideas, events, and characters into realistic narratives. Her work preceded and influenced Gabriel García Márquez's famous magic-realist novel, *One Hundred Years of Solitude*.

An important turning point in Garro's life came in 1968, when she spoke out against the Mexican government after government troops massacred students during a political demonstration. Garro not only antagonized the government with her comments but also outraged fellow intellectuals by suggesting that they had played a role in the tragedy. Garro was briefly jailed and then went into a self-imposed exile. After more than a decade of silence, Garro began to publish again. While living in Spain and France, she wrote memoirs and fiction. The themes of her writing revealed her conflicted feelings about Mexico. Like the characters in *A Solid Home*, Garro was at once alienated from and wistful for her home.

A Final Homecoming

In 1991, Garro visited Mexico for the first time in many years. Her three-week tour was marked by a public celebration of her literary achievements and political principles. One of her plays was performed by a troupe of indigenous actors. After years of living and writing in exile, Garro was finally acknowledged as an influential force in Mexican and Latin American letters. Garro returned to Mexico in 1993 and lived and wrote there until her death from a heart attack in 1998.

Background to A *Solid Home*

Two distinctly Latin American traditions—one literary and one cultural—are integral to Garro's 1957 play *A Solid Home*. The play incorporates the elements of a school of writing called **magic realism**. As noted earlier, magic realism includes supernatural or surrealistic elements, such as ghosts, dreams, and fantasy, in narratives that often seem otherwise realistic. In magic realism, readers may encounter ghosts existing among the living, children born with green hair, or corpses talking among themselves. Magic realism also affects the way in which narratives are told. Time may be stretched out or shortened. Characters may live hundreds of years, or decades may pass in an instant. Magic realism presents an alternative understanding of existence beyond purely logical reality to reveal larger truths about life and death.

Dia de los Muertos

The Mexican tradition of the Day of the Dead (*Dia de los Muertos*) is also reflected in Garro's play. The Day of the Dead is celebrated each year in Mexico on November 1 and 2. It is a ritual that celebrates the dead with parades and feasts. On November 1, the souls of deceased children are believed to return to their families. In their honor, children are given sugary treats, like skull-shaped cookies and candy, and gifts. On November 2, families gather and proceed to cemeteries to visit the graves of their deceased loved ones. People scatter marigold petals, light candles, and leave the deceased's favorite foods on the gravesites in order to attract loved ones' spirits and to keep evil at bay. The gravesites of loved ones are cleaned, and families hold a vigil. The celebration often concludes with a costume ball in which people dress as skeletons or adorn themselves with images of death. The point of the tradition is to celebrate the living, to honor the dead, and to accept death as a natural stage in the process of life. Garro honors this tradition in *A Solid Home* by imagining how the dead might remember and respond to events in the living world.

A Solid Home

Elena Garro

Translated by **Francesca Colecchia and Julio Matas**

CHARACTERS

Don Clement, sixty years old
Doña Gertrude, forty years old
Mama Jessie, eighty years old
Katie, five years old
Vincent Mejía, twenty-three years old
Muni, twenty-eight years old
Eve, a foreigner, twenty years old
Lydia, thirty-two years old

Scene. Interior of a small room with stone walls and ceiling. There are neither windows nor doors. To the left, imbedded in the wall and of stone also, are some berths. In one of them, MAMA JESSIE in a nightgown and a lace sleeping cap. The stage is very dark.

Voice of Doña Gertrude. Clement! Clement! I hear footsteps!

Voice of Don Clement. You're always hearing footsteps! Why must women be so impatient? Always anticipating what isn't going to happen, predicting calamities!

Voice of Doña Gertrude. Well, I hear them.

Voice of Don Clement. No, woman, you're always mistaken. You're carried away by your nostalgia for catastrophes. . . .

Voice of Doña Gertrude. It's true . . . but this time I'm not mistaken.

Voice of Katie. They're many feet, Gertrude! (KATIE *comes out dressed in an ancient white dress, high black shoes, and a coral necklace. Her hair is tied at the nape of her neck with a red bow*). How nice! Now nice! Tra-la-la! Tra-la-la! (*She jumps and claps her hands.*)

Doña Gertrude (*appearing in a rose dress of the 1930s*). Children don't make mistakes. Aunt Katherine, isn't it true that someone is coming?

Katie. Yes, I know it! I knew it from the first time that they came! I was so afraid here all alone. . . .

Don Clement (*appearing in a black suit with white cuffs*). I believe that they're right. Gertrude! Gertrude! Help me find my metacarpuses.[1] I always lose them and I can't shake hands without them.

---

1. **metacarpuses:** the five bones between the wrist and the fingers; the fact that Don Clement is looking for the bones of his hand is the first clue that characters in the play have been dead for some time.

Vincent Mejía (*appearing in a uniform of an officer of Benito Juárez*). You read a lot, Don Clement, that's why you have the bad habit of forgetting things. Look at me, perfect in my uniform, always ready for any occasion!

Mama Jessie (*straightening up in her berth and poking out her head which is covered with the lace sleeping cap*). Katie's right! The steps are coming this way. (*She puts one hand behind her ear as though listening.*) The first ones have stopped . . . unless the Ramirezes have had a misfortune. . . . This neighborhood has already been very disappointing to us!

Katie (*jumping*). You, go to sleep, Jessie! You only like to sleep.

> Rock-a-bye Jessie,
> on the tree top.
> When the wind blows,
> the cradle will rock.
> When the bough bends,
> the cradle will fall.
> And down will come Jessie,
> cradle and all.

Mama Jessie. And what do you want me to do? If they left me in my nightgown . . .

Don Clement. Don't complain, Mama Jessie. We thought that out of respect . . .

Doña Gertrude. If it had been up to me, mama . . . , but what were the girls and Clement going to do?

[*Many footsteps which stop and then start again are heard overhead.*]

Mama Jessie. Katie! Come here and polish my forehead. I want it to shine like the North Star. Happy the day when I went through the house like lightning, sweeping, shaking the dust that would fall on the piano in deceptive gold mists. Then when everything shone like a comet, I'd break the ice on my buckets of water left out in the night air and bathe myself with water full of winter stars. Do you remember, Gertrude! That was living! Surrounded by my children straight and clean as lead pencils.

Doña Gertrude. Yes, mama. And I also remember the burnt cork you used to make circles under your eyes with, and the lemons you'd eat so that you'd look pale. And those nights when you would go with papa to the theater. How pretty you looked with your fan and your drop earrings!

Mama Jessie. You see, daughter, life is short. Each time that I would arrive at our box. . . .

Don Clement (*interrupting*). For pity's sake, now I can't find my femur![2]

Mama Jessie. What a lack of courtesy! To interrupt a lady!

[*Meanwhile,* KATIE *has been helping* JESSIE *arrange her nightcap.*]

Vincent Mejía. I saw Katie using it for a trumpet.

Doña Gertrude. Aunt Katie, where did you leave Clement's femur?

Katie. Jessie, Jessie! They want to take my bugle away from me!

Mama Jessie. Gertrude, let this child alone! And as for you, let me tell you for a grown woman you're more spoiled than she is. . . .

Doña Gertrude. But, mama, don't be unjust. It's Clement's femur!

Katie. Ugly! Bad! I'll hit you! It's not his femur, it's my little sugar bugle![3]

Don Clement (*to* GERTRUDE). Could she have eaten it? Your aunt's unbearable.

Doña Gertrude. I don't know, Clement. My

broken clavicle[4] got lost. She liked the little streaks left along the scar a lot. And it was my favorite bone! It reminded me of the walls of my house, covered with heliotrope.[5] I told you how I fell, didn't I? The day before, we'd gone to the circus. All of Chihuahua was in the stands to see the clown, Richard Bell. Suddenly a tightrope walker came out. She resembled a butterfly. I've never forgotten her. . . . (*A blow is heard above.* GERTRUDE *interrupts herself. Continuing:*) In the morning I climbed the fence to dance on one foot, because all night I'd dreamed that I was she. . . . (*Overhead a harder blow is heard.*) Of course, I didn't know that I had bones. As a little girl, one doesn't know anything. Because I broke it, I always say that it was the first little bone that I had. It takes you by surprise!

[*The blows follow one another more rapidly.*]

Vincent Mejía (*smoothing his mustache*). There's no doubt. Someone's coming. We have guests. (*He sings.*)

When in darkness
The moon glimmers
And on the pool
The swallow sings . . .

Mama Jessie. Be quiet, Vincent! This isn't the time to sing. Look at these unexpected guests! In my day people announced themselves before dropping in for a visit. There was more respect. Let's see now whom they're bringing us, probably one of those foreigners who married my girls! "God overwhelms the humble!" as my poor Raymond, may God have him in His glory, used to say. . . .

Vincent Mejía. You haven't improved at all,

---

2. **femur:** a thighbone; the longest and heaviest bone in the human body.
3. **sugar bugle:** candy in the shape of a trumpet given to children on the first part of the Day of the Dead celebration; this is also a clue that the characters are deceased.

---

4. **clavicle:** collarbone, or bone that connects the shoulder to the sternum.
5. **heliotrope:** flowering plant that turns its head to follow the sun.

Jessie! You find defects in everything. Before, you were so agreeable. The only thing you liked was to dance polkas! (*He hums a tune and dances a few steps.*) Do you remember how we danced at that carnival? (*He continues dancing.*) Your pink dress spun around and around, and your neck was very close to my lips . . .

Mama Jessie. For heaven's sake, cousin Vincent! Don't remind me of those foolish things.

Vincent Mejía (*laughing*). What would Raymond say now? He was so jealous. And you and I here together, while he rots there alone in that other cemetery.

Doña Gertrude. Uncle Vincent, be quiet. You're going to cause an argument!

Don Clement (*alarmed*). I already explained to you, Mama Jessie, that at the time we didn't have the money to transfer him.

Mama Jessie. And the girls, why don't they bring him? Don't give me explanations. You always lacked tact.

[*A harder blow is heard.*]

Katie. I saw a light! (*A ray of light enters.*) I saw a sword. St. Michael's coming to visit us again! Look at his sword!

Vincent Mejía. Are we all here? Now then, easy does it!

Don Clement. Muni and my sister-in-law are missing.

Mama Jessie. The foreigners, always keeping away!

Doña Gertrude. Muni, Muni! Someone's coming. Maybe it's one of your cousins. Aren't you happy, dear? You'll be able to play and laugh with them again. Let's see if that sadness leaves you.

[EVE *appears, blond, tall, sad, very young, in a traveling dress of the 1920s.*]

Eve. Muni was around here a moment ago. Muni, dear! Do you hear that blow? That's the way the sea beats against the rocks of my house. . . . None of you knew it. . . . It was a rock, high, like a wave, always beaten by the winds that lulled us to sleep at night. Swirls of salt covered its windows with sea stars. The walls in the kitchen had a golden glow which radiated from my father's hands, warm as the sun. . . . During the nights, creatures of wind, water, fire, and salt came in through the fireplace. They would huddle in the flames and sing in the water that dripped into the washstands. . . . Drip! Drop! Drip! Drop! Drip! Drop! . . . And iodine spread itself about the house like sleep. . . . The tail of a shining dolphin would announce day to us, with this light of fish scales and corals!

[*With the last sentence,* EVE *raises her arm and points to the torrent of light that enters the crypt when the first stone slab is moved above. The room is inundated with sunlight. All the luxurious clothes are dusty and all the faces pale. The child* KATIE *jumps with pleasure.*]

Katie. Look, Jessie! Someone's coming! Who's bringing him, Jessie? Lady Diptheria[6] or Saint Michael?[7]

Mama Jessie. Wait, child. We're going to see.

Katie. Lady Diptheria brought me. Do you remember her? She had fingers of cotton and she wouldn't let me breathe. Did she frighten you, Jessie?

---

6. **Lady Diptheria:** personification of diphtheria, a disease that is characterized by the formation of thick membranes that block the air passages; Katie describes the membranes as Lady Diptheria's choking fingers.

7. **Saint Michael:** the archangel who, according to Christian tradition, is the patron of soldiers and the protector of the dead at the time of their death; he carries a flaming sword as a symbol of his power.

Mama Jessie. Yes, little sister. I remember that they took you away and the patio of the house remained strewn with purple petals. Mama cried a lot and we girls did too.

Katie. Dummy! Didn't you know that you were going to come to play with me here? That day, St. Michael sat down beside me and wrote it with his sword of fire on the roof of my house. I didn't know how to read . . . and I read it. And was the school of the Misses Simson nice?

Mama Jessie. Very nice, Katie. Mama sent us with black ribbons. . . .

Katie. And did you learn to spell? That's why mama was going to send me. . . .

Muni (*comes in wearing pajamas, with a blue face and blond hair*). Who can it be?

[*Overhead, through the fragment of the vault open to the sky, a woman's feet are seen suspended in a circle of light.*]

Doña Gertrude. Clement, Clement! They're Lydia's feet. What a pleasure, daughter, what a pleasure that you've died so soon!

[*Everyone becomes silent. The descent of* LYDIA, *suspended on ropes, begins. She is stiff, wearing a white dress, her arms crossed on her chest, her fingers in the form of a cross, and her head bowed. Her eyes are closed.*]

Katie. Who's Lydia?

Muni. Lydia's the daughter of my uncle Clement and my aunt Gertrude, Katie. (*He caresses the girl.*)

Mama Jessie. Now we have the whole bunch of grandchildren here. So many brats! Well, isn't the crematory[8] oven more modern? As far as I'm concerned at least it seems more hygienic.

Katie. Isn't it true, Jessie, that Lydia isn't for real?

Mama Jessie. I wish it were so, my dear. There's room here for everyone except my poor Raymond!

Eve. How she grew! When I came she was as little as Muni.

[LYDIA *remains standing, in the midst of all of them, as they look at her. Then she opens her eyes and sees them.*]

Lydia. Papa! (*She embraces him.*) Mama! Muni! (*She embraces them.*)

Doña Gertrude. You're looking very well, daughter.

Lydia. And grandmother?

Don Clement. She can't get up. Do you remember that we made the mistake of burying her in her nightgown?

Mama Jessie. Yes, Lili, here I am, lying down forever.

Doña Gertrude. My mother's notions! You already know, Lili, how well groomed she always was.

Mama Jessie. The worst thing will be, daughter, to present myself this way before God, our Lord. Doesn't it seem a disgrace to you? Why didn't it occur to you to bring me a dress? That gray one with the brocade[9] ruffles and the bouquet of violets at the neck. Do you remember it? I'd put it on for formal occasions . . . but no one remembers the old people. . . .

Katie. When Saint Michael visits us, she hides.

Lydia. And who are you, precious?

Katie. Katie!

Lydia. Of course! We had your picture on the piano! Now it's in Evie's house. How sad it was to look at you, so melancholy, painted in your white dress. I'd forgotten that you were here.

_____

8. **crematory:** furnace for cremating, or burning, dead bodies.

_____

9. **brocade:** rich cloth with a raised design woven into it; brocades are associated with nineteenth-century apparel, which gives a clue to the period in which Mama Jessie lived.

Vincent Mejía. And aren't you pleased to meet me, niece?

Lydia. Uncle Vincent! We also had your picture in the living room, with your uniform and your medal in a little red velvet box.

Eve. And don't you remember your Aunt Eve?

Lydia. Aunt Eve! Yes, I just barely remember you, with your blond hair spread out in the sun . . . and I remember your purple parasol[10] and your faded face under it, like that of a beautiful drowned woman . . . and your empty chair rocking to the rhythm of your song, after you had gone.

[*From the circle of light a* VOICE *comes forth.*]

Voice. The generous earth of our Mexico opens its arms to give you loving shelter. Virtuous woman, most exemplary mother, model wife, you leave an irreparable void . . .

Mama Jessie. Who's speaking to you with such familiarity?

Lydia. It's Don Gregory de la Huerta Ramírez Puente, President of the Association of the Blind.

Vincent Mejía. What madness! And what do so many blind people do together?

Mama Jessie. But why does he address you in such intimate terms?

Doña Gertrude. It's the style, mama, to address the dead familiarly.

Voice. Most cruel loss, whose absence we shall feel in time. You leave us forever deprived of your boundless charm. You also leave a solid and Christian home in the most terrible neglect. The homes do tremble before inexorable Death. . . .

Don Clement. Good God! But is that blustering fool still running around there?

Mama Jessie. What's useless abounds.

Lydia. Yes, and now he's president of the bank, of the Knights of Columbus, of the Association for the Blind, the Flag Day and Mother's Day Committees.

Voice. Only irrevocable faith, Christian resignation, and pity . . .

Katie. Don Hilary always says the same thing.

Mama Jessie. It isn't Don Hilary, Katie. Don Hilary died a trifling sixty-five years ago. . . .

Katie (*not hearing her*). When they brought me, he said, "A little angel flew away!" And it wasn't true. I was here below, alone and very frightened. Isn't that so Vincent? Isn't it true that I don't tell lies?

Vincent Mejía. You're telling me! Imagine, I arrived here, still stunned by the powder flashes, with my wounds open . . . and what do I see? Katie crying: "I want to see my mama! I want to see my mama!" What trouble she caused me! Believe me, I'd rather have fought the French. . . .[11]

Voice. Rest in peace!

[*They begin to replace the stone slabs. The scene becomes dark slowly.*]

Katie. We were alone a long time, weren't we, Vincent? We didn't know what was happening, but no one came anymore.

Mama Jessie. I've already told you, Katie, we went to the capital, then the revolution came along. . . .[12]

---

10. **parasol:** decorative umbrella carried by women to protect themselves from the sun; this too is an accessory from the nineteenth century.

11. . . . **I'd rather have fought the French:** reference to Mexico's war with France in the 1860s. French Emperor Napoleon III established rule through King Maximilian from 1863 until 1867, when Mexican forces under Benito Juarez overthrew foreign rule and reestablished republican rule.

12. . . . **then the revolution came along:** reference to the Mexican Revolution (1910–1917).

Katie. Until one day Eve arrived. You said, Vincent, that she was a foreigner. . . .

Vincent Mejía. The situation was a little tense and Eve didn't say a single word to us.

Eve. I too was restrained . . . and besides I was thinking of Muni . . . and of my home. . . . Everything was so quiet here.

[*Silence. They place the last slab.*]

Lydia. And now, what'll we do?

Don Clement. Wait.

Lydia. Still wait?

Doña Gertrude. Yes, daughter. You'll see.

Eve. You'll see everything you want to see, except your home with your white pine table and the waves and the sails of the boats through your windows.

Muni. Aren't you happy, Lili?

Lydia. Yes, Muni, especially to see you. When I saw you that night lying in the courtyard of the police station, with that smell of urine that came from the broken flagstones, and you dead on the stretcher, between the feet of the policemen with your wrinkled pajamas and your blue face, I asked myself, "Why? Why?"

Katie. Me too, Lili. I hadn't seen a blue dead person either. Then Jessie told me that cyanide[13] has many artists' brushes, but only one tube of color, blue!

Mama Jessie. Don't bother that boy any longer! Blue looks very good on blonds.

Muni. Why, cousin Lili? Haven't you seen stray dogs walk and walk along the sidewalks looking for bones in the butcher shops full of flies, and the butcher, with his fingers drenched in blood from cutting up the meat? Well, I no longer wanted to walk along atrocious sidewalks looking through the blood for a bone, nor look at those corners, shelters for drunks and urinals for dogs. I wanted a happy city, full of sunlight and moonlight. A solid city like the home we had as children, with sunshine in every door, moonlight for every window, and wandering stars in the rooms. Do you remember it, Lili? It had a labyrinth of laughs. Its kitchen was a crossroads; its garden, source of all the rivers; and all of it, the birthplace of Man. . . .

Lydia. A solid home, Muni! That's just what I wanted. . . . and you already know, they took me to a strange house. And in it I found only clocks and eyes without eyelids that looked at me for years. . . . I polished the floors so as not to see the thousands of dead words that the maids swept in the mornings. I shined the mirrors in order to drive away our hostile glances. I hoped that one morning the loving image would face me in the looking glass. I opened books in order to open avenues in that circular hell. I embroidered napkins with linked initials in order to find the magic, unbreakable thread that made two names into one. . . .

Muni. I know, Lili.

Lydia. But it was all useless. The furious eyes didn't stop looking at me ever. If I could find the spider that once lived in my house—I used to tell myself—with the invisible thread that unites the flower to light, the apple to fragrance, woman to man, I would sew loving eyelids to close the eyes that look at me and this house would enter into the solar order. Each balcony would be a different country. Its furniture would bloom. From its glasses jets of water would spurt. The sheets would turn into magic carpets in order to travel to sleep. From the hands of my children, castles, flags, and battles would come forth . . . but I didn't find the thread, Muni. . . .

Muni. You told me that at the police station. In that strange courtyard, forever far from the other courtyard, in whose sky a belltower counted for us the hours that we had left to play.

---

13. **cyanide:** extremely poisonous substance that, when ingested, turns the skin blue.

Lydia. Yes, Muni, and with you I put away forever the last day that we were children. Afterward, only a Lydia seated, facing the wall, waiting, remained.

Muni. I couldn't grow, either, and live on the street corners. I wanted my home. . . .

Eve. Me too, Muni, my son, I wanted a solid home. A house that the sea would beat every night. Boom! Boom! A house that would laugh with my father's laugh full of fish and nets.

Muni. Don't be sad, Lili. You'll find the thread, and you'll find the spider.

Don Clement. Lili, aren't you happy? Now your house is the center of the sun, the heart of every star, the root of all the grasses, the most solid point of every stone.

Muni. Yes, Lili, you still don't know it, but suddenly you won't need a house, nor a river. We'll not swim in the Mezcala River, we'll be the Mezcala.

Doña Gertrude. At times, daughter, you'll be very cold, and you'll be the snow falling on an unknown city or gray roofs and red caps.

Katie. What I like most is being a piece of candy in a little girl's mouth. Or a sty, to make those who read near a window weep!

Muni. Don't grieve when your eyes begin to disappear, because then you'll be all the eyes of the dogs looking at absurd feet.

Mama Jessie. Ah, child! May you never be the eyes of the blind, of a blind fish in the deepest abyss of the seas! You don't know the terrible feeling that I had. It was like seeing and not seeing things never thought of.

Katie (*laughing and clapping*). You also were very frightened when you were the worm that came in and out of your mouth.

Vincent Mejía. Well, for me, the worst thing was being a murderer's dagger!

Mama Jessie. Now the gophers will return. Don't shout when you yourself run along your face.

Don Clement. Don't tell her that. You're going to frighten her. It's frightening to learn to be everything.

Doña Gertrude. Especially because in the world one scarcely learns to be a man.

Lydia. And will I be able to be a pine tree with a nest of spiders and build a solid home?

Don Clement. Of course! And you'll be the pine tree and the staircase and the fire.

Lydia. And then?

Mama Jessie. Then God will call us to his bosom.

Don Clement. After having learned to be all things, St. Michael's sword will appear, center of the universe, and by its light the divine armies of angels will come forth and we'll enter into the celestial[14] order.

Muni. I want to be the fold of an angel's tunic.

Mama Jessie. Your color will go very well. It'll give beautiful reflections. And I, what'll I do dressed in this nightgown?

Katie. I want to be the index finger of God the Father!

All Together. Child!

Eve. And I, a wave sprinkled with salt, changed into a cloud!

Lydia. And I the sewing fingers of the Virgin, embroidering . . . embroidering . . . !

Doña Gertrude. And I the music from the harp of St. Cecilia![15]

Vincent Mejía. And I the rage of the sword of St. Gabriel![16]

Don Clement. And I a particle of the stone of St. Peter![17]

---

14. **celestial:** of the heavens, divine.
15. **St. Cecilia:** early Christian martyr whose body did not decompose after more than a thousand years in the grave; according to Catholic tradition, she is the patroness of church music.
16. **St. Gabriel:** archangel and divine messenger and intermediary; like Michael, Gabriel also carries a sword.
17. **St. Peter:** one of Jesus' twelve apostles; Jesus called him "the rock" on which the Christian church would be built.

Katie. And I a window that looks at the world!

Mama Jessie. There'll no longer be a world, Katie, because we'll be all that after the Final Judgment.[18]

Katie (*weeping*). There'll no longer be a world. And when am I going to see it? I didn't see anything. I didn't even learn the spelling book. I want there to be a world.

Vincent Mejía. Look at it now, Katie!

[*In the distance a trumpet is heard.*]

Mama Jessie. Jesus, Mary Most Pure! The trumpet of Final Judgment! And me in a nightgown! Pardon me, my Lord, this immodesty!

Lydia. No, grandma, it's taps.[19] There's a barracks[20] near the cemetery.

Mama Jessie. Ah, yes, they had already told me! And I always forget it. Who had the bright idea of putting a barracks so close to us? What a government! It lends itself to so much confusion!

Vincent Mejía. Taps! I'm going. I'm the wind that opens all the doors that I didn't open, that goes up the stairs that I never went up in a whirl, that runs along new streets in my officer's uniform and lifts the skirts of the pretty, unknown girls. . . . Ah, coolness! (*He disappears.*)

Mama Jessie. Rascal!

Don Clement. Ah, rain on the water! (*He disappears.*)

Doña Gertrude. Wood in flames! (*She disappears.*)

Muni. Do you hear? A dog howls. Ah, melancholy! (*He disappears.*)

Katie. The table where nine children eat supper! I'm the game they play! (*She disappears.*)

Mama Jessie. The fresh heart of a head of lettuce! (*She disappears.*)

Eve. I'm the flash of fire that sinks into the black sea! (*She disappears.*)

Lydia. A solid home! That's what I am! The stone slabs of my tomb! (*She disappears.*)

Curtain.

---

18. **Final Judgment:** also known as *Last Judgment*, which, in Christian tradition, is the day on which Jesus will return to earth and decide which souls go to heaven.
19. **taps:** bugle call used to signal the end of the day in a military camp; also played at military funerals.
20. **barracks:** buildings used to house soldiers.

Acknowledgments

For permission to duplicate copyrighted material, grateful acknowledgment is made to the following sources:

Applause Theatre & Cinema Books: "The Flying Doctor" by Molière, translated by Albert Bermel, from *Theatre for Young Audiences: Around the World in 21 Plays*, edited by Lowell Swortzell. Copyright © 1997 by Lowell Swortzell. International copyright secured. All rights reserved.

Arcade Publishing, New York, New York: "The Spy" from *Fear and Misery of the Third Reich* by Bertolt Brecht. Copyright © 1957 by Suhrkamp Verlag, Berlin; translation copyright © 1983 by Stefan S. Brecht.

James Ene Henshaw: "The Jewels of the Shrine, a Play in One Act" from *This Is Our Chance, Plays from West Africa* by James Ene Henshaw. Copyright © 1956 by James E. Henshaw.

Harold Ober Associates Incorporated: *A Doll's House* by Henrik Ibsen from *The Plays of Ibsen*, Volume I, translated by Michael Meyer. Copyright © 1965, 1974, 1980 by Michael Meyer. CAUTION: This play is fully protected, in whole, in part or in any form under the copyright laws of the United States of America, the British Empire including the Dominion of Canada, and all other countries of the Copyright Union, and is subject to royalty. All rights including motion picture, radio, television, recitation, public reading, are strictly reserved. For professional rights and amateur rights all inquiries should be addressed to the Author's Agent: Robert A. Freedman Dramatic Agency, Inc., 1501 Broadway, New York, NY 10036.

Oberon Books Limited: *Medea* by Euripedes, translated by Alistair Elliot. Translation copyright © 1992 by Alistair Elliot; Introduction copyright © 1993 by Nicholas Dromgoole. All rights whatsoever in this play are strictly reserved and application for professional performance should be made before commencement of rehearsals to Peters Fraser & Dunlop Group Ltd., 503/4 The Chambers, Chelsea Harbour, London SW10 OXF. Application for amateur performance should be made before commencement of rehearsals to Samuel French Ltd., 52 Fitzroy Street, London W1P 6JR.

Smith and Kraus, Inc.: "The Proposal" from *Chekhov: "The Vaudevilles" and Other Short Works*, translated by Carol Rocamora. Translation copyright © 1998 by Carol Rocamora.

University of Pittsburgh Press: "The Man Who Turned Into a Dog" by Osvaldo Dragún and "A Solid Home" by Elena Garro from *Selected Latin American One-Act Plays* edited and translated by Francesca Colecchia and Julio Matas. Copyright © 1973 by University of Pittsburgh Press.

Viking Press, a division of Penguin Group (USA) Inc.: "Antigone" by Sophocles from *The Three Theban Plays*, translated by Robert Fagles. Copyright © 1982 by Robert Fagles.

Photo Credits